WITHDRAWN
UTSA LIBRARIES

RENEWALS 458-4574

D1739306

The Sephardim
of Sydney

Coping with Political Processes
and Social Pressures

I dedicate this work to my late parents
Sasson and Farcha Hella,
*immigrants who instilled in their ten children the
motivation to achieve and succeed, but at the
same time taught us to open our
hearts and help others to make
our world a better place.*

The Sephardim of Sydney

Coping with Political Processes and Social Pressures

NAOMI GALE

sussex
ACADEMIC
PRESS

BRIGHTON • PORTLAND

Copyright © Naomi Gale, 2005

The right of Naomi Gale to be identified as author of this work has been asserted in accordance with the Copyright, Designs and Patents Act 1988.

2 4 6 8 10 9 7 5 3 1

First published 2005 in Great Britain by
SUSSEX ACADEMIC PRESS
Box 2950
Brighton BN2 5SP

and in the United States of America by
SUSSEX ACADEMIC PRESS
920 NE 58th Ave   Suite 300
Portland, Oregon 97213-3786

All rights reserved. Except for the quotation of short passages for the purposes of criticism and review, no part of this publication may be reproduced, stored in a retrieval system, or transmitted, in any form or by any means, electronic, mechanical, photocopying, recording or otherwise, without the prior permission of the publisher.

British Library Cataloguing in Publication Data
A CIP catalogue record for this book is available from the British Library.

Library of Congress Cataloging-in-Publication Data
Gale, Naomi.
    The Sephardim of Sydney : coping with political processes and
    social pressures / Naomi Gale.
        p. cm.
    Includes bibliographical references and index.
    ISBN 1-84519-035-1 (hardcover : alk. paper)
1. Jews—Australia—Identity. 2. Sephardim—Australia.
3. Ashkenazim—Australia. 4. Australia—Social conditions.
5. Australia—Ethnic relations. I. Title.
DS135.A882S924 2005
305.892'409441—dc22
                                                                    2004020674
                                                                    CIP

Typeset & Designed by G&G Editorial, Brighton
Printed by The Cromwell Press, Trowbridge, Wiltshire
This book is printed on acid-free paper.

Library
University of Texas
at San Antonio

Contents

List of Tables, Figures and Maps   vii
Preface   viii
Acknowledgements   xiii

I   Ethnicity, the Ethnic Group and Ethnic Identity   I
Research Trends   1
Ethnic Identity: Operational Definitions   2
Acculturation, Assimilation, Pluralism and Multiculturalism   6
Ethclass Subculture   15
Problems of Identity Crisis   17
Summary and Conclusions: Are the Sephardim of Sydney   19
   a Social or an Ethnic group?

2   The Sephardim of Sydney   22
Socio-Ethnic Structure   22
Ethnic Division and the Organizational Structure   24
The Sephardic Communities of the Middle East and Asia   27
   The Jews of Egypt   30
   The Jews of Iraq   35
   Social Changes and Religious Orientation in Iraq,   39
      Egypt and Turkey
   The Jews of India   42
   The Jewish Community in Cochin   42
   The Jews of Bombay   43
   The Jews of Calcutta   45
Summary and Conclusions: Past and Present Degrees of   45
   Communality and Religiosity

3   The Immigration of Sephardic Jews to Australia   47
Australian Immigration Policy   48
The Executive Council of Australian Jewry   50
Summary and Conclusions: Facing up to the Wider   60
   Australian Society

4 The Sephardic Family — 62
The Social Structure — 65
Divorce: Past and Present — 67
Choosing a Partner — 75
Relationships between Family Members — 82
Familial Authority Today — 86
The Socialization of Children — 87
Occupation and Socialization — 89
Kinship Relationships — 92
Summary and Conclusions: Changes in Kinship Ties — 94

5 Residence, Social Mobility and Ethnic Identity — 96
Socio-Geographical Distance and Patterns of Kin Contact — 98
Upward Mobility and "Ashkenization" — 106
Change of Reference Groups — 111
Summary and Conclusions: Becoming a Minority within a Minority — 113

6 Religious Organization and Secular Power — 117
The Rabbi: A Socio-Political Figure — 118
Control of Liturgy — 119
The Clash between Religious Law and Social Norms — 121
Segregation of the Sexes in the Synagogue — 121
Dominance by the Laity: The Sunday School Curriculum — 123
The Naming Ceremony for a Baby Girl — 124
Religious Rituals for the Birth of a Boy — 126
Intergroup Conflict – Intergenerational Power Struggle within the Executive and the Religious Committee — 126
The Generation Gap and Acculturation — 128
The Youth Organization — 128
An Inter-ethnic Conflict — 129
Religious Observance — 130
Summary and Conclusions: The Dilemma of Continuity, Identity and Power — 136

7 Conclusion: A Paradoxical Community — 141
Status Anxiety and Marginality — 142

Appendix: Methods Used in the Collection of Data — 150
Notes — 155
Bibliography — 166
Index — 183

Tables, Figures and Maps

Tables

4.1	Marriage and Divorces among the Sydney Jewish Community	68
4.2	Marriage and Divorces Registered in the Sydney Sephardic Synagogue	72
6.1	Cross Tabulation of Frequency of Synagogue Attendance by Length of Time in Australia	131
6.2	Jewish Ritual Observance	133
6.3	Cross Tabulation of Age and Ritual Observance	134

Figures

2.1	Ethnic Division	23
4.1	Marriage and Divorces among the Sydney Jewish Community	69
	Patterns of Interaction:	
5.1	The Sadik Family	103
5.2	The Shasha Family	104
5.3	The Zamir Family	105
6.1	Cross Tabulation of Frequency of Synagogue Attendance by Length of Time in Australia	132

Maps

5.1	Sephardic Residence in the Eastern Suburbs	100
5.2	A Typical Pattern of Family Dispersion	101

Preface

The natural attractiveness of Sydney is amplified by the diversity of its population, which comprises immigrants from the Far East and the Middle East, from northern and southern Europe, as well as English-speaking countries. Indeed, over the past fifty years, Sydney has developed into a truly multicultural community, each group choosing its own territory and building its own ethnic, social and religious institutions.

The Sydney Jewish community is dynamic and vibrant, with many communal, social and religious institutions. Of the 110,000 Jews who live in Australia, fifty thousand live in Sydney, and about five thousand of them are Sephardim, or Jews from Spanish and Arabic-speaking lands. The Sephardic community differs little from the city's other ethnic groups, in that members of each community have congregated in their own areas. In the early days of the Sephardic immigration, the newcomers lived in the inner western and northern suburbs of the city, but its members have began gravitating toward the lower- and middle-class eastern suburbs, where a majority of Sydney's Ashkenazi Jews live. However, as most Sephardim are in the lower- and lower-middle classes, their largest concentration is still in Sydney's international and multicultural inner-city "ethnic belt," where lower-class pockets allow many immigrants to make their home.

There are twenty-one Orthodox, two ultra-Orthodox Hasidic and two Progressive or reform congregations in Sydney, as well as several Jewish schools attached to these congregations. A majority of these are located in the eastern part of the city, where the Jewish population is concentrated. Thus, over 40 percent of Jewish children attend congregational schools. The Orthodox Moriah, Massada and Mount Sinai colleges cater to children from kindergarten age through high school. Liberal Jews send their children to the Emanuel School, and Yeshivah College caters to Sydney's Hassidic community. About 50 percent of the Sephardic youth attend Yeshivah College, with another 10 percent going to Moriah College. In addition, the Jewish Board of Education plays an active role in seeing that Jewish students in the eastern suburbs' state schools – where they form a high percentage of the population – receive some form of Jewish education at school. The Board also runs Sunday schools in congregational halls and synagogues to teach about Judaism and instill Jewish pride in the next generation.

The Jewish community of Sydney is a very vibrant group. It is not only active, but it is generally recognized that its members contributed to the development of post-war Australia, disproportionate to their small numbers, especially in the economy, the media and academia.

What particularly struck me upon my arrival in Sydney in mid-1979 was the small number of Sephardim in Australia – about 7 percent of the Sydney Jewish community and only about 4 percent of the Jewish population in Australia. I had come from Israel where, at the time of this research, Sephardim accounted for well over 65 percent of the Jewish population. It was questions about their immigration, integration and intra-Jewish relations into such an overwhelming "other" community that led me to study the Sephardim of Sydney. From them I learned a great deal about Jews in the Diaspora and the intricacies of their relationship to one another.

The current work deals with the Sephardic community of Sydney – their history, their experiences as new immigrants in a host society, as well as the changes they have undergone since they arrived in Sydney. A prime purpose is to evaluate their position and self-evaluation *vis-à-vis* the Ashkenazi Jewish and larger Australian society.

There is no doubt that the history and traditional lifestyle of Sephardim in their countries of origin – Iraq, Egypt and India – have influenced the extent to which they have been able or willing to adapt to Australian society. The fact that most of them have emigrated from non-Western countries has made the transition to a more sophisticated society slow and painful. This, together with their experiences in the new country, has obstructed their ability to acculturate and successfully integrate into the Australian way of life. This incapacity has been a crucial factor in the poor image their ethnic group has developed among the larger society as well as in their own feelings of marginality.

The manifestations of marginality and unworthiness uncovered in this study result not only from the Sephardim's relationship with Australian society, but from that with their Ashkenazi co-religionists as well. Australia's ethnic communities, particularly those that are visibly ethnic, generally suffer from alienation. This is the case with the majority of first-generation Australians, who do not share their parents' experiences of the old countries and wish to be considered one hundred percent Australian, but who are nevertheless still viewed as belonging to the same category as their parents.

The usual method of studying ethnic groups is to examine their position *vis-à-vis* the host society. The influence of this interaction is crucial to the formation and redefinition of their identity in the host society. What makes the Sephardic group so sociologically interesting is that they constitute an immigrant community whose members share some cultural features but differ from each other in a great many ways. For this reason, we view the Sephardim of Sydney as a social rather than an ethnic group. This does not imply that there is a conflict between "ethnic" and "social" (by definition, all ethnic groups are social groups, but not all social groups are ethnic groups). It does, however, emphasize the cultural heterogeneity of the Sephardim in Sydney, whose members share diacritical cultural features – primarily religion.

This work also differs from studies of other ethnic groups in that the Sephardim represent a minority within a minority: a small group of Oriental Jews within a larger pool of those with European backgrounds. Thus, the changes in the Sephardic social and religious institutions in the new social order are viewed through the prism of their relationship to both the Ashkenazim and the larger Australian society, that is, the Anglo-Saxons, whom I view as the second reference group for the Sephardim, after the Ashkenazim. However, while the direction of acculturation is largely toward the Ashkenazi community, Sephardim rejected by this reference group seek acceptance by the larger society. Thus, in terms of degree of acculturation or assimilation, the Ashkenazim may also be viewed as a buffer between the Sephardim and Australian society.

The main theme that arises throughout this study is the rejection, marginality and negative ethnic identity of Sydney's Sephardic Jews, an internal rejection that denotes a repudiation and denial of their cultures and traditions, which in turn contributes to their negative self-identity – an individual psychological state that results in negative implications for the group as a whole. What the study really delineates, then, is a triple rejection: by the Ashkenazim, by the Australians (who treat the Sephardim as Asians due to their physical characteristics), and by themselves. In the end, the internal and external rejections cannot be separated, for members of rejected groups cannot develop a positive image of themselves unless their own sense of personal worth and the environment's evaluation of them (as they perceive it) strengthen each other.

Most Sephardic identity problems derive from and are enhanced by the lack of agreement and commonality within the group itself, which stem from the group encompassing several different ethnic backgrounds, with different histories and traditions. This not only makes it difficult for them to present themselves as one united group to the larger society, but also prevents them from manipulating their norms, customs and traditions to gain acceptance by the Ashkenazim, whose background and therefore lifestyle is so very different. Thus, while focusing on the changes in their ethnic identity, this study also evaluates the conceptualization of the Sephardic identity in both traditional and modern societies.

Chapter 1 briefly discusses the theory and history of ethnicity in Australia, the United States and Israel, with a brief explanation of the Canadian experience. The conditions under which ethnic groups can successfully acculturate and assimilate into a host society are examined. An explanation is put forward to show why, despite the fervent desire of most Sephardim to acculturate and be counted as Australians, their success in accomplishing this has been limited – particularly for those of Asian appearance. This issue has been rendered particularly relevant since 1988, when a move to restrict Asian immigration began to occupy a prominent position in the Australian media.

The Sephardic community of Sydney is introduced in **chapter 2**, along with the history of the group before immigration to Australia, beginning in 1850. The socio-religious structure of the community in their countries of origin is discussed in terms of its minority status and its members' relationship to the larger society.

Chapter 3 deals with the immigration of Sephardim to Australia, highlighting their struggle to gain entry. This struggle is reflected through the community's relationship to the Ashkenazi community and to Australian society of the late 1940s and early 1950s.

Chapter 4 illustrates the changes within the Sephardic family after immigration to Australia, highlighting practices of marriage and divorce. Comparison of the old familial patterns with the new highlights the increased status of women in the Australian situation and the consequent waning of the husband/father's absolute authority, as well as the effect that this has on familial and marital relationships.

Chapter 5 looks at the relationship between upward residential mobility and the weakening of Sephardic identity. The family cases studied underline the socio-economic division among members of each family and illustrate how degree of economic success has influenced social relationships among siblings.

Chapter 6 examines the religiosity of Sydney's Sephardim as compared with their degree of Orthodoxy in the countries of origin. The power struggle for religious supremacy is shown to take place on many levels: between old and young; among Orthodox, traditionalists and the non-religious; as well as among different ethnic groups within the community itself, whereby leaders of, for example, the Iraqis and the Indians each endeavor to gain social superiority through religious supremacy.

The concluding **chapter 7** relates the material presented to the main argument: it explains why Sydney's Sephardic Jews experience difficulty in acculturating and assimilating into Australian society, and in being accepted by the larger Jewish community. It seems that the primary reason is their poor self-image, which has been enhanced by the rejection at the hands of both these groups.

An Appendix provides information on the research method adopted, the time period of the research (1979–89), and the results obtained.

Acknowledgements

I received encouragement and support from many people within Sydney University and outside it, and I am indebted to all of them. I would like, first, to thank Dr. Richard Basham, who encouraged me throughout. Richard Basham played an important part in the completion of the doctoral thesis on which this book is based. His mastery of anthropological concepts and his continual constructive criticism helped me formulate my ideas and clarify my thoughts. I thank him for his unlimited patience and the valuable knowledge I have gained from him.

I am also indebted to the late Professor Peter Lawrence, who read parts of my thesis, and who assisted me as co-supervisor while Dr. Basham was on leave. I wish to extend my thanks to Professor Michael Allen, who at the time of this research was the head of the Department of Anthropology for his constructive comments.

I owe special thanks to members of the Sephardic community of Sydney for opening their hearts and conveying intimate details of their lives. To this particular group I wish to express my gratitude and thanks. I also wish to thank them for their hospitality, for accepting my family and for their wonderful friendship, which I hope will continue for many years.

I would also like to mention Dr. Myer Samra, a prominent member of the community who also researched the Sydney Sephardic community. We conducted our fieldwork at the same time, albeit independently of each other.

I would like to thank the Ashkelon Academic College for its contribution and in particular I would like to mention Professor Moshe Mannie – President of the college, Professor Shimon Sharvit – Academic Head, and Adv. Pinchas Haliwa – Director general.

The material on which this work is based was gathered between 1979 and 1986 through participant observation and formal and informal interviews, and has been substantiated by a "blind" questionnaire largely based on Encel and Buckley's 1972 study of the Jewish community in New South Wales. The theoretical material is based on data residing in the Australian National Archive, the Judaica Archive, and the Australian Bureau of Statistics, as well as the libraries at universities in Australia and Israel.

My fieldwork benefited greatly from the willingness of Sydney's Sephardic Jews to open their hearts and minds to me and for allowing me into their community as both participant and observer. I have taken all reasonable care to disguise the identities of those who trusted me with the details of their lives. Therefore, I have used pseudonyms in all chapters except for some sections of chapter 3, which deals with the immigration of Sephardim to Australia and utilizes information from the Australian Archives, since this information had already been released under the Freedom of Information Act.

The Sephardim of Sydney

Coping with Political Processes and Social Pressures

1

Ethnicity, the Ethnic Group and Ethnic Identity

Research Trends

Over the past several decades, ethnicity has developed into a major academic concern.[1] This chapter explores past and contemporary theories of immigration and current empirical research on ethnic Sephardic communities, and in particular the emergence of ethnic enclaves within the Sephardim in Sydney and the source of conflict and tension amongst the various ethnic groups within the Sephardic community.

Most of the numerous definitions of "ethnicity" and "ethnic group" emphasize common origin, language, cultural tradition[2] and a sense of group continuity.[3] The common usage often equates ethnic with lower-class or marginal minority groups since "everyone in a subordinate position is potentially an ethnic, it being the privilege of the dominant group to assign roles and lay down rules. Dominant groups rarely define themselves as ethnics".[4]

The phenomenon of ethnicity was triggered in the Western world by international migration. It became increasingly important in the political and socio-economic arena. The cultural traditions of groups in the modern world have changed dramatically from their original manifestations in the homelands.

The gaining of power by ethnic groups often serves to strengthen their positive sense of ethnic identity. Those groups for whom the struggle for a place in their society's power structure is futile tend to experience a sense of desperation and a consequent weakening of ethnic group identity. This in turn further discourages individuals from active participation in their group, which promotes negative ethnic identity and feelings of marginality. Such individuals seek other reference groups to fulfill their expectations, even though these groups, too, are likely to reject them. Indeed, Glazer and Moynihan (1975:15) refer to those who "pass out" into another ethnic group – a type of behavior that Peterson-Royce (1982:5) calls "long-term identity switching" or "passing, from an inferior position to improve their situation".

Glazer and Moynihan treat ethnic groups as political or interest groups who use their ethnic identity as a vehicle for political mobilization.[5] In their book *Beyond the Melting Pot,* they emphasized how interest binds members of the group together. Thus, as cultures, languages and, to some extent, religions began to fade away after the second generation of immigrants, ethnic groups reorganize themselves into interest groups. The group develops "new attributes that the original immigrants would never have recognized as identifying their group".[6]

Ethnic Identity: Operational Definitions

There are many definitions of ethnic identity but there is consensus on the two basic concepts: self-identification and identification by others – albeit that scholars are divided on the issue of which of these predominates. Barth (1969:13) terms ethnic identity as "self-ascription" and "ascription by others", emphasizing the former and minimizing the latter. De Vos (1990a) and Roosens (1989a) have paid particular attention to the psychological dimension of ethnic identity. A. L. Epstein (1978:90) views ethnic identity as a product of "the interaction of external and internal perceptions and pressures". Skinner and Hendricks (1979:37) emphasized the "people's choice" influenced by the "larger society". Thus here too the inner and the outer are closely interwoven.

De Vos (1975:17), however, views self-identification as the main factor in defining one's ethnicity. He notes that ethnicity is strongly linked to a "feeling of continuity with the past". De Vos (1990a:18) speaks of "people that share a past", highlighting the role of psycho-cultural factors in building ethnic identity. Rossens (1989a:16) goes even further claiming that, "those who do identify with an ethnic category can find psychological security . . . a feeling of belonging . . . ".

Rhedding-Jones (2001:150) speaks of "Shifting Ethnicities", ethnics whose life style "is of transit and flexibility", who function synchronically in "actual space" and "cyberspace".[7] Children of migrants visit their country of origin, or alternatively are educated in schools where the curriculum highlights their own culture and tradition. Consequently, individuals may feel as part of the majority in the country of origin and as part of the minority in the host society, "'minorities' may be majorities". One may speak of "shifting ethnic identities", because ethnic identity did not disappear as was predicted by many sociologists. On the contrary, ethnic identity persists side by side with the development of national identity; the global added to the local.

In the modern world, globalizations undoubtedly influence our lives. It is possible to find in immigrant societies individuals who have allegiance to three identities: to the country of origin, to the culture that has developed in the host society, and to the national identity of the host society. In the case of Jews, they develop allegiance to the culture of the ethnic group that has developed as a minority in the host society, and to the national identity of the host society. Some Jews, in addition to the above, develop allegiance to Israel, particularly in cases where they were previously refugees.

Ethnic struggle and competition is manifested largely in the areas of property and resource allocation. However, although Glazer and Moynihan continue to emphasize the importance of ethnic groups, they do not deny the ongoing process of assimilation. Moreover, they argue that even though "the cultural content of each ethnic group [has] become very similar to that of the others", the emotional attachment to the ethnic group seems to persist, thus acknowledging the emerging symbolic nature of ethnicity.[8]

With the emergence of a new ethnicity in Israel, many second-generation individuals know little of their culture and tradition, but they maintain a strong sense of belonging to the group.[9] Even in Australia, with a Jewish population of only 110,000, of which about 5,000 are Sephardim,[10] ethnicity plays a role in all state and national elections. Two days prior to the 1987 national election, the Sephardic community celebrated its Silver Jubilee at a cocktail party attended by politicians from both the Labor and the Liberal parties. The political dignitaries posed for photographs for the *Sydney Morning Herald*, the local papers (the *Eastern Herald* and the *Wentworth Courier*) and the *Australian Jewish Times*. They signed the Silver Jubilee Book and mingled with the crowd. Here it is clear that the Sephardim received as much publicity as the politicians. The Sephardim also benefited from the presence of political power brokers to enhance their image as an organized ethnic interest group.[11]

Bell and Newby (1975:156) regards ethnicity as a confusing term and an oblique social force,[12] and Jupp (1988:163) views it as "a slippery sociological concept". And O. Patterson argues that "most definitions . . . have been descriptive and static". In sum, ethnicity is "a confusing approach because it emphasizes culture and tradition as the critical elements, which "are of no intrinsic interest from a dynamic structural perspective". In other words what is important about the Jews in immigrant societies "is not their worship but the function of these rituals for the group" that "sustains and enhances identity . . . and establishes social networks and communicative patterns of behaviour".[13]

Similarly, A. L. Epstein and others[14] argue that the meaning attached to the practices and the function they fulfill for the ethnics are important. Thus, for a Jew, membership in the synagogue symbolizes affiliation with the group and enhances Jewish identity, utilizing the use of religious symbols.

A. Cohen (1974:ix) suggests an operational definition of "ethnic group" that emphasizes interaction as a major component in the existence of such groups.

Although Glazer and Moynihan, and A. Cohen, note that ethnic groups are interest groups, Cohen stresses the political aspects of ethnicity whereas the former focus on economic interest. All, however, view the political and economic aspects of ethnicity as closely related, and all offer an analysis of "ethnic groups" that emphasizes the perpetuation of religious rituals by minority groups in primarily secular societies,[15] which fulfill a social function. Thus whereas in the past Passover fulfilled a mainly religious function and was observed as a religious ritual, for the majority of today's Jews it serves more as a social function and an affirmation of Jewish identity.

While A. Cohen clearly stresses the instrumental aspects of ethnicity, he equates it with religion, arguing that religion is an ideal vehicle for mobilizing secular interests. However, in making this equation, he risks confusing "ethnicity" with "social group". One may argue that, unlike most other groups, the Jews represent a special case since their historical relationship with both Christians and Muslims has placed them in a status more akin to race or caste than to ethnicity. One may also argue that culture is the most important concept for most people and that religion is not necessarily ethnically exclusive. The Jews are unique because religion is the main component of their definition of their ethnic identity. Even when Jews choose to minimize their Jewish identity, "others" do identify them and refuse to let them "escape" this identity. Only in Israel, where "Jewishness" is the assumed norm, is ethnicity more salient socially than religion.[16]

A. L. Epstein (1978:95) disagrees with the assumption derived from A. Cohen and Glazer and Moynihan – that ethnic behavior is governed by rational calculation. According to him, this behavior expresses the degree of affection rooted in the unconscious.[17]

In his classic discussion *Ethnic Groups and Boundaries,* Barth (1969:14) stresses the boundary that separates groups rather than the "cultural stuff". "[T]he fact that 'dichotomization between members and outsiders' continues, highlights the importance of ethnic boundaries not the 'cultural stuff'".However Barth's position, that "an ethnic group is whatever anybody says it is", is extremely ambiguous. For, "anybody" can include both members of the group in question and outsiders. According to him, the "common culture" should be viewed as "an implication or result, rather than a primary and definitional character-istic of ethnic group organization". Evidently, he does not give culture much importance.[18]

In her criticism of Barth, Peterson-Royce (1982:7) argues that Barth stresses "boundaries at the expense of content". She adopts the "middle ground", that is one should examine content and boundary, symbols and behavior, since boundaries cannot be maintained without symbols, and "a symbol system without boundaries cannot continue to exist."

In his criticism of Barth, Van den Berghe (1981:18) opts for analysis based on structural reality as perceived by the outsider, rather than on the psychological reality of those involved. For example, in the early stage of its formation, many Sephardim resented being lumped together as "Sephardim" with other "Oriental Jews". Nevertheless, as time passed, some have internalized their social position as ethnics in the light of how they are viewed by Australians and Ashkenazim. Today the "psychological reality" of the majority of Sydney's Sephardim seems to coincide with academic "structural reality", and counter to Australian and Ashkenazi perceptions: they do not see themselves as an ethnic group – and this study therefore does not view them as such. The minority who have accepted and internalized a self-perception as an ethnic group are, for the most part, members of the NSW Association of Sephardim. Moreover, even though the members of this small group view themselves as ethnics, they cannot agree on a common goal, or on policy and division of power. What seems to bind them together is the mere fact that they are not of Ashkenazi origin. However, these factors do not constitute a sufficient basis for viewing them as an ethnic group.[19]

The difficulty with Barth's position is that one can find many indi-viduals within the Sephardic community who would willingly "pass" for either Ashkenazim or "old" Australians, even though they have not yet been accepted socially by the Ashkenazim. The question, then, is whether we should accept self-identification as an Ashkenazi as the reality, or whether it is not necessary for the Ashkenazim to accept Sephardim socially before the latter can be considered as such. Of course, Barth might reason that he is speaking not merely of individual identification, by those involved, but of "group" consensus, following Durkheimian notions.[20]

This leads us to Warner's study (1963:38–45) that defines class based on *participation in*, and *acceptance by*, the *reference group*. According to Warner, participation in the activities of a chosen reference group does not imply an automatic acceptance by that group's members. Warner's thesis of social stratification also seems to suit ethnic classification. For, just as a person who is born into the lower classes finds difficulty in being accepted into higher classes, when he or she has succeeded in attaining the financial wherewithal that would seem to warrant this, a person born into an ethnic group, who achieves high standing within the community, cannot change ethnic origin, particularly for ethnics who are visibly different from the group of their choice.

Van den Berghe (1981:xi, 6) views ethnicity and race as extensions of kinship. His definition of ethnicity is based on a combination of genetic and environmental factors and includes culture as an important part of the environment: an "impressive bag of tricks . . . ".

Consequently, in the competition for resources ethnic groups become political, social and economic forces. However, there is some doubt whether a person will act in accordance with his "ethnic" interests when these clash with his other interests.

Acculturation, Assimilation, Pluralism, Multiculturalism

Scholarly theories can be divided broadly into three groups: (1) assimilation, (2) pluralism and (3) symbolic ethnicity. In recent years there has been a salient trend of multiculturalism theory propelled by academics and politicians.

The "Anglo-conformity", an assimilative theory, assumes that immigrants should renounce their ancestral culture in favor of the behavior and values of the Anglo-Saxon core group. This would mean migrants would eventually leave the ethnic institutions and enclaves that they tended to establish upon arrival. In Australia, as in America earlier, immigrants were expected to assimilate into the Anglo-Celtic culture, and in Israel Sephardim were expected to assimilate into the established Ashkenazi culture.

Anglo-conformists in America attempted to strip immigrants of their "native culture and attachments and make [them] over into an American along Anglo-Saxon lines – all this to be accomplished with great rapidity". It was an attempt at pressure-cooking assimilation.[21] With regard to acculturation, it seems that this goal "has been achieved partially" with regard to acculturation, "especially with the children of the immigrants [where] this process has been overwhelmingly triumphant".[22] Indeed, acculturation of the young was so triumphant in immigrant societies that often the young were alienated from their family and their tradition. Similar processes took place in other migrant societies as Australia and Israel.[23]

In America, Australia and Israel cultural assimilation was quite successful over the generations. However, structural assimilation did not take place to the same degree.[24] For, instead of allowing the immigrants entry into their organizations, institutions and clubs, the WASP excluded them along with other ethnics. This in America not only militated against Anglo-conformity, but also encouraged ethnic minorities to establish equivalent social organizations such as B'nai Brith and Jewish hospitals to accommodate Jewish doctors who were unable to attain positions at most other hospitals.[25] The Anglo-conformists were most successful in promulgating behavioral assimilation. Nevertheless, complete assimilation was not possible without massive structural changes in ethnic institutions.[26]

The Australian experience was similar to the Americans' when Australia was bound-up in the preservation of the European standards of living, institutions and traditions.[27]

In the aftermath of World War II more than three million immigrants settled in Australia. This represented an even higher percentage of Australia's total population than was experienced by the United States in the late nineteenth and early twentieth centuries. Yet, despite this, Australians expect immigrants to conform to the mixture of English–Irish–Scots cultural pattern, which has dominated Australian society.[28]

Israel has not escaped absorption problems. The *Zionist Record* of 4 May 1954 noted that, "For the vast majority of new arrivals immigration to Israel meant a complete revolution in their lives". Cahnman (1965:210) argues that European settlers – including a good part of the academic community – believed that immigrants to Israel should abandon their customs and traditions in favor of those of the "veteran" community (*yishuv*).[29] "Ethnics" were encouraged actively to deny their origins and identity and even change their names. For example, a Lebanese woman told me how she came to be known as Leah. Born in Turkey with the name Lulah, her parents immigrated to Lebanon when she was very young. When she began school in Beirut, her Muslim teacher told her parents that Lulah had an "unusual un-Arabic sound" and suggested the name Liela, a common Arabic name. She was called Liela until the early 1960s, when she was thirteen years old and the family immigrated to Israel. Her Israeli teacher then suggested that, now that she lived among Jews, in a Jewish state, she should change her name to one that had a "Hebrew sound". And what better Jewish name was there than a Biblical one like Leah, particularly as it was very similar to her Arabic name. This same phenomenon is evident today in Australia, where most Asian immigrants have adopted English names for use outside their own community.

In general, the first generation of immigrants to the United States, Australia and Israel has attempted to shed visible cultural aspects of its ethnicity such as religious and ceremonial practices and folklore, in the course of behavioral acculturation. Thus, what began as behavioral acculturation ended up with real acculturation for the second genera-tion, resulting in much of their culture and traditions slowly dying. This was a "cultural sacrifice" that they felt was necessary to either achieve occupational mobility, or to prepare the ground for their children. Hence most individuals opted for social mobility and class in lieu of ethnic integrity and identification. Spiro (1955:1243) states that social mobility "is a threat both to the group's social solidarity and to its cultural survival".

The *Melting Pot* theory was advocated by Zangwill (1908) at the begin-ning of the twentieth century, and was based on Turner's (1893) frontier thesis promoting the formation of a composite nationality for the American people. However, the immigrants' experiences showed that this was not the case. Instead, they established a religious-based Melting Pot in which intermarriage took place across national but not religious boundaries.

The Melting Pot was more a political than an academic concept. Political activists adapted this concept to suit their own interests. Clearly, the Melting Pot concept was a popular analogy aimed at expounding one strategy – the preferred strategy for most of the "old" Americans, "old" Australians and "old" Israelis involved in the politics of immigration – to cope with an influx of immigrants. The Melting Pot strategy placed the social hegemony and the political power in the hands of the "Whites" and the dominant group to decide the combina-tion of cultural ingredients that should form the new culture. One must keep in mind that the concept is merely a metaphor.[30]

The *straight-line theory* advocated by Sandberg (1974) suggests that ethnicity has declined throughout the generations, and views accultur-ation and assimilation as secular phenomena in which the final product is the absorption of ethnic groups into the dominant culture. This theory fails to distinguish between religious groups (like the Jews) and national groups (like the Italians and Poles), or between religious and secular cultures. It also does not treat class factors at all. In the view of Warner and Srole and others[31] ethnicity is largely a working-class phenomenon, and the behavior described as "ethnic" is a working-class behavior. This calls the validity of the straight-line theory into question since it assumes homogeneity within ethnic groups and considers all such groups similar. The Sephardim of Sydney, in this context, have seen themselves and were seen by others as lower class. The same division occurs in Israel. As Weingrod (1965:39) puts it: "Ashkenazim are ranked higher than . . . Sephardim. To come from Poland or Britain is, 'ipso facto' to be more prestigious than to have one's origins in Egypt or Iraq. This rift is fundamental, and it runs throughout the society."[32]

Stressing the importance of religion and culture Gans (1979:2–3) notes that in the Western world, "While acculturation and assimilation have affected both sacred and secular cultures, they have affected the latter more than the former". Patterns of religious observance have changed, and there has been a decrease, particularly among Jews.

Glazer and Moynihan (1970) and Abramson (1973) criticize the straight-line theorists for having predicted the eventual absorption of ethnic groups when in fact the opposite has been the case. For, not only are ethnic cultures and ethnic institutions still functioning, ethnic groups continue to act as political interest groups, and ethnic pride and identity remain strong in America, Israel, Canada and Australia. Herberg (1955) agrees that ethnic differences tend to disappear in the third generation, resulting in religious identity without ethnic–national identity. This resulted in a kind of triple Melting Pot: Catholic, Jewish and Protestant in which religion fulfills an important social function among the third generation after the ethnic groups and residential sub-communities have disintegrated.[33] Lenski (1961:40), who tested Herberg's generation thesis, found that only among Jews was the second generation less religiously active than its parents were. Second-generation white Protestants attended church with the same frequency as their parents, and Catholics "showed a marked increase in attendance over the first [generation]". He claimed that the prevalent pattern was of increasing religious activity linked with increasing Americanization and decreasing ethnicity.

It seems that what Lenski took for "religious involvement" was membership in religious organizations rather than actual involvement in and observance of religious traditions. However, while increased levels of synagogue or church membership may be significant, this in itself does not suffice to demonstrate an increase in religiosity. For example, about seven hundred and forty people belong to one of the Sephardic congregations in Sydney, but only about sixty of them attend services every Sabbath.[34] While the gathering of people during such important holidays as Passover may fulfill a religious function for some, for the majority it is primarily a social duty. By assuming there is one pattern that operates in the same way for all groups, and to which all groups respond in a similar fashion, we ignore the dynamics of change.

The difficulty in accepting Lenski's conclusion parallels with the major differences between pluralism and "symbolic ethnicity". Whereas *pluralism* suggests maintenance of the ethnic group, and even increasing ethno-religious behavior, *symbolic ethnicity* implies the utilization of religious and ethnic symbols to express distinctiveness. Thus, whereas pluralism may attempt to demonstrate the persistence of ethnicity, symbolic ethnicity suggests that ethnic identity persists but that ethnicity – in the sense of cultural content – does not.

During the past few decades, the concept of "pluralism" has been central to the discussion emphasizing the tolerance of cultural heterogeneity. But the terms ethnics and ethnicity are defined by the superior perception of dominant groups. Consequently, dominant groups have the political power to propagate those values that best serve their interests. As Guilleremo (1995) argues, while the valorization of cultural diversity is important, it is necessary to examine its application. He claims that:

> This is an illusion . . . If the rubric of cultural diversity will only function as an ideological smokescreen to conceal more sophisticated forms of politico-economic domination and racism, then certainly it will prove beneficial only to some but deleterious to the interests of large, dominated populations in different countries all over the world.

Some scholars use "cultural pluralism" referring to the preservation of the immigrant culture.[35] Others focus on "structural pluralism" or the persistence of communal structures and organizations that enable the separate functioning of ethnic groups. Finally, some scholars distinguish between so-called "traditional" and the "new" ethnicity in which the "new" represents ethnic symbols selectively chosen from tradition.[36]

According to Gordon, immigrants become completely assimilated after several generations, because cultural pluralism cannot survive without structural pluralism, however, in the end cultural assimilation eventually occurs.[37] Consequently, what ethnic groups are left with is structural pluralism only at the organizational and institutional level – of churches, synagogues, Jewish schools, Christian clubs, etc. – to limit structural assimilation and intermarriage. Thus, structural pluralism is the major key to the understanding of the ethnic make-up of immigrant societies – what matters in identifying ethnic groups is not their culture, which disappears, but the boundaries that distinguish them from others.[38]

G. J. Patterson (1979) argues that the "new ethnicity" is not a true revival or survival of ethnic culture, since acculturation has stripped away much of the authentic culture. What the new ethnicity does evince is the emergence of ethnic symbols derived from old cultural patterns. Schneider expresses it strongly by referring to "cultural markers" as "symbols empty of elaborate social distinctions . . . maintaining a distinct cultural symbolic identity as markers".[39]

A considerable amount has been written on the subject of pluralism and multiculturalism in Australia.[40] While Zubrzycki (1968:27) advocates a modest commitment to cultural diversity by encouraging the study of the culture of Australia's immigrants, he makes it clear that structural assimilation is the ultimate goal. However, although Grassby's (1973a) comprehensive work, *A Multicultural Society for the Future,* promoted cultural pluralism, this program was followed only in the area of education. As Martin (1978:55) notes, "No official statement has gone on to develop the position that [Grassby] sketched out". Walter Lippman (1979:37–45) – chairing the Commonwealth Committee on Community Relations, cautiously supported the "pluralistic concept of integration", recommending that community relations should be restructured so dominant groups can play an active role in the encouragement of cultural and social diversity within the context of national unity. This is to enable ethnic groups to establish their own cultural and social structures, achieving the ends of pluralistic integration.

The pluralists viewed what had been considered problems inherent in assimilation, in terms of race and ethnic relations. Thus, Martin (1976:26) coined the term "robust pluralism" to denote a "cultural pluralism [that] is dependent on some kind of structural pluralism" and to distinguish from "emasculated pluralism", i.e., ethnic solidarity developed to counter the hostile attitudes of the host society. On the other hand, "genuine ethnic pluralism" is based on promoting a distinct ethnic identity out of ethnic pride.[41]

In general, the pluralistic model predicts acculturation, at the same time as it assumes that groups will remain structurally separated. This process differs from that expected in the Anglo-conformity and Melting Pot models, in that group boundaries persist even though acculturation takes place.

Gans (1979:7) coined the term "symbolic ethnicity", to explain trends in American ethnicity. He argues that people tend to use religious and cultural symbols to express ethnic distinctiveness. Accordingly, although pluralism may indicate the persistence of ethnicity, "symbolic ethnicity" suggests that ethnic identity may persist but ethnicity does not. Hence, symbolic ethnicity fills the vacuum in the acculturated world of the second and third generations. The symbols borrowed from the "real culture" of the old country allow individuals and groups to sustain only symbols that are crucial to the manifestation of their ethnic identity. Roosens (1989a:19) goes even further by defining "symbolic ethnicity" as "ethnicity that manifests itself superficially and temporarily, to the comprehensive commitment of the ethnic leader figure who professionally organizes the interethnic struggle".

According to these authors, the search for identity is a necessary factor for a sense of orientation in a highly sophisticated world in which anonymity dominates most spheres of life and when interaction with others is largely restricted to secondary relationships. They see ethnic persistence only as a matter of individual choice only.

While symbolic ethnicity cannot exist without the freedom to express one's ethnicity in one's own way, "the most important factor in the development of symbolic ethnicity was probably the awareness . . . that neither the practice of ethnic culture nor participation in ethnic organizations were essential to being and feeling ethnic".[42] Gans seems confident that society will continue to encourage such ethnicity.

Roosens (1989a:19–20) emphasizes the elasticity of the expression "ethnic identity", as ethnic symbols which combined socio-cultural and psychological characteristics and are manipulated as such.

As in America and in Australia, there was a period when the Melting Pot ethos was also fashionable in Israel. When this ethos failed, ethnicity and pluralism were glorified in popular and academic writing. These periods were followed by an increased role being assigned to symbolic ethnicity. In the early years of mass immigration, Israeli authorities made every effort to denigrate persistent ethnic pluralism, especially in the education system, where an attempt was made to "melt" the cultures of approximately eighty ethnic groups into one "Israeli culture".[43] This indoctrination of the children in schools generated a wide gap between children and their parents, and led to confusion as to what "Israeli culture" really was. Was it the culture and way of life brought from Russia by the first groups of modern pioneers? Was it European-Jewish culture? Or should it perhaps be a new amalgamation that allowed room for Sephardic customs as well?[44] In a similar fashion, Rhedding-Jones (2001) demonstrates how white dominated pedagogical fields and anti-minority practices go unremarked. It appears quite clearly in the three societies that whites dominate people of color. The latter are more softly named as ethnic minorities.[45]

When it became apparent that neither the "Ashkenazi conformity" nor the Melting Pot model was working, Israeli leaders sought the somewhat more appealing concept of pluralism, which fulfilled the need for self-identity and unity of the nation. "Ethnic revival" at the beginning of the 1970s was encouraged by Israeli politicians and by government policies, much as Stein and Hills (1977:182) found was the case in America: "Whereas one's ethnic origins might once have been a source of shame, that shame has now become, under the cult of ethnicity, transfigured into a radiant pride."

While mass immigration in the 1940s turned Australia into a much more ethnically diversified country than it had been,[46] the ethnics of other than Anglo-Saxon ancestry still represent a clear minority. Blainey claims that about 75 percent of Australia's population was born either in Australia or in the United Kingdom, or have at least one parent of British stock. In contrast, a 1980s Department of Immigration, Local Government and Ethnic Affairs report states that only 26.1 percent of Australia's population was born in other countries.[47] Thus, Blainey, it seems, underestimated the number of people whom he defines as of Anglo-Saxon stock. In light of Australia's very small non-white population – including the 250,000 Aborigines who constitute 1.4 percent of the population – it turns out to be not such a diverse society, especially when compared with the United States or Israel. Nonetheless, the popular conception within Australia is that it is a diverse society. As Stannard (1987:74–75) puts it:

> We are no longer a predominantly Anglo society, at least in the population mix. And yet, in our institutions and structures that is not fully reflected . . . There is a growing acceptance that other people, Asian people, do have something to offer. It's not a total acceptance and probably never will be.

Martin (1976: 21) noted that the myth of Australian pluralism afforded those in power a means of avoiding embarrassing questions related to access to power. It enabled the reply that "members of ethnic minorities participate in the political process as 'individuals'" – and they enjoy equal rights as individuals but not as members of ethnic groups. In other words, Australian politicians attempted to foster the myth, that ethnic pluralism and multiculturalism were encouraged. Martin, however, noted a quite different reality: migrants of non-English-speaking origin rarely occupy decision-making positions, and pluralism is tolerated because of mutual ignorance.[48]

The origin of *multiculturalism* in Australia was associated with issues of equity. Multiculturalism rejected not only the attempt to promote amalgamation of culture, but also the need for Anglo-Saxon superiority and the conformity to English-oriented cultural patterns. In Zubrzycki's (1995) view, multiculturalism can contribute to the social fabrics of the Australian society.

> Ethnic groups often provide people with a sense of belonging, which can make them better able to cope with a new society . . . Ethnic loyalties . . . do not, detract from wider loyalties to community and country . . . therefore . . . migrants should be encouraged . . . to preserve and develop their culture . . . can become living elements in the diverse nature of Australian society.[49]

The attempt to follow Canada's multiculturalism policy was made in 1973 by Al Grassby the then Minister for immigration, who spoke of a multi-cultural ideology highlighting pluralism and diversity. This was followed in 1977 by the announcement of Australia as a Multicultural Society, emphasizing equality of opportunity, and cultural identity.

In contrast to this optimistic spirit about multiculturalism, others stated that it is difficult to balance between ethnic identities and national identity. Furthermore, in my opinion, national identity has become an instrument of hegemony and dominance, of inclusion and exclusion by ruling groups. Guillermo[50] (1995) argued that the ruling political/ economic elite gives the dominant definition of multiculturalism, having the power to marginalize, oppress, and diminish the rights of particular groups, therefore perpetuating inequality. In her view there is a need to dismantle the old power structures, which would be followed by development of political consciousness within ethnic communities – only then will ethnics enjoy equal rights and relative autonomy within the national framework, resisting full assimilation.

At the beginning of the third millennium, one might say that multiculturalism is a reality. It is not a policy, which treats all cultures as equal; it is rather a strategy that promotes that ethnic groups should live side by side – a society which can accommodate and respect differences. Those who advocate multiculturalism argue that in this era of global migration, the world must reconcile cultural diversity with national goals, because this is the only constructive way of building a nation. That means that multiculturalism advocates the perpetuation of identity of minorities within a national identity.

Multiculturalism nevertheless has its drawbacks. In the name of multiculturalism, dominant groups categorize ethnic groups in the allocation of power. Rhedding-Jones (2001:146) put it even more robustly by stating that, "In racist discourses of ethnic disadvantage, dominant whites, non-immigrants and Christians [and I would add Ashkenazim] see themselves as the norm against which all others must measure up." In Australia, a metaphor was created for non-white, the "native" that represents the "other", which was to establish institutional hegemony of the whites. Consequently "native" becomes all persons who are not white and they are forced into subordination. In the case of Sephardim, it is clear that this dichotomy of "us" and "other" drew a wedge between Ashkenazim and Sephardim in the same way it did during the most formative years of the State of Israel. In Australia and in Israel all these dichotomies had strong political connotations in terms of superiority–inferiority relations between "them" and "us"; between white and non-white; between "us" and "natives",[51] and all in the name of multiculturalism and ethnic and cultural diversity.

Hirst (1990) differentiates between "soft" and "hard" multiculturalism. By "soft" he means the tolerance displayed in Australia toward migrants, and on the other hand the satisfaction of observing migrants participating in Australian life. "Hard" multiculturalism means an active governmental policy to correct wrongdoing and provide support as the policy for migrant cultures. By "soft", the author means that the people advocate multiculturalism whereas the government observes the changes and gives little encouragement. By "hard", the author means that multiculturalism is activated by a massive vigorous governmental policy, aiming at narrowing the current gaps between dominant groups and underprivileged migrant ethnic groups.

In contrast Gray (2000:169–85) argues that multiculturalism is the denial of cultural diversity because it aims to preserve the inundated relics "as public spectacles". After all nothing remains stagnant and untouched. Some critics say multiculturalism is destructive, divisive or erodes the nationhood. Migrants lost their cultures and tradition through policies of the host societies, beginning with assimilation, going through melting pot theory and pluralism. However, the structural ethnic boundaries have remained – and in most cases, not because ethnics of the second and third generation wish to preserve them; it is because they were and still are excluded by the dominant hegemonic political groups, who preferred to exclude members of these groups from the ruling power. In short, multiculturalism arrived too late, and currently it can do more harm the good.

Thus, to conclude, one can see that even within this innovation of multiculturalism, there is no common agreement as to the definition, meaning, principle, purpose or rationale that stands behind these notions.

The above highlights the historical development of theories and definitions of ethnicity, ethnic identity and ethnic groups. It demonstrates that definitions can be extremely elastic, as influenced by place, society, historical concepts and political circumstances.

Ethclass Subculture

According to Gordon's classic study (1964:51–54), when cultural differences disappear, ethnicity (in its new form) combines with class to form an "ethclass" structured society. A. L. Epstein (1978:92) hypothesizes that assimilation and modernization combine to bring about "an increasing emphasis on achievement . . . in the definition of social status".

Ethclass results from the meeting point between vertical stratifications of ethnicity with the horizontal stratifications of social class. Examining the variables of group identity, social participation and cultural behavior, and their manifestation Gordon (1964) finds that (1) social class differences are more important and decisive than ethnic differences; (2) people have a tendency to confine social participation in primary groups and primary relationships to their own social class segment within their own ethnic group – in other words, to the ethclass; and (3) there are two types of group identification: (3.1) a sense of peoplehood, and (3.2) a sense of feeling comfortable only with a particular social class segment of those people.

Gordon concluded (1964:52) that, while people may circumscribe their social activities by ethnic group and social class borders, "the attribution of ethnic group membership by itself is a powerful pattern in our culture – a pattern generated both by pressure from within the ethnic group and from without". He then distinguishes between two types of psychological identification – historical and participational – the former referring to the sense of peoplehood and ethnic culture, and the latter to behavioral similarities. "The only group which meets both of these criteria is people of the same ethnic group and the same social class."[52]

Scholars have generally assumed that once ethnic differences disappeared, class would dominate the social arena and individuals would be mobilized in accordance with their level of achievement rather than ethnic origin. However, as this has not yet happened, what we see is group mobilization along ethnic lines within the class system. This indicates ethnicity is still a relevant force determining boundaries which are meaningful in the power relations between groups and are becoming – whether the individual wants or not – fundamental in individuals' life.[53]

In contrast to "traditional" ethnicity, the "new ethnicity" is perceived as a dynamic phenomenon, which acknowledges ethnic groups' positions and maintains substantial structural differentiation, but can still become highly acculturated to the host society. This can be compared to Rhedding-Jones's (2001) definition of "Shifting Ethnicities", where the urban population includes many who have more than one nation or home. These people "have shifted language and way of being, and have the knowledge and skills of diversity". In her opinion "transnationals and hybrid ethnicities takes up the habits of the "other" and might become the 'other'".

The recent glorification of ethnicity and emphasis on pluralist policies or multicultural policies was largely a reaction to structural problems. Policies toward ethnic minorities were often bound up with longstanding problems with "racial" minorities: American blacks, French Canadians and Israelis of Sephardic background. As Deshen 1975:281–309) and others explicitly maintain, the political focus on ethnicity in the United States was largely a reaction to its racial situation.[54] In Israel, where the attempt to melt Sephardim into the Ashkenazi pot has failed, ethnicity has also become a political issue. In a sense, each of these nations of immigrants has converted the inability to structurally – and in some cases, culturally – assimilate minorities to a virtual as well as a political matter, attempting to reward them by acts of, for example, "positive discrimination".

In Australia and in other western countries there is a trend to recognize the hybridism and the composite characteristic of the ethnic make-ups, by giving a place to "multiculturalism". However, the cultural differences are still "cultivated and polarized, with immigrants and their offspring marginalized and excluded".[55] This type of multiculturalism results in residential segregation, class and ethnic differences, which might relate to poverty.

Problems of Identity Crisis

In any interethnic contact, both groups suffer a certain level of cultural erosion. But when one of the groups involved is small and relatively poor, the erosion is likely to be almost completely one way. Consequently, the group may adopt or develop new social identities.[56]

The situation of the Sephardim in Sydney is considerably different from that of their brethren in Israel. Whereas they have always been regarded as Oriental, Asian or North African Jews – i.e., Sephardim – their appearance often leads to their being identified as Arabs or Indians. This leads many Sephardim to highlight their Jewish identity, as they view the Sephardic identity as more advantageous than the Indian, Arabic or Asian etc.

On arrival in Sydney, my family and I lived in the Eastern Suburbs "Jewish" neighborhood. Since I have a dark complexion, I was advised by an Ashkenazi Jewess, a fellow student, "Jenie", to wear the Star of David in order to make it clear that I was not an Arab.

Nevertheless, the Jewish side of the Sephardic identity can also prove to be a disadvantage. Thus, in the eyes of the Lebanese non-Jews among whom "Alex" worked as a psychologist, he was identified as Muslim because of his oriental look and his Arabic-sounding surname. Alex was often told that he was "one of us". He did not disclose his Jewish religion, especially because he began working with them at the time of the Six-Day War. Alex's appearance and name worked to his advantage. When his identity was disclosed by a medical officer years later, members of the Lebanese community met him with deadly silence, until one of them finally blurted out: "You are still one of us; after all we are brothers. We have the same culture, but not the same religion."

Many Sephardim downplay their Sephardic origins with Ashkenazi Jews, adopting the stance that, "We are all Jews". These Sephardim view their identity as an obstacle to their desperately sought acceptance into Ashkenazi social circles.

Individual Sephardim may stress their ethnic identity in some economic or other social activities where they view it as an asset, but minimize it when it is seen as a liability.[57] Both Deshen and P. Cohen claim that the same is true in Israel. Thus, politicians of North African origin emphasize their identity to gain political power, but when they marry Ashkenazim they usually attempt to downplay their Sephardic identity.[58]

Weber's definition of ethnic identity combines self-identification and identification by others. It is therefore more flexible, and can be manipulated to the advantage of each person. Weber viewed identity as an ongoing process influenced by historical events and by the individual's past and present dynamic interaction with others, rather than as primordial and static.[59] De Vos (1975:18) goes further than Weber by distinguishing between three types of ethnic identity: past-oriented, present-oriented and future-oriented. While he views ethnic identity as essentially subjective he goes on to explain that, "like any form of identity, [it] is not only a question of knowing who one is subjectively, but also of how one is seen from the outside" (1975:37). Similarly, Herberg (1955:25) and Devereux (1975:42) categorize ethnic identity as a form of role attribution in which the internal and external aspects reflect, sustain and illuminate each other.

Cooley (1902:151–52) and Mead (1934:154) stressed the importance of primary groups in the development of individual personality, which is the product of interacting with others, defining it as "looking-glass self": "Each to each a looking-glass reflects the other that doth pass." In *The Presentation of Self in Everyday Life*, Goffman (1959) followed Cooley and Mead, with his similar interpretation of "self" and "other". He also suggested that an identity is the product of the mixture between how society views the individual together with his own conscious ideas about himself.[60]

A. L. Epstein (1978:90) labeled identity a product of the interaction between "external and internal perceptions and pressures", viewing external perceptions as socio-cultural forces external to the group or individual, and internal perceptions as those derived from the individual's own life experience. For Skinner and Hendricks (1979:37), ethnic identity is determined by the people's choice and the influence of categories that have meaning in the larger society. In this context, it seems that a Sephardic living in Sydney has four extra-familial audiences: ethnic groups (Iraqi, Indian, Egyptian or other), Sephardim, Ashkenazim, and Australian society. One's behavior differs considerably depending on the audience for which one is "performing".[61]

From the religious point of view, the Sephardim of Sydney operate within the context of two majority groups: one within Judaism (the Ashkenazim) and the other within the wider Australian society (Anglo-Australians). At different times, they highlight the values and ideas of these groups at the expense of their own values and ideas in order to gain acceptance. What makes this task even more difficult are the internal cultural differences between the ethnic groups within the Sephardic community, who do not agree on what constitutes proper religious conduct.

The negative ethnic identity of Sephardim in both Sydney and Israel has developed partly because of the larger society's negative view of them.[62] There are, however, instances where external factors have promoted a positive sense of identity. In the case of Melbourne's Jewish community, Medding (1968:6–7) strongly suggests that positive in-group solidarity "has thus been reinforced by persecution . . . anti-Semitism, social rejection, and economic and occupational barriers".[63]

For those operating from the psychological vantage point, ethnicity can be best understood by examining the subjective forces that underlie and define group identity, persistence and continuity. To them such forces as social structure and cultural history are insufficient for the understanding of the nature of ethnic identity. Thus, Erikson (1968:205) refers to the "psychological core" of individual self-perception as "primarily an unconscious phenomenon that results from a series of childhood identifications, and passes through the crisis period of adolescence". Dashefsky (1975:12) stated that, "identity is a continuing quest . . . it proceeds at the unconscious as well as the conscious level".

A. L. Epstein (1978), too, denies that ethnic behavior is governed by rational calculation. Like Erickson and Dashefsky, he sees it as rooted in the unconscious. In his view, while strong attachment to one's group may lead to certain types of behavior – including behavior in the political and economic arenas – these do not determine the intensity of an individual's attachment to his or her group; this intensity is rooted in the unconscious. Recognizing the existence of both positive and negative ethnic identities, Epstein suggests (1978:99) that: "Negative identity exists where the image of self rests chiefly on the internalized evaluations of others", whereas "positive identity is built on self-esteem, a sense of worthiness of one's own group's ways and values, which is manifested in one's attachment to them".

In my view, the formation of ethnic identity is based on both sociological and psychological factors. Thus, I believe that positive ethnic identity is the result of inner strength and a positive evaluation of one's identity, in combination with group cohesion, culture, tradition and myth. Negative ethnic identity, on the other hand, is a product of the individual's anxiety about his position and an anomic group structure, as well as the sense that one is following an emasculated or irrelevant cultural tradition.

Summary and Conclusions: **Are the Sephardim of Sydney a Social or an Ethnic Group?**

Unlike cultural groups, the members of social groups need not have a common language, history, culture, shared traditions or territory. Social groups must have a common cause that brings their members together. As time passes, other groups in the society come to accept social groups, until they become independent entities, which their members relate to as a reference group, and outsiders identify them by cause.

In his study of Marx's general and middle-range theories of social conflict, L. Benson (1979:194) speaks of "non-social" and "social" groups, where in "social" he refers to "the quality of relationships among individuals grouped together". Members of social groups are identified by specified attributes that have "some significant degree of association, alliance, sociability, or communality".

Benson divides social groups into three types: interest or associational groups, quasi-communal or limited-communal groups, and communal groups. Mormons, Hasidic Jews and Sephardic Jews are members of communal groups. But in the sociological literature, "cultural group" also refers to one or more of four related kinds of attributes: ethnic, linguistic, religious and territorial. Here one can see a very clear distinction between social and cultural groups, although social groups with some of these attributes can be defined as cultural groups. Benson (1979:195) specified that: "At the least, members of a cultural group share some significant degree of consciousness of kind based upon the previous existence of a distinctive cultural system."

Mercer and Wanderer (1970:122) defined a social group as one with: a mutual awareness among the members; some form of communication among the members; some degree of prediction of the behavior of one another by the members; behavior to some degree regularized according to social norms; some reasonable persistence over time. In other words, they view social groups as being created by people whose behavior is anticipatory and judgmental, unlike ethnic groups into which one is born. Basham (1977:176–84) has drawn parallels between ethnic groups and total institutions, claiming that the former attains its membership through birth. Similarly, Breton and Pinard (1960) argued that, "A person does not belong to an ethnic group category by choice. He is born into it and becomes related to it through emotional and symbolic ties."[64]

Van den Berghe (1981:27) argues that "historical reality" provides a crucial aspect of an ethnic group's self-definition. "Ethnicity can be *manipulated* but not *manufactured, and* ethnicity cannot be created *ex nihilo*." In contrast, as Selvin (1975:348) notes, "for social groups . . . histories are largely irrelevant. In classifying types of groups, all that matters is the observable set of group properties at the moment of constructing the classification."

In my view, the Sephardim of Sydney form a social group whose members have similar ethnic and cultural backgrounds. However, since the cultural and sub-ethnic groups within the community differ from one another, the members of each sub-group have tended to adopt close-knit and tight social relationships within their own group. They have not yet fully come to terms with the fact that other ("European") Jews view them under the classification of Sephardim. This poses problems in their definition of their own identity as Sephardim. In a very real sense, the Sephardim of Sydney constitute a social category rather than an ethnic group; it is their religion with its all-encompassing manifestations that at least led their elders to adopt the solidarity that is generally associated with ethnic groups, in the sense that De Vos and Suarez-Orozco (1990:249) see ethnicity as being group-specific and past-oriented selfhood.

In this respect, the Sephardic community of Sydney is unique. For classical studies of ethnic groups have usually been made on groups with a common origin, common language and common culture (although the culture and language may have disappeared through acculturation). However, although many of them spoke English prior to immigration, the Sephardim of Sydney did not have a common language. And, although there were broad similarities in their cultures, they came from countries with different mores and traditions. Yet, Jews from Iraq, India, Singapore, Burma, Egypt, Spain, Morocco and Yemen have gradually formed a group that some of them characterize as an ethnic group, even though the patterns of community leadership and social organization, as well as Jewish practices and rituals, differed considerably from one homeland community to another.

The question then is, on what basis have the members of these different groups come to form a "group" in Sydney? These were people who were thrown together due to political circumstances and events beyond their control, who sought refuge in Australia. They came together as a group with a non-specific history and unclear goals. Furthermore, they became a group as a result of double rejection by Ashkenazim and the wider Australian society.

In the present work, the Sephardic community of Sydney is viewed as a social category comprised of individuals from different ethnic groups. Since its establishment, there have been numerous conflicts and power struggles among these groups for political power and religious supremacy within the "community" – particularly among the Iraqis and the Egyptians whose cultures differ most markedly. These struggles have resulted in the emergence of an identity crisis at the individual and the communal levels, as well as in concomitant cultural erosion among all Sephardic ethnic groups in Sydney. They have a "brokered history", a corporate history based on the fact of their being outsiders *vis-à-vis* the Ashkenazim. Their lack of a common past, and the rejection they suffer from both Ashkenazim and Anglo-Australians, renders their future as a group very doubtful – especially among the younger generation.

2

The Sephardim of Sydney

After World War II, and following the independence of India in 1947, establishment of the State of Israel in 1948 and the Suez Crisis of 1956, the position of many Jewish communities in Arab lands and in the East became precarious. Many of those uprooted and dislocated belonged to communities more than two thousand years old. Over 800,000 Jews from these countries emigrated during this period. The majority went to Israel, but the families who found their way to Australia settled in Sydney, Melbourne and Adelaide, but mainly in Sydney.

Of the approximately 3,000 Sephardic Jews who lived in Sydney, at the time when this study was conducted 540 belonged to the New South Wales (NSW) Association of Sephardim, and 250 to the Eastern Jewish Association (EJA).[1] The Jewish community of Sydney comprises eighteen Orthodox and two Liberal congregations. Both the NSW Association of Sephardim and the EJA are registered as Orthodox congregations, and both organizations are affiliated with the Orthodox Beth-Din (Jewish Ecclesiastical Court), and seek its jurisdiction when necessary.

Socio-Ethnic Structure

In the context of Australian society, the majority of Sydney's Sephardim would be classified as lower middle class, although a handful of them are engaged in such middle- and upper-class professions as medicine and law. The most common occupations for males are those of bookkeeper and salesperson, and few in these occupations hold executive positions. The majority of women spend the first few years after marriage as housewives. After their children enter school, many return to part-time positions, mostly as salespeople in shops or clerks in offices, although several younger members of the community are teachers.

The large majority of Sydney Sephardim are of either Indian-Iraqi or Egyptian origin. While small numbers migrated from Singapore, Burma, Indonesia and Shanghai, China, all of these are of Iraqi ancestry. Most members of the NSW Association of Sephardim and the Eastern Jewish Association emigrated from India, but their ancestors went to India from Iraq several generations earlier. Many of the ancestors of those who emigrated from Egypt are of Spanish origin, and went to Egypt from Turkey or Italy. Of those who went to Sydney from Egypt, some had resided in Singapore before coming to Australia. The third and smallest group emigrated either directly from Iraq, or from Israel, where they had lived for several years.

Members of the Egyptian group almost invariably regard themselves as superior to the Iraqi and the Indian-born Sephardim. They see their group as more modern and more advanced than the others and form a distinct clique, socializing little with those outside their own group. In addition, they claim "pure" Sephardic heritage because most of them have their origin in Spain. In Egypt, their contact with Muslim locals was limited and, like many upper-class Egyptians, they were highly Europeanized. Although born and brought up in Egypt, they too tended to be more fluent in French, Italian or English than in Arabic.

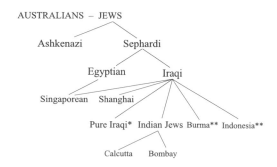

Figure 2.1   Ethnic Division

Members of the Iraqi group who emigrated directly from Iraq consider themselves superior to Indian-Iraqis, whom they regard as a lower class of Jew. In contrast to the Egyptians, Iraqi Jews adhered strictly to their religion, although they were well acculturated into Iraqi society.

There are two distinct divisions within the Indian-Iraqi group: the Calcutta and the Bombay Iraqis. Although the majority of both groups originated in Iraq, the founder, religious leader and first president of the Calcutta Jewish community, Moses Duek Cohen, immigrated to India from Aleppo, Syria. The two groups differ slightly from each other insofar as liturgy: members of the Bombay group adhering to the Iraqi liturgy, while Calcutta Jews follow the liturgy that Cohen brought with him. There are very few Bene-Israel and Cochin families in Sydney.

Figure 2.1 shows the ethnic divisions within the Sephardic community of Sydney.

Since less than a third of Sydney's Sephardim are members of either the NSW Association of Sephardim or the Eastern Jewish Association, one wonders what has happened to the remaining Sephardim. It seems that the majority of Iraqi or "pure Iraqi" Jews do not belong to any congregation, since they consider the Sephardic synagogue in Sydney too low-class for them. As one Indian-Iraqi Jew explains, it is "below their dignity to become members of our organization". Some Iraqi and Egyptian families are members of Ashkenazi synagogues.

The most important reason for the dearth of Sephardic participation or affiliation is sociological: in their countries of origin, one did not "join" a synagogue. In these traditional societies, synagogues were usually built and maintained by wealthy families, and all Jews could participate in services without having to pay a fee or make a formal statement of membership. Sephardic Jews find the notion of membership dues anathema. One person put it candidly: "It is absolutely disgraceful that in order to be able to come and pray in a house of God I have to pay money." In Australia, however, most of the funds for the rabbi's salary and the upkeep of the synagogue are generated from membership fees and donations. One member of a synagogue executive had the following to say about low synagogue membership:

> We never know how many Sephardim are in Sydney. We meet them only when they come to us to bury their dead. They do not want to know us or to acknowledge our existence in their joyful events such as birth, *Bar-Mitzvah* and marriage, but they know their place very well when they lose a member of their family. In this respect, we might just as well become a *Chevra Kadisha* [Jewish Burial Society].

Ethnic Division and Organizational Structure

The NSW Association of Sephardim has a Board that has ranged between thirteen and eighteen members. Five of these are members of the inner executive (because it is Orthodox, all members of the inner executive are men): the president, two vice-presidents, the treasurer and the secretary. In 1980, some 20–25 percent of the Board members were from Egypt, the rest coming from India and Iraq. However, by the time

I concluded my fieldwork in 1984, the entire executive was of Indian-Iraqi or Iraqi origin. Although the Eastern Jewish Association is also registered as a congregation, the only Sephardic synagogue in New South Wales is that of the NSW Association of Sephardim, located at Bondi Junction in Sydney's eastern suburbs. Most members of EJA are affiliated with the NSW Association of Sephardim for most of the year, since the EJA functions as a congregation only on high holidays, when they hire a hall for services.

Social functions are conducted mostly by women. At the beginning of my study there were two women's organizations: the Ladies Auxiliary and the Young Ladies Guild. The former had a membership of about sixty elderly women, of whom the majority was not active, social functions being organized by a small group who met monthly to plan activities. While, in 1980, two members of this working group were of Egyptian origin, by 1984 there were no Egyptians in this group or in the organization, and functions organized for the elderly by the working group had ceased. However, the working group was still meeting to organize social and communal functions in 1993.

During the years of my research, all members of the Young Ladies Guild were in their early to late twenties and were born in India. No "young ladies" from Egypt participated. Guild activities and functions were directed toward young families, and activities were organized for children, particularly on the Jewish holidays. Organization members met on a monthly basis, but attendance was so poor that the group disbanded in 1980. And, although the Sunday school was functioning on a weekly basis at the beginning of my research, that, too, closed within the year. Many subsequent attempts to organize an effective Sunday school have failed, including a school that opened with forty children in 1984 upon the arrival of a new rabbi, but had only nine by the end of that year. Those who attended the Sephardic Sunday school were forced by their fathers to do so. Despite several attempts to establish a successful youth group, that too failed, since most children attended Yeshiva or other Jewish schools and spent free time with school friends.

The Eastern Jewish Association (EJA) has no socio-religious center. Mainly run by the two Musleah brothers from Calcutta and their families, the organization was in the hands of four people: the two brothers, the wife of one of them and one of the sons. The son, who is a qualified rabbi and medical doctor, has acted as the organization's rabbi, for the most part during *Rosh Hashana* and *Yom Kippur* – the most important religious holidays in the Jewish calendar. During the rest of the year, he concentrates on his medical practice. During my fieldwork, his father served as either president or vice-president of the EJA, these positions being rotated among the three male family members active in the organization. The major function of this small group is to organize a prayer hall for its members twice a year for the high holidays – usually in the Hillel kindergarten in Old South Head Road. In 1984, the final year of my research, there were several attempts by the two Sephardic organizations to amalgamate as one group. However, despite ongoing negotiations toward this end, no progress had been made by January 1994. Though relationships between members of both organizations are quite relaxed and friendly, there is still hesitation and old feelings of mistrust between the leading families of both groups.

The first Sephardic religious service for the high holidays in Sydney took place in 1947, in a room of the Jewish War Memorial. A similar service was held in 1948, in the small hall of the old Central Synagogue. The first attempt to organize Sydney Sephardim into a formal group occurred in 1950, when there were about three hundred Sephardim in the city. A meeting of those involved, on 21 of May 1951, resulted in the formation of the NSW Hebrew Association. In December 1953, the Sephardim joined the State Zionist Council and sent representatives to the Zionist Conference. In 1954, the NSW Hebrew Association changed its name to the Association of Sephardim. Until 1959, the community used hired halls mostly in the Central Synagogue, to conduct its religious affairs. By then, when the need for a synagogue and socio-religious center became urgent, the Aaron family began a campaign to raise funds for the purchase of land and building for a synagogue.

But here too the Sephardic community of Sydney was divided, this time over the trusteeship of a piece of land in the East Sydney suburb of Woollahra, which Jacob Aaron (uncle of the founder Aaron Aaron, first president of the NSW Association of Sephardim), donated for a synagogue. According to the donor's family, there was a misunderstanding regarding the office of trustee. The donor had been advised that he was to nominate two of the four members on the Trusteeship Board, the other two members to be from the Association executive, and the president of the NSW Board of Deputies to sit as arbitrator. But, during the NSW Annual General Meeting in December 1959, a bitter argument broke out over the exact make-up of the trusteeship committee.[2] It seems that a group, led by Myer Musleah, feared that the donors' family, which was already quite influential, would take over the synagogue and dominate the community – a process that often occurred in similar situations among traditional societies from the East. Even though a majority of the Board agreed with the donor that the trusteeship committee should include two of their nominees to guarantee that the land would be used for the purpose specified no agreement could be reached. At the monthly Board meeting of January 1960, the secretary of the NSW Association of Sephardim was informed that the forty-nine members who were against the donor had resigned. After the split, the donor withdrew his offer, and the land was subsequently sold.

In mid-1961, the NSW Association of Sephardim was accepted as an affiliate of the Federation of Orthodox Synagogues of NSW on the understanding that it would recognize the ecclesiastical authority of the *Hakham* in London who heads Sephardim within the Commonwealth countries. The Association and the NSW Jewish Board of Deputies attempted to reconcile the two groups, but to no avail. In December 1961, the "breakaway" group – the Eastern Jewish Association – was accepted as an affiliate of the NSW Board of Deputies.[3]

The cornerstone of the Sephardic synagogue was laid on the 15 of July 1962 (the thirteenth day of the Hebrew month of *Tammuz*, 5722), by the same Jacob Aaron who had originally offered the land, but who now donated instead 3,000 pounds sterling for its construction. The first Sephardic synagogue in Australasia opened on 24 September 1962.[4] The congregation's first rabbi, Rabbi Simon Silas, arrived in Sydney from London in September 1963. Rabbi Silas, who was born in Calcutta, was trained by and had worked under the Chief Sephardic Rabbi of the Commonwealth in London before coming to Sydney where he was religious leader for seventeen years. While in Sydney, Rabbi Silas also participated in the Sydney Beth-Din as the Sephardic *Dayan*. It is important to note that, although he is Sephardic, Rabbi Silas studied at and graduated from an Ashkenazi rabbinical college, which hindered his ability to understand the Sydney Sephardic community.

A brief history of Jewish communities in the Middle East may shed some light on the present socio-religious structure of the Sydney Sephardic community.

The Sephardic Communities of the Middle East and Asia

The majority of Sephardim in Sydney immigrated to Australia because of social and political upheavals that restricted their freedom and livelihood in their homeland.[5] This chapter provides a historical account of the three major groups of Oriental (or Sephardic) Jews living in Sydney – those from Egypt, Iraq and India. It discusses the political, social and economic changes, as well as changes in the educational system and the demographic evolution within these Jewish communities during the past hundred years. The majority of the community is of Indian-Iraqi origin, and since their ancestors came from Iraq two or three generations earlier, institutions and changes within the Indian community are linked with those in Iraq.

To examine the recent history of the Jews in Iraq and Egypt, we must first understand the socio-political systems under which these Jewish communities existed and operated. Throughout most of their long diasporas under Islam, they lived under the hegemony of the Ottoman Empire, which ruled most of the Middle East from 1231 until 1924. The Ottomans organized the minorities under their rule into *millets*, or communities, in which life was regulated by the communities' religious functionaries. In the case of the Christian groups, it was the patriarch; the *Hakham Bashi* or Grand Rabbi was the ultimate authority for the Jews.[6] The Muslims tolerated religious minorities as long as these minorities acknowledged their subordinate position in the Empire, particularly the Jews, who posed no threat to Islam. This situation lasted for some seven hundred years. But from the end of the eighteenth to the second half of the nineteenth century, the Muslim attitude toward all minorities, and particularly toward Jews, became increasingly autocratic, Muslims viewing them with the contempt of a "master toward his slaves".[7]

Researchers tend to agree that, during the period of the Ottoman Empire, people of distinct identities lived together in a "relatively peaceful atmosphere" and that the Jews achieved a high level of cultural eminence and social acceptance under Islam.[8] On the other hand, scholars like Grunebaum[9] argue that: "[I]t would be just as easy to cite a long inventory of persecutions, arbitrary confiscations, attempts at forcible conversion and pogroms." That Ottoman subjects were not content with this rule has been pointed out by Hunt and Walker (1974:245), who report that, "The maintenance of order was marred by massacres, and even in peaceful years the minorities experienced discrimination."

One of the consequences of Islamic rule was the reinforcing of identity between religion and ethnicity, as religion was viewed as a matter of ancestry rather than personal choice. Thus, while ethnicity was not wholly subsumed within religion, the development and social organization of the *millets* was based on religion. Not only was there explicit separation between the Muslim groups and the *millets*, but Muslim domination was an unpleasant fact for all minorities living in the Empire. Moreover, separation was implemented among the *millets* as well as among the Muslim minority groups and the Ottoman ruling class, and was perpetuated by a high rate of marital endogamy, differential rights as citizens, as well as differences in religious beliefs. Most peasants and military and political officers were Muslims, whereas the Jews and Christians were more active in commerce and the professions. The Ottoman Empire also required its minorities to pay higher taxes (*jizya*) than the dominant group, although Jews and Christians were partially compensated by being exempt from military service. Finally, while the leaders of each *millet* were usually chosen by their own communities, the Caliphate had to approve all appointments. Thus, the *Nagid*, or head of all Jewish communities in Egypt, who was chosen by the Caliph, was not always popular among Egypt's Jews.[10]

As long as the Turks maintained full power, there was relatively little pressure against non-believers. Nevertheless, the ebbing of their power saw a concomitant erosion of tolerance for minorities among the locals. To counter this, the Turks replaced local regimes after 1835 in favor of direct administration, a move that helped protect Jews and other minorities from the hostile indigenous population until 1917.[11]

The Jewish population of Iraq, which was 135,000 in 1948, was reduced to 400 by 1974, to a mere 200 by 1991, and to just a few by 2003.[12] Jews lived in Iraq since biblical times. Iraq being the oldest Jewish Diaspora community with the longest continuous history, from 586 BC to AD 1949.[13] The Jews lived relatively well in Iraq, even after the Muslim conquest of AD 634, when they began to undergo some persecution – but persecution grew. Between AD 800–850 Jews were subject to heavy taxation and severe oppression and were forced to wear a yellow patch on their clothing. Between 1750–1830 persecution of Jews led many to flee to Persia, India, Egypt, Syria and Israel.

During the period 1835–1917, known as the period of direct rule of the Turkish Wallis, the position of Jews and other minorities in Iraq improved considerably. Unlimited religious freedom encouraged Torah studies, and many *Yeshivot* religious seminaries were established. The socio-economic position of the Jews was elevated and Jews not only controlled industry and commerce, but many rose to high positions in the administration of Baghdad and Basra. After the Turkish Revolution of 1908, many Jews were elected to the Turkish Parliament. Although all minorities were officially declared equal and given some freedom, beginning with the reign of Sultan Abed-Al-Magid in 1839, and although Abed-Al-Magid's policies were endorsed by the Young Turks in 1908, it was not always easy to actualize these declarations due to the hostility of the Muslims. Thus, Madhat Pashas, who ruled between 1869 and 1872, reinforced equal rights for all citizens; he established hospitals and educational institutions for all minorities. His regard for the Jews was so great that they called him "Father of the Peace". Madhat Pasha's policies were carried forward by Seri-Camal Pasha (ruled 1889–92) and Hagi-Hasan Rafic-Pasha (1892–96), who was so good to the Jews that they called him "father, patron, defender and savior".

This period of protection and advancement in Iraq was rudely interrupted during the reign of Mustafa Azem Pasha (1887–89), a brutal and cruel ruler who accused the Jews of endless crimes. He encouraged the already hostile indigenous people to torture and kill Jews. It was during his brief period that many Jews fled Iraq to India. However, sultan

Abed-al-Hamid did not take steps to replace him until several influential Jews complained to the British government, who threatened the
sultan with intervention if he did not do something to ease the plight of
the Jews in Iraq. Obviously, the sultan was impressed by the British
threat, since his next appointee was Seri-Camal Pasha who began his
regime by investigating all the baseless accusations that Jews had been
blamed for, such as ritual murders and other crimes, and clearing them
of these accusations.

The prosperity, religious freedom and progress that was generally the
case during direct Ottoman rule began to break down with the rise of
nationalism, particularly in the years 1914–17, when the British came to
power.[14]

After Turkey was defeated in World War I, and the Ottoman
Caliphate was ended even in Turkey, there was a new social order in
which the emphasis in the newly independent Arab countries shifted
from religious uniformity as such to nationalism. This deprived the
minorities of the protection of the *millet* system and they were left
exposed to governments committed to the welfare of their Muslim
population, which exhibited little of the pluralistic tolerance of the
Ottoman rule.

The growing tension in Palestine, the rise of the Zionist movement
toward the end of the Ottoman Empire and the establishment of the
State of Israel led to a sharp decline in the position of Jews in Arab lands.
In a new Exodus, over six hundred thousand Jews were expelled or fled
from the Arab lands where they and their ancestors had lived for many
centuries. Those who fled did so out of fear of renewed discrimination
and oppression. Thus, Jewish and Arab nationalisms brought to a close
a coexistence that had lasted for hundreds of years.[15]

To conclude, the Ottoman rulers readily accepted the Jews expelled
from Spain in 1492, allowed them to observe their religious obligations
and gave them wide latitude insofar as how they chose to earn their
livelihood. Indeed, the Ottoman pattern of ethnic relations, and its
survival throughout the centuries, is testimony that a system can be
devised under which different groups can dwell in the same national
territory. The *millet* system under which Iraqi Jews lived so long may be
a historical reminder of the need to respect ethnic identity within a
larger national framework.

The Jews of Egypt

The flourishing and self-sufficient, middle-class Egyptian Jewish community that had enjoyed a sense of relative security shrank from some
seventy-five thousand in the first half of the twentieth century to a mere
three hundred by the beginning of the 1980s.

There has been a Jewish community in Egypt for the past 1,900 years, but there were "non-community" Jews in Egypt much before that, the earliest reference to them being in Egyptian monuments of 1220 BC.[16] During the eighteenth century, however, with the gradual decline of the Ottoman Empire, and the growing influence of the European powers, Jews and other minorities in Egypt began to evince increasing interest in the European way of life and customs. When the Alliance Israelite Universelle opened schools in Egypt, many Jews began to adopt French and other European languages for everyday use. More decisive in the Europeanization of Egyptian Jews was the consequent loss of tradition and the granting of extra-territorial privileges to foreigners, which allowed European consuls the power to juridicate over civil matters regarding their own nationals.

Many Jews expelled from Spain in 1492, who were welcomed by the Ottoman Empire, chose to settle in Ottoman-ruled Egypt after having lived in Italy. Other Spanish exiles and their descendants came to Egypt from Corfu, the Greek coast and the Aegean archipelago. Of Italian nationality, they spoke both Italian and Ladino (Judeo-Spanish).[17]

When the Khedive Ismael came to power (1863–79), there were six thousand Jews in Egypt. Ismael initiated large-scale economic development plans to ease Egypt's debt, and foreigners were encouraged to come to Egypt to help carry out these plans.[18] By 1897, the number of Jews had quadrupled to 25,000, of whom 12,507 were foreign nationals. The 1917 census reflected another jump, to 59,581, of whom 34,601, or 58.07 percent, were foreign nationals.[19] During the nineteenth century, more and more middle- and upper-class Jews acquired foreign nationality. This tendency was so extreme that, in 1900, the Jews of Alexandria registered their community's statutes with the Austrian consul general. The status of foreign nationals allowed the majority of Egyptian Jews to receive their consul's protection, to enjoy economic and legal advantages, and to be exempted from taxation. This general freedom, together with the Khedive allowing foreigners to acquire land after 1858, as well as the persecution they were suffering in Eastern Europe, Morocco and the Balkans, encouraged an increasing number of Jews to move to Egypt.[20]

Egyptian Jewry swelled during the eighteenth and nineteenth centuries by Iraqi Jews who took advantage of Khedive Ismael's economic initiative to escape their socio-economic oppression in Iraq. This strengthened the local Jewish religious and social institutions, particularly in Cairo. Since foreign nationality was an asset during that period, a majority of foreign and local Jews living there sought to gain nationality from Austro-Hungary, the Italian principalities, France or Great Britain. When the Austro-Hungarian representative granted their protection there was an influx of Jews from Europe, which formed the basis of a separate Ashkenazi community in Egypt. The French mission, too, was quite forthcoming, especially regarding the descendants of Jews who professed an Algerian background. The British, however, were far more demanding, consular officials in Egypt carefully checking the testimonials of the many Jews who professed British nationality.[21]

At the outbreak of the Arab–Israeli conflict in 1948, the number of Jews in Egypt stood at between 75,000–80,000, of whom 30,000 were foreign nationals and 40,000 without any nationality. Only about 5,000 (7 percent) possessed Egyptian nationality.[22] Nine years later, after the Suez Canal crisis of 1956, the Jewish population stood at a mere 15,000. By the Six-Day War of 1967, only 2,560 Jews were left in Egypt, and this number had shrunk to one hundred by 1993.[23] Those who wished to leave were forced to surrender their homes and other possessions to the government – events recalled vividly by my Egyptian informants in Sydney.

Since 1948, Egypt's Jews have been concentrated in Cairo and Alexandria, the Jewish population of the provinces that had lived in peace with local Muslims having completely disappeared. Although the Jewish community councils of Cairo and Alexandria did not have a legal status, they received de facto recognition by the government. From the Ottoman period on, the government officially recognized the Rabbi of Cairo as the Chief Rabbi of Egypt.

Jews began to occupy central positions in the socio-economic sphere, particularly in banking, almost as soon as they arrived *en masse*. "Nowhere in the Muslim world did the urban concentrations of the Jews even approximate the extent it manifested in Egypt."[24] This was because a majority enjoyed foreign nationality even before Khedive Ismael invited Jews to come to Egypt in the 1860s.

The British ushered in a period in which the Jews of Egypt – unlike those elsewhere in the Muslim world – were closer in occupational structure to those in Europe than to local Muslims. This included a relatively high percentage of Jewish women being employed in commerce, industry and clerical work, as well as in the practice of medicine. Not surprisingly, Egyptian Jews were quite well educated. Their literacy rates in 1947 were 89.7 percent for Jewish males over five years of age and 75.95 percent for all Jewish females. Educated in foreign schools in which the curriculum was taught in French, Italian or English (Arabic was taught as a foreign language), middle-class Jews – together with other foreigners and some westernized Muslims – distanced themselves from the mass culture. Lower-class Jews, however, felt Egyptian, spoke Arabic and lived like any poor Muslim or Copt.[25]

While Egyptian independence, in 1922, brought no immediate changes in the political situation of the Jews, signs of Jew hatred, particularly among Christians, became evident in the 1930s. Thus, from being represented in the Egyptian Chamber of Deputies and Senate (between 1924 and 1952), and having one of their members serve as Minister of Finance, the Jews began to be accused of "blood libels" against Christians.[26]

Beginning in 1938, when Jews were accused of active association with the Zionists in Palestine, anti-Jewish riots were organized by the Young Egypt movement. Synagogues were bombed, several Jewish institutions in the heart of the Jewish quarter were destroyed and many people were killed. As the Jewish quarters began to be unsafe, many Jews emigrated from Egypt. By 1947, by which time the Palestine issue was being given prominence in the Egyptian media and the authorities had joined forces with the press in condemning Zionism, even those Jews inclined toward Zionism were afraid to participate in any Zionist activity. However, the fact is that, until they felt unsafe in their countries of origin, most Jews in Arab countries were indifferent or even hostile to Zionism, which they viewed as a European movement of which they wanted no part. They were not "converted" to Zionism until anti-Semitism and persecution in their countries grew unbearable after Israel's establishment.[27]

Employment and economic opportunities for Jews began to be curtailed in 1947, and in 1948 much Jewish property was confiscated and hundreds of Jews arrested. November 1948 witnessed violent demonstrations organized by the Muslim Brotherhood against foreign-owned and Jewish business houses. With the United Nations partition declaration on the 29 November 1947, the Jews of Egypt became the scapegoat for all of the country's economic and political ills. The first sign of this came in July 1947, when a "company law" was introduced requiring company directors to be Egyptian nationals. At that time, only about 15 percent of the Jews were Egyptian nationals; some two-thirds were stateless and 20 percent held foreign nationality.[28] In 1929, when the Egyptian government had wished to encourage Egyptian-born nationals who held foreign nationality to become Egyptian citizens, it passed the Egyptian Nationality Law. The law stated that every resident who applied for citizenship would be granted it unless he or she retained another nationality. At that time, Jews did not avail themselves of Egyptian nationality, not attaching any importance to it. And later, in the early 1940s, when the law was amended to include only those who could prove that their grandfathers were born in Egypt, or that their families had been in Egypt since 1848, the majority of Jews were no longer eligible and thousands remained stateless.[29]

On 25 May 1948 all citizens were prohibited from leaving Egypt without a special permit. Jews were generally denied these permits, those who did receive them had the letter "J" stamped in red in the center of the document. On 30 May, an order was issued to the effect that the property of those whose activities were deemed detrimental to the state would be confiscated. Although Jews were not mentioned specifically, the majority of the more than 100,000 individuals and companies whose properties were confiscated were Jewish. When the Wafd government came to power in 1950, Egypt's policy toward its Jews became somewhat more lenient, and the Jews were permitted to resume normal socio-economic activity. While the revolution of July 1952 and the deposing of King Faruk brought no tightening of policy, the overthrow of General Nagib by Gamal Abd-al-Nassar in November 1954 again brought difficult times to the Jews. Jews were arrested and sentenced to death for allegedly spying for Israel; two Jews were hanged in 1955. Anti-Jewish publications increased and Jews were again denied the right to leave the country.[30]

During the Sinai Campaign of 1956, there were no anti-Jewish demonstrations and no harm came to Jews. But after Israel won the war, and the reality of defeat became apparent, Egypt became increasingly dangerous for its foreign residents, especially Jews. This was when foreigners began their exodus from Cairo. But now the Jews experienced additional difficulties in leaving, hundreds (including some of the wealthiest and most respected members of the Jewish community) were arrested and their property transferred to the Director General. Between November 1956 and September 1957, in less than a year, 21,012 Jews were expelled from Egypt. Still others left voluntarily, since they no longer had any way to earn a livelihood.[31]

Many members of Sydney's Egyptian Jewish community arrived in Australia as stateless persons with little money. They had been allowed to take 40 Egyptian pounds, jewels up to the value of 140 pounds and unlimited amounts of clothing when they were expelled. By the beginning of 1960, some 36,000 Jews had left Egypt, the majority immigrating to Israel. Out of the 40,000 Jews living in Egypt in 1956, only about 8,500 remained in 1960. Of this number, only a few hundred came to Australia after the Sinai Campaign in 1956. All those who left, except for British and French nationals who were compensated in accordance with agreements Egypt had with those countries, lost their property. The Jews, who left between the Sinai Campaign and 1960, left about 24.2 million Egyptian pounds behind.

Many of the 3,000 Jews still in Egypt in June 1967 – including the rabbis of Cairo and Alexandria – were arrested in the wake of the Six-Day War and sent to concentration camps. They were freed in July 1970, and by mid-1972 most of them had left Egypt except for some 300, for the most part elders, who remained in Cairo. When Chief Rabbi Hayyim Duwayk left for France in 1972, Egypt was left without a rabbi.

The Jews of Egypt were reputed to be mainly financiers, moneylenders, moneychangers and pawnbrokers during the eighteenth and nine-teenth centuries. Few engaged in manual labor. The 1937 census showed no Jews engaged in farming and only 18–19 percent in industry and crafts, in contrast to other Jewish communities in the East. Most (59.1 percent) engaged in commerce or general administration and public service, including medicine and law. Large-scale trade was monopo-lized by Christians, the Jews for the most part owning shops in bazaars. The low birth rate, the low illiteracy rate and the fact that more Egyptian Jewish women were the breadwinners of their families than was the case in any other community in the East, meant that there were far fewer dependents per worker than in any other Jewish community in the region.[32]

Egyptian Jews began to become large-scale financiers after the British arrived in 1882. They contributed substantially to the economic devel-opment of the country, helping to develop the sugar industry and railroad, and assisting in founding the National Bank of Egypt and the cotton exchange. The offspring of these people – many of whom became doctors, lawyers or engineers – tended to lead increasingly Western-oriented lives, which led to their alienation from the rest of the population. Moreover, the widening gap between newly rich and poor Jews resulted in serious social tensions between indigenous Jews, who were mainly poor, and "foreign nationals" who never considered them-selves Egyptians.[33]

Despite these changes, however, the majority of Egypt's Jews remained artisans and small traders. Fortunes fluctuated, and a crisis on the stock exchange – such as that of 1907 – could cost both poor and rich Jews their savings and/or employment. Nonetheless, many Jews con-tinued to deal on and influence the stock exchanges well into the first half of the twentieth century. By 1920, the community's fortunes had undergone a transformation that turned it into the richest of all Eastern Jewries.

The Jews of Iraq

Prior to immigration, there were two major Jewish communities in Iraq: Baghdad and Basra, Baghdad's 77,000 Jews comprising one quarter of its total population. The legal status of Jews improved under the direct Turkish Empire (1832–1914). They ceased paying poll tax, but paid a collective tax that exempted them from military service. This tax, too, was abolished in 1909, when Jews became subject to military service.[34] Under the Turks, the Jews also flourished economically; many were very rich, most of the pharmaceutical industries being in their hands. In addition, Jews had representatives in the first parliament in 1909, and held positions in the government law courts, district and municipal councils and the civil service. By 1920, with the first Iraqi provisional government, there were four Jewish judges in Baghdad.[35] Under the Turks, the Jews felt much more secure and began moving away from Jewish quarters to mixed neighborhoods, and from Baghdad to other places where Jews had never lived before.

Between the beginning of World War I until the British occupied Baghdad in 1917 and Kirkuk, Mosul and Arbil in 1918, Iraqi Jews again faced a difficult period. Many were recruited into the army and were posted to the front lines during the war. Others were tortured and money extorted from them to finance the army.[36] The British occupation (1917–21) and the entire mandatory period (1918–32) brought the Jews freedom, security and almost complete equality of rights with Muslims. Many Jews worked for the British administration.[37] King Feisal, who reigned between 1921 and 1933, was liberal-minded and sympathetic to Jews. He even signed an agreement with Chaim Weisman regarding a Jewish home in Palestine in 1919. Minority rights were ensured in the Iraqi Constitution of 1924, when the Jews were given five seats in the Iraqi parliament, later changed to four deputies and a senator.[38]

During Feisal's reign many Jews in high positions were very close to the King. Among the Jewish administrators during this period were first Minister of the Treasury, Sir Sasoon Yehezkel; Chief Administrator of the Treasury Abraham-al-Kabir, considered to be the most brilliant economist in Iraq; Post Office and Telegraph Manager, Salim Tarzi; Train Authority Deputy Manager, Moshe Shahat; and High Court Deputy President, David Samra. The first Iraqi pilot was a Jew. Eighty percent of the workers in banks were Jews. Most of the railway workers in Iraq were Jews. Seventy percent of the radio musicians were Jews. The number of Jews in high status professions such as judges, lawyers, doctors, pharmacists and others was considerably high.

Iraqi Jews filled most of the places in law and medical schools. They also had a great influence on the media and on Arabic literature. Their high education and business abilities gave them almost a monopoly on the export–import trade. Most shops in Baghdad were owned by observant Jews who did not conduct business on the Sabbath. Thus, even Muslims closed their shops on that day. In short, Jews contributed enormously to the Iraqi administration and economy. Opening branches of their businesses from London and Manchester in the West, throughout Europe, and as far East as China and Japan, they contributed millions of pounds sterling annually to the Iraqi Treasury.

With the outbreak of disturbances in Palestine in August 1929, Iraqi authorities began their active struggle against Zionism, but little harm came to the Jews of Iraq until 1933, when the Mandate ended. The position of Iraqi Jews began to deteriorate seriously in 1932 with independence.[39] Jews were dismissed from government positions and forbidden to travel to Palestine. The teaching of Hebrew was prohibited, and Arabic was made compulsory in Jewish schools, which were placed under government control. This initiated a period of the "Arabization" of Iraqi Jews, when Jewish writers and poets began to write in Arabic (rather than Hebrew), seeking to prove their loyalty to the Arab regime. However, efforts in this direction notwithstanding, after the death of King Feisal in 1933, discrimination only increased.[40] Although no laws were introduced to restrict their rights, a nationalistic group led by a consortium of refugees from Syria and Palestine, in conjunction with Iraqi officials, began promulgating Nazi propaganda at this time, which encouraged attacks against Jews.[41]

By 1934, many Iraqi Jewish youth doubted that they would ever be able to live in Iraq as equal citizens. Their fears were only enhanced between then and 1939, when several military revolts brought about a further deterioration in their position. In this context, the 1937 government of Nuri-al-Said led to a wave of bomb-throwing in the Jewish quarters of Baghdad. In the riots of late spring 1941, during the Jewish holiday of *Shavuoth,* between 170 and 180 people were killed in three days of riots and looting aided and abetted by the army and the police. Baghdadi Jews were stunned by the riots, the first they had experienced since the middle of the nineteenth century. Less serious outbreaks also occurred at Basra, Mosul and other places in the provinces.[42] Nevertheless, the majority of Jews resumed their normal activities during the next two years, when discrimination against them was suppressed by the authorities. During this same period, however, they were forced to contribute to support the Palestinian national struggle, and the president of the Jewish community was ordered to issue a declaration on Arab rights in Palestine. As the political situation worsened, and Iraqi Communists held demonstrations with banners saying, "Long live our Jewish brethren, and death to Zionism, the enemy of the Jews", the Jewish *Haganah* in Palestine established a branch in Iraq, where it operated as an underground movement.[43]

The community's last five years in Iraq (1945–50) were the worst yet. As the Palestine problem intensified, many Arabs sought active measures against the Jews, but they were restrained by the Minister of the Interior. Between 1946 and 1949 the *Mujtahid*, the highest-ranking minister of the *Shi'ite* sect, joined the anti-Jewish campaign, promulgating religious laws against the sale of land to Jews. Jews were again subjected to physical and property damage. These events, together with the establishment of the State of Israel, led to mass emigration. From 1949 to 1952, 123,371 Iraqi Jews were airlifted directly to Israel in what came to be known as *"Operation Ezra and Nehemia"*. This led to an official decree, in March 1950, confiscating the property and bank accounts of Jews leaving for Israel. Nonetheless, by 1955 over 126,000 Iraqi Jews had immigrated to Israel. Those who stayed were put under heavy restrictions and left to the mercy of the rulers. By February 1958, all Jewish community property, including schools and hospitals, were transferred to the state. Approximately two million pounds sterling of Jewish property was confiscated by the government between August 1948 and June 1965.[44]

After the State of Israel was established, Jews were arrested daily. Their homes were searched, families were harassed, the heads of families arrested and many Jews were exiled from Baghdad to other cities in Iraq. On 23 January 1952, two Jews were hanged for spying for Israel. One was an employee in the synagogue. Another was an international lawyer and officer in the Iraqi reserves. All this took place under martial law. Jews active in the *Haganah* and underground Zionist movement were arrested and tortured, some managing to escape to Iran with the help of the *Hechalutz* Zionist movements or by paying Arab smugglers. Between 1949 and 1952, the Jewish population was decimated. Of the 130,000 Jews residing there in 1949, only 6,000 remained by 1953.

The situation of the remaining 6,000 Jews became increasingly precarious. Many were arrested on charges of spying for Israel, nine being sentenced to death and hanged publicly in 1969 for this alleged offense. Others were accused of all sorts of horrific crimes. It was not until mid-1971 that pressure by foreign governments resulted in the Iraqi government ceasing its persecution of Jews and allowing many to emigrate, again after forfeiting their property and money.[45]

Unlike the Jews of Egypt, Lebanon and North Africa, to whom speaking French was a matter of pride and status, Iraqi Jews from all walks of life had always spoken Arabic – and were proud of it – although not exactly the same version that was spoken by the non-Jewish population. In Iraq's many small towns, the Jews interacted daily with their Muslim neighbors, communicating in the local dialects so it was generally difficult to distinguish them from the rest of the local population. Many among Baghdad's large Jewish community – especially women, who were mainly at home – had little contact with Arabs and were not proficient in the Muslim dialect. The only Baghdadi Jews who had complete command of this dialect were those who studied in a state secondary school or had daily business contact with Muslims.[46] In the middle of the nineteenth century, the majority of Iraq's Jews were engaged in crafts, sales and small commercial businesses, those in Kurdistan also engaging in agriculture. Few were involved in foreign trade, which existed on a limited scale during that period.[47] During the Ottoman period, Iraqi Jews found little employment in the civil service. It was only after the opening of the Suez Canal on 17 November 1869, when Baghdad and Basra began to play an important role in trade with the Far East, that the Jews began making their dramatic contribution to the country's growing foreign trade. This growing class of businessmen and merchants began to excel in foreign languages and to establish connections with Iraqi Jews who had settled in Manchester and India, which helped them seize control of Iraqi's foreign trade.[48]

In contrast to the much improved economic situation of the Jews of Baghdad and Basra, there was no change in the economic situation of the Kurdish Jews during that period. Their economic situation and that of the Jews of Mosul worsened considerably. "The Mosul Jews and those of the Kurdistan area suffered badly from the famine prevailing in the region at the end of the nineteenth century, and required financial assistance from abroad, in 1884 the number of the needy in the Vilayit [district] of Mosul was estimated to be 1,782 out of the 4,732 Jews there."[49]

Between 1918 and 1932, the period of the British Mandate, Iraqi Jews increased their control of wholesale business and foreign trade. Not only did they have a large share in commercial companies, banks, the railroad administration, the Basra post office and the Iraqi oil companies, but also educational expansion had brought many Jews to the free professions and academia. Thus, the Jews who fled Iraq after World War II and the establishment of Israel were a middle-class group that had barely existed prior to 1914.[50]

Social Changes and Religious Orientation in Iraq, Egypt and Turkey

Beginning with the twentieth century, there was a considerable move away from religiously oriented lifestyles among the Jewish communities in Middle Eastern countries. During the preceding one hundred years, Jews had not been pressured to convert to Islam, and very few did. Moreover, since Islamic law forbade intermarriage, marriages between Jews and Christians were non-existent, except in those few instances where Jewish girls converted to marry Muslim men.[51]

In 1908, when the Young Turks came to power, they did so under a banner of secularization. This was when Turkish Jews, who had been religiously observant as a matter of custom and family tradition, began acquiring a secular education, although the Jews of Iraq still clung to tradition. The first group of Jews who were influenced by the secular movement were engaged in civil service and began to work on the Sabbath and other Jewish holidays – although Jewish business owners did not. When the British occupied Iraq in 1918, and hired many Iraqi Jews, tradition began to break down. Those who worked for the British worked on the Sabbath and some even worked on the high holidays. The move toward secularization was further hastened in the late 1920s, when Jews were allowed to study in state schools, which held classes on Saturdays and Jewish holidays.[52]

Many Jewish intellectuals now began to view religious customs and observance as outdated. The majority of Jews, those who maintained tradition, seemed to do so mainly to uphold the ethnic differences between themselves and Islamic society. Faur (1972:6) argues that the Sephardim "captured the stimuli of their times and adapted them to the specifics of the community."

Changes in the status of women became apparent with their acquisition of education, which brought about changes in occupation and attire, and raised the age at which they were married. Thus, from an average marriage age of eight in Turkey and twelve to thirteen in Egypt, by the 1940s Egyptian women were not entering matrimony until at least sixteen years of age. But traditional Jewish conservatism in sexual matters meant that relationships between the sexes were little affected by the new secularization and education.

The birth of a daughter was not welcomed by any religion in Eastern countries including Judaism. Until the beginning of the twentieth century, Jewish girls were sent to *cheder* with their brothers only until the age of four. In Baghdad, in the 1930s, girls were sent to Jewish or state kindergartens and then to co-educational schools until the age of nine or ten, when they stopped their education because there was no state or Jewish school to cater for them. Although by the end of the 1930s, Iraqi girls of all religions were eligible to study in institutions of higher education, few Jewish women entered high school or university even as late as 1950.[53]

The education of Egyptian Jewish women, and their consequent employment, exceeded that of their sisters in all of the Middle Eastern countries. Polygamy had become almost extinct by 1937, and divorce was more frequent in Egypt than in other Middle Eastern countries – 1.8 percent of all Egyptian marriages ended in divorce, compared with 0.8 percent of all Iraqi marriages – perhaps because Egyptian women received an education and worked outside the home.[54]

Along with educational progress in the Jewish communities of the Middle East came an improvement in the Jews' socio-economic condition. The Alliance Israelite Universelle and other foreign schools – where a majority of Egyptian, Syrian and Lebanese Jewish children studied between 1860 and 1960 and where Iraqi, Iranian and Turkish students were enrolled prior to World War I – played an important role in this advancement. These schools taught foreign curricula, in foreign languages, which brought their students closer to Europe and reinforced their sense of being foreigners in the local society. It should be noted that, while their education differed greatly from that of their parents, no real "generation gap" was created, and they did not rush to assimilate, although their education did alienate them from religious observance.[55]

Jewish publications, which had been almost entirely restricted to religious works in the second half of the nineteenth century, were concentrated by the twentieth century in the fields of science and literature. Hardly any religious works were produced, even by rabbis. These works were written in a variety of languages, including Persian, Turkish, Arabic and European languages. Iraq, which had been the center of many outstanding *yeshivot* – between the thirteenth and eighteenth centuries, had to rely on congregational rabbis for their religious learning since these institutions were closed by the authorities in the mid-1940s. Unlike other Middle Eastern countries, Baghdad's religious leaders opposed the teaching of secular subjects in the two boys' schools set up in that city, in 1832 and 1907. That and the poor teaching standard in these schools led the majority to seek modern education in the Alliance schools.[56] One of the incentives for Jews to complete their education was that those who held a matriculation certificate were released from army service. Prior to World War I, many Iraqi Jews graduated from the faculties of medicine, pharmacy and law in Istanbul. After World War I they studied in England, France, Turkey, India, Egypt, Syria, Lebanon and the United States.

Jewish education in Egypt underwent a dramatic change in the second half of the nineteenth century. With increased European influence and the introduction of foreign languages into the schools, religious learning and practice declined. It should be noted that these changes came about without pressure from the authorities and were not unique to Jews. Indeed, the secular curriculum introduced in 1939 increasingly attracted both Muslims and Jews. Muslim and Jewish schools were susceptible to the French influence since the French government invested eight hundred thousand francs in operating Catholic institutions and the Alliance Israelite Universelle sponsored a parallel school network for Jewish children. By 1914, one hundred twenty thousand youngsters from Egypt to Turkey were receiving their education in these French schools. It is interesting that Jewish girls tended to study in Christian schools, while boys mostly attended Jewish schools. One possible explanation for this might lie in the desire to see that Jewish boys received a Jewish education in order to maintain Judaism. For, as the head of the family, they and only they could ensure the perpetuation of Jewish culture and religion. While the women stayed at home and within the bounds of the community, men interacted with outsiders through business and social contacts. It was therefore crucial to give them a solid foundation in Judaism to avoid their assimilation.[57]

The literacy level of Egyptian Jews was higher than that of the general population – and higher than that of all other Jewish communities in the

Middle East. Jews were admitted to the universities in both Cairo and Alexandria, where they were generally successful in their studies due to their familiarity with the foreign languages in which they were taught.[58]

Egypt's two spiritual Jewish centers, Alexandria and Cairo, each had its own chief rabbi, the smaller communities falling under the jurisdiction of one or the other of these centers. However, since Egypt lacked *yeshivot* or rabbinical seminaries, spiritual and religious leaders were brought to Egypt, mainly from Jerusalem, with a few from Italy and Morocco. But these rabbis, who were unfamiliar with the general social dynamics in Egypt, were not able to provide the leadership that would have kept Egyptian Jews within traditional Jewish society. Thus, Egyptian Jews were less tradition-bound than the Jews of North Africa, and far less so than Iraqi Jews.[59]

The Jews of India

The Indian Jewish community comprised many quite diverse groups, although the overwhelming majority belongs to the Bene-Israel community and resided in the Bombay region. Most of those who settled in India after 1800 came from Iraq, some also emigrating from Iran, and a few from Afghanistan. Large numbers of the more recent arrivals settled in Bombay and Calcutta.[60]

The majority of Sydney Sephardim are descended from Indian Jews who originated in Iraq and who had immigrated from Calcutta or Bombay. Iraq was also the origin of most of those who came to Sydney from Burma, Singapore, China, Indonesia and Hong Kong. My data indicates that Jews from Singapore, Rangoon, Shanghai and Indonesia relied on the authority of the Baghdadi, Calcutta and Bombay Jewish leaders prior to immigration. Thus, they followed the customs and traditions of Iraqi Jews.

The Jewish Community in Cochin

The Cochin Jewish community was the smallest – 2,500 Jews at its peak – and the oldest – dating back to the twelfth century – in India. Those who originated in Spain and Portugal settled in the southwestern tip of India, in the Cochin and Malabar areas in the region of Kerala. The community was rigidly divided into three sub-castes, "white", "black" and "brown" endogamous groups, with each sub-group having its own synagogue and tradition, and little intra-group contact or intermarriage. The "whites" are believed to be the offspring of Jews from Spain, Holland, Germany and Syria. The "blacks" are the offspring of the native Indians and Jews. The "brown" are the offspring of slaves who were set free in the late 1920s.[61]

After the State of Israel's establishment, most Cochin Jews immigrated to Israel, leaving 200 in the Cochin and Malabar areas by 1971. Only 8 percent of Indian Jews were of European origin.[62]

The Jewish population of India was 6,951 in 1833, of which 5,255 (75.6 percent) were Bene-Israel, 1,039 (14.9 percent) Cochin Jews and 657 (9.5 percent) Baghdadi Jews. By 1899, the population had increased to 12,009, 9,023 residing in Bombay, 1,370 in Cochin and 989 in Calcutta. And by the mid-twentieth century this number had again doubled, to 25,392. After the mass migration to Israel, however, a mere 6,200 remained in India, mostly concentrated in New Delhi. And by 1991, this number was further reduced to 4,700. Only a few hundred Iraqi Jews remained in Bombay in the 1970s. And Calcutta's Jewish population, which had reached a peak of some 5,000 during World War II, had dwindled to less than 500 by 1969. The partition of India in 1946 and the bloody riots coupled with the fear of a socialist government pushed the Calcutta Jews who were very close to the partition line with East Pakistan, and who felt especially threatened, to leave India. This is one of the reasons why the Jews of Calcutta left India a few years earlier than the Jews of Bombay.[63]

Gist and Wright (1973:157) note that, like the Armenians, the Jews represented Western-oriented minorities in India. These groups integrated successfully into the economic system of Indian society, through achievement in business and the professions. Thus the majority did not leave India in response to discrimination, but because they felt themselves foreigners and were treated as Westerners by Indians.

The Jews of Bombay

The Bene-Israel were the first Jews to settle in the city of Bombay, gradually moving north from the Konkan coast thirty miles south of Bombay County where they had been living for several centuries. They believe they are the descendants of the lost ten tribes (II Kings 17:6). The community was divided along caste lines into "black" (Kala) and "white" (Gora) Jews. According to tradition, the "white" Jews are the descendants of the fourteen survivors of a ship that was wrecked on the shores of the Konkan over two thousand years ago, in 175 BC. The "black" Jews are the offspring of the white men and native women. Until the independence of India in 1947, the division between these two groups was rigidly maintained.[64]

Prior to the end of the sixteenth century, when they began moving north to Bombay, the Bene-Israel were oil crushers, on the bottom rung of the caste system. Upon arrival in Bombay, they became carpenters and builders. Many were said to be outstanding soldiers and officers in the British Army. They were so assimilated and acculturated to the

Indian caste system that they were known as the Saturday Tali (the caste that did not work on Saturday). Unlike other Jews in India, the Bene-Israel were considered lower caste by other Indians.[65]

Jews settled in Bombay at the beginning of the eighteenth century, and built their first synagogue in 1796. The next wave of Jewish immigrants was that of Jewish merchants from Syria and Mesopotamia. This Arabic-speaking community was augmented by an influx of Jews from Surat, who migrated to Bombay in the middle of the nineteenth century out of economic necessity. The Jewish settlement in Bombay reached "a turning point" when Baghdad Jewish merchant, industrialist and philanthropist David Sassoon arrived in 1883. Sassoon, who soon assumed the leadership of the Jewish community, built schools and other educational, cultural and civic institutions, as well as synagogues and a Jewish hospital for both Iraqi and Bene-Israel Jews. With his arrival, Iraqi Jews became leaders among the Jewish population of Bombay. Most of the Iraqi Jews in Bombay dealt in foreign trade, working for Sassoon firms in Bombay and the B.N. Elias Company in Calcutta, acting as intermediaries, agents, storekeepers and petty traders.[66]

The Baghdadis played an important role in the nineteenth-century religious revival of the Bene-Israel by providing an example of Jewish orthodoxy. Since the Baghdadis enjoyed not only religious superiority, but also prosperity and prestige, it is not surprising that the Bene-Israel strove to be accepted by them. The Arabic-speaking community at first continued to speak Iraqi Arabic, later adopting English. Although they began to emulate Europeans, and were politically and economically independent of the Jewish community in Iraq, they continued to regard Baghdad as their spiritual and religious center.[67]

Six of Bombay's eight synagogues were Bene-Israel and two were Iraqi. Although Bombay's synagogues were theoretically separated into three strands – Orthodox, Conservative and Liberal – membership in each synagogue was in reality based on socio-economic status, and all synagogues followed Orthodox traditions.[68]

The Iraqi Jews built two Jewish schools with government aid, one strictly for their children and the other for the children of the Bene-Israel. This followed the sub-ethnic stratification of the community, in which the lower class was primarily composed of impoverished Bene-Israel, the middle class mainly of Iraqi Jews, and the upper class of European Jews and a few well-to-do Iraqi Jews.[69] Despite their rejection by the Iraqi Jews, the Bene-Israel made great efforts to associate with them at the beginning, but ceased to do so when they realized the Iraqis did not want to mingle with them, because the Iraqis doubted their origin as true Jews. When the Bene-Israel immigrated to Israel, they had to struggle and prove they are true Jews. The inquiry into their origin by the Chief Rabbinate of Israel lasted almost four years (1961–64), when finally it was decided to accept them as full-fledged Jews.[70]

The Jews of Calcutta

Calcutta Jews, too, viewed Baghdad as their spiritual center. They formed a flourishing community of some five to six thousand people at its peak in the 1940s and provided the basis of the Jewish settlements in Rangoon and Singapore, which depended on its leaders in religious matters. As in other Jewish communities in Asia, the Calcutta community relied on wealthy benefactors – like the Kadouris – to pay for construction of social, educational, health and religious institutions.[71]

Moses Duek Cohen, who is often referred to as the leader and founder of the Calcutta Jewish community, was elected its first president in 1825. As honorary rabbi, minister, *mohel* and *mekkadesh*, his guidance was sought in all disputes and he performed circumcisions and marriages until his death in 1861. His grandson, Elias Moses Duek, became a minister of synagogue Nevah-Shalom, winning representation for the synagogue on the Council and Board of Deputies of British Jews in London, and established a Jewish school in 1881.[72] Duek was also editor and printer of the Jewish weekly *Paerach*, published in Arabic between 1878 and 1889, which provided a link between the Calcutta community and Jewish communities throughout the world.

Many Calcutta Jews of Iraqi extraction became important in the export–import business, but none of them acquired the fortune or fame of the Sassoons. Others prospered in real estate, at which some continue to do well in Sydney.

Summary and Conclusions: Past and Present Degrees of Communality and Religiosity

The three main groups of Jews that make-up Sydney's Sephardim lived in vastly different socio-economic, political and cultural spheres in their homelands. Although both the Iraqis and the Egyptians lived under Muslim social systems, Iraq was isolated socially and geographically from Europe and remained a traditional society within an autocratic polity, while Egypt was exposed to heavy Western influence. These influences were especially evident in the degree of religious observance in the two communities. Additionally, although the Iraqi Jewish community preserved an ancient tradition of Hebrew religious learning, culturally and linguistically it had integrated quite profoundly into Iraqi society.

The Jews of Egypt followed an entirely different pattern. For example, religion played a minor role in the lives of most of its middle and upper class, who considered themselves superior to the indigenous population and preferred to speak Italian or French rather than Arabic, and educate their children in foreign-language schools. This group was the most secularized of all Middle Eastern Jewish communities.

Although the Iraqi Jews of India regarded the Iraqi rabbinical authorities as their own, they took a path quite different from that of their Iraqi co-religionists in Iraq. While Jews in Iraq became completely socially acculturated while remaining strictly observant, the Iraqi Jews in India were neither acculturated into their host society nor strictly observant of their own religion.

With the defeat of Turkey in World War I, and the rise of nationalistic groups in the Arab countries, the relative religious freedom enjoyed by minorities under the Ottoman Empire was drastically curtailed. The *millet* system that had protected minorities and given a certain amount of power to their leaders was abolished, exposing the Jews to the vagaries of local politics. While Jews received a greater degree of civil and political security during the brief period of Anglo-French dominance, their involvement, however, with the Western powers contributed to their downfall when the foreign powers left. As Lewis (1984a:52) states, at this stage, the historical hostility to Jews began to assume a "radically different character". Their decline was further hastened with the development of Zionism and the establishment of Israel.

The Iraqi Jews of India considered themselves superior to their indigenous Jewish brethren. However, when a newly independent India gave them the opportunity to remain and assume Indian nationality, a majority chose to emigrate to the West or to Israel.

This comparison of the past and present degrees of communality and religiosity illustrates that the Sephardim of Sydney do not share a common language, culture or history. It seems that their immigration to Western countries such as Australia has brought with it a high degree of secularization and acculturation, if not assimilation. While the processes of acculturation and modernization were already underway in varying degrees in the homelands, many elders of the Sydney Sephardic community blame modernization and "Ashkenization" for the acculturation. However, data from the literature and information collected from Sydney Sephardim indicate that this, as well as diminished religious observance, had begun before emigration. The diversity of perspective within the Sephardic community, together with imperfect knowledge of local, traditional Sephardic religious culture, has compounded the difficulty of transmitting an alien tradition to children raised in an open society such as Australia.

3

The Immigration of
Sephardic Jews
to Australia

Many Sephardic Jews attempted to immigrate to Australia since World War II, to make it their home. However, governmental restrictions like the quota system and the White Australian policy has made this exceedingly difficult for any Jew, especially dark-skinned Sephardim. With such a small number of Sephardim, who are still anxious to be accepted by the Ashkenazim, it is no wonder that this community is viewed by others and views itself as a marginal aberration within an Ashkenazi minority.[1]

In 1851, there were 1,887 Jews in Australia, or 0.47 percent of the total population. By 1921, this number had grown to 21,615, accounting for some 0.4 percent of the total population. And in 1966, some 70,000 Jews were divided among Sydney (30,000), Melbourne (34,000) and Perth (3,000).

Although only 62,217 persons declared themselves as Jews or Hebrews in the 1981 census, if the percentage of "undeclared" Jews is similar to that of the general population (21.7 percent), the number of Jews would be about 80,000. Thus, while the 1986 census lists some 69,000 Jews in Australia, demographers estimate that there are at least 90,000 and perhaps as many as 120,000 Jews. [2]

In 1987, the Sephardic Jewish community in Sydney numbered some 3,000 individuals, only 640 of whom belong to the New South Wales Association of Sephardim and 100 are members of the Eastern Jewish Association. While some Sephardim are affiliated with Ashkenazi congregations, the majority are non-affiliated.

At the beginning of the twentieth century, there were fifteen Iraqi families in Australia, who had immigrated there after a brief sojourn in India. By the early 1940s, forty Sephardic families were living in Sydney alone. After the establishment of the State of Israel in 1948 and the independence of India in 1947, there was a massive wave of emigrants from Arab countries and India. Although most of those who fled immigrated to Israel, a portion went or tried to go to Australia. Other post-war Sephardic immigrants to Australia included a segment from Jewish communities in Asia that had began to disintegrate, particularly Jews from Singapore and Burma where some of them had been prisoners of war. The Jews of China, who had numbered 3,000 Sephardim and Ashkenazim before the war – this number was increased by some 19,000 Ashkenazim who found asylum from Nazi persecution in the late 1930s – began to feel unsafe when China began its political upheaval and the Chinese Nationalists wanted to expel them because they were stateless.[3]

With the independence of India, a majority of its Jews chose to immigrate to other countries.[4] While a majority immigrated to Israel, as well as to England since they held British passports, many decided to settle in Australia. The Jews of Calcutta were the first to leave, when trouble broke out in the Bay of Bengal area in 1947 upon Britain's departure. The Jews of Bombay and other parts of India soon followed.[5]

The majority of Egyptian Jews left after the Sinai War of 1956, a small group opting to make their home in Sydney.

The treatment of those Sephardim who wished to immigrate to Australia can be examined through their relationships to two groups: (1) The Australian government and society (in particular the Immigration and Interior departments, which were responsible for issuing visas and landing permits); and (2) the Jewish community in Australia (in particular the Australian Jewish Welfare Society, to which the Sephardim turned for assistance in their immigration attempts).

Australian Immigration Policy

The immigration policy of the Australian government before, during and after World War II was one based on doing everything possible to keep Australia white, British and homogeneous. "'White Australia' was an early idea . . . used to prevent non-Europeans from coming to Australia."[6] With the rise of Nazism in Germany, many Jews attempted to leave Europe even prior to the war. The response from Australia, in common with countries throughout the world, was lukewarm to say the least: the Australian government allowed 15,000 Jews to immigrate for "humanitarian reasons", between 1938 and 1940 – a scandalously low number considering Australia's sparse settlement and need for migrants. "Australia had enormous construction projects, a manpower shortage, and what we wanted essentially was factory fodder . . . there was a nice fit between compassion and economic requirements."[7] Yet Australian officials applied stringent conditions to Jewish applicants for entry.[8] The authorities considered German Jews the most desirable Jewish immigrants since they had lived in Germany for generations and had assimilated to the German culture, way of life and business ethics. Polish Jews, on the other hand, were regarded as "the worst type of Jew in Europe".[9]

The Australian Jewish Welfare Society (AJWS) was established in 1937 to assist German Jews wishing to enter Australia. This organiza-tion was authorized by all the state Jewish executives in Australia to deal with the Immigration and Interior departments on matters concerning Jewish refugees and their settlement.[10] When the Executive Council of Australian Jewry (ECAJ) was established in 1945, it handed complete authorization to the AJWS. When the government agreed to accept 15,000 European Jews, the AJWS was authorized to assist 500 to enter Australia each year. However, implementation of this policy was halted when war broke out in September 1939 and the authorities suspended immigration from enemy territory.[11]

Government policy statements concerning racial issues are in them-selves influential. "They change as a response to public opinion and the pressures of small but influential groups. Once changed, they tend to become socially accepted."[12]

In September 1938, an Australian who had been living in America for nineteen years wrote to the Prime Minister:

> I have studied and observed the results of unrestricted immigration . . . the Jews present a more serious problem and one that will be serious in Australia if they are admitted . . . Mr. Lyons, I have no racial or national prejudices and I certainly do not condone Jewish persecution as practiced in Germany, but if the truth were known probably a lot of this was caused by the Jew himself . . . The American Jew is an exploiter . . . they stay in the background and make others do the work but they reap the benefit. It is also common knowledge that most of the brothels in this country are run by Jews . . . Keep [Australia] white, English-speaking and Gentile.[13]

Another document on file in the Australian Archives is a letter from Australian citizen Peter Ferrier, dated 11 February 1938: "As an elector of Australia I . . . contend that we have far too many [Jews] here already . . . Germany, since she has scraped off her human ticks – dipped herself in fact, has never been so progressive and strong." Ferrier concluded with: "All the very worst criminals in every sphere of crime are Jews. If permitted into Australia, the Jews would be like rats from a sinking ship, swarming over the country, taking over its medical and legal profes-sions, and congregating in ghettos in the capital cities".[14]

A letter sent by member of Parliament H. B. Gullett to the *Melbourne Argus* on 12 February 1947, headed "Admittance of Jews", included the following:

> The arrival of additional Jews is nothing less than the beginning of a national tragedy and a piece of the grossest deceit of the Parliament and people by the Minister of Immigration Mr. Calwell and his department . . . The people should demonstrate . . . their opposition to immigration of this sort. In the last fifty years these people have swarmed all over Europe . . . they are European neither by race, standards, nor culture. They are in fact, an Eastern people . . . They secured a stranglehold on Germany after the last war during the inflation period, and in a very large part, brought upon themselves the persecution which they subsequently suffered.[15]

Although this letter may seem extreme, it and many similar ones which appeared in Australian newspapers or were sent to the Australian Department of Immigration highlight the paranoia and anti-Jewish propaganda that prevailed among Australians, including many members of Parliament. In particular, the notion of an international Jewish conspiracy enjoyed widespread currency among Australians and incited feelings against the Jews. This anti-Semitism, coupled with the White Australia policy, made the immigration of Sephardim extremely difficult.

In the immediate post-war period, there was reasonable cooperation between the AJWS and the Minister for Immigration Arthur Calwell. By 1946, two thousand Jews had received landing permits on a humanitarian basis. However, Calwell's lenient policy led to an outcry against Jewish refugees who were blamed for, among other things, the housing shortage. This outcry, which came from parliamentarians like H. B. Gullett from Victoria and other important officials as well as Australians in the street, led Calwell to stiffen entry requirements for Jewish refugees.[16]

In an article called "Not All Refugees Are Jews", which appeared in the *Melbourne Sun* on 10 October 1947 in response to charges that most post-war "reffos" [refugees] were Jews, the chairman of the Executive Council of Australian Jewry pointed out that Australian Jews bitterly resented the impression that Jews were receiving preferential treatment. He continued to say that nothing was said of the 150,000 Roman Catholic and other refugees who were entering Australia each year.

The change in immigration policy became more extreme in the months prior to the December 1949 election, when Calwell stated that he was "deeply perturbed" by the large number of Jews who had immigrated to Australia and those still requesting entry. This statement was aimed at the Australian public, only 17 percent of whom approved of Jews as immigrants in a survey of Australian attitudes toward migrant groups conducted in 1948.[17] A similar survey, carried out in Melbourne, in 1948, demonstrated that more than 50 percent of the respondents wanted to keep out all Jews.[18] In August 1949, Calwell publicly instructed the Department of Immigration to delay admitting Jews. As

Rutland (1991:40) states: "The Commonwealth Migration Officers (CMOs) were instructed to follow these 'pin pricking methods to drastically restrict the number of such permits issued'." The severe measures instituted by Calwell were continued by the next Minister of Immigration, Harold Holt, between 1950 and 1955.[19]

While it was maintained that "official immigration policy" treated all Jews on the same basis as those holding other religious beliefs, a confidential Department of Immigration document dated 26 July 1954 emphasized that, "(1) All Jews who are British subjects *and of European origin*, [my emphasis], are permitted to enter Australia subject to the same conditions as any other European British Subjects; (2) Nationals such as Netherlands, German, Scandinavian, Austrian, Belgian, Danish, Finnish, French, Swiss, United States of America and citizens of Luxemburg are eligible for admission on direct application (Form 47) without sponsors in Australia."[20]

The following paragraph deals with the undesirability of Middle Eastern Jews: "(3) In regard to Jews of the Middle East origin [sic], it has been found that a proportion of them show distinct traces of non-European origin and their admission is generally restricted to the wives and minor children of residents of Australia. Applications for the admission of this class of persons, whether of British or alien nationality, should be referred, accompanied by evidence that they are at least of 75 percent European origin, as in the case of Eurasians who are not Jews."[21]

When some Jews of Middle Eastern and Oriental origin attempted to gain entry visas to Australia during this period, letters labeled "Top Secret" were directed to consular officers instructing them to turn down Asians, including Sephardim who otherwise met the conditions set by the Department of Immigration. The following is one such letter. It was sent by the Head of the Immigration Department, T. H. Heyes, to the Department of External Affairs on 20 January 1949:

SECRET

The Minister holds the view that persons who are not of pure European descent are not suitable as settlers in Australia and it is his desire that those wishing to make their homes in this country be not granted facilities to do so, even though they are predominantly of European extraction and in appearance. [P]ersons of Jewish race of Middle Eastern descent are not eligible, under the existing Immigration Policy, for entry to Australia. It should be impressed on these Officers that the Minister wishes his ruling to be kept strictly secret.[22]

Despite this blatant discrimination against them, many Jews living in the Far East and India viewed Australia as a natural site for resettlement because of its proximity, climate and membership in the British Commonwealth. But Iraqi-Indians, who held British passports, and considered themselves British subjects, were threatened with deportation when they attempted to enter Australia. Subjected to official humiliation and degradation, they were forced to realize that Australians divided British citizens into two types: whites and non-whites.[23]

Australia's "White Australia" policy irritated most Asian governments. A report by Indian researcher C. Kondapi was particularly embarrassing to the Australian government. In reaction to Kondapi's "Indians Overseas", J. Horgan of the Department of Immigration submitted a report to the Immigration Advisory Council on 18 May 1954, which highlighted the plight of the Asians. Among other things, Horgan recommended that, "Australia should adopt an immigration quota for the entry of non-Europeans as a token of good will to 'satisfy the aspirations of Asian countries, which were concerned mainly with the question of the prestige of their nationals in the international sphere'."[24]

Mr. Kondapi condemned the exclusion of Indians and other Asians, on racial grounds, pointing out that racial discrimination is inherent in quota systems based on national origin, which are in violation of democratic principles, Christian ethics and the United Nations, calling "the colour bar" an "economic weapon and political power in the hands of the whites and their governments to exclude Indians and Asians". He called on Australia to "adjust herself to the new concept of geography and security that draws Australia into the orbit of Asia and the Indian Ocean Region and not into Europe". He warned that there were already strong international reactions to her racial policies and that history might not give Australia a second chance to rejoin the liberal societies of the world.

Nonetheless, in 1966, Minister for Immigration Hubert Opperman declared that "our primary aim in immigration is a generally integrated and predominantly homogeneous population".[25] By 1972, Labor Party leader Arthur Calwell had veered so far from his original enlightened policy as to say that no "red-blooded Australian" wanted to see "the creation of a chocolate-colored Australia".[26] In addition, a migrant attitudes survey conducted by the Australian government found that: "Significant minorities in both public and private housing in Sydney rated too many Asian and/or Middle Easterners in their neighbourhood as a concern, namely 21 percent overall."[27] There was no doubt that Asians continued to be viewed as unassimilatiable because they were visually and culturally different. This discriminatory attitude, especially against Indians, led some Iraqi-Indians to seek admission to Australia on the basis that they were not native Indians, but whites.

On several occasions, the Jewish associations of Calcutta and Singapore intervened on behalf of Sephardim already in Australia who were experiencing difficulties in bringing over their wives and children. In this context, Secretary of the Calcutta Jewish Association Mr. B. V.

Jacob, wrote to the then Minister of Immigration Calwell of the anguish being experienced by Sephardim in Australia. First, Mr. Jacob informed the Minister that Sephardic Jews in India were of Spanish heritage and had not intermarried with Indians. Then he added that the people in question were "of some economic and social standing, and apart from the smallness of their numbers [about 100], they are not likely to lower the standard of living of the Australian people". The Minister's reply stated that, "Applications for entry into Australia are considered on their own individual merits and that any permission granted to enter the Commonwealth does not extend to the applicant's relatives whose names are not included in the application".[28] However, Immigration Department head Mr. T. H. Heyes' follow-up letter to Mr. Jacob informed him that the cases brought to his attention had been reviewed and could not be approved under existing rules.

As an increasing number of Sephardim sought entry into Australia, a pattern developed that made the Immigration Department's distinction between "white" and "non-white" Sephardim clear. Contemporary correspondence between government departments indicates that those that have complexion light enough to appear "European" qualified as white. Here, government policy underlined the principal reason why Ashkenazim in Australia suffer such severe status anxiety *vis-à-vis* Sephardim. Since the Ashkenazim themselves suffered from being Jewish even though they were white, one can see why they did not wish to have their difference emphasized by any connection with non-white Jews.[29]

A great deal of Department of Immigration correspondence was devoted to the Aaron family, one of the most prominent families among the Sephardim in Sydney. After younger brother Reuben Aaron arrived in Sydney in 1947 from Calcutta, he made application for his sisters. In assessing this application, the immigration officer stated that Reuben had previously requested entry on behalf of his older brother and the brother's wife, and that this application had been refused. If, the officer argued, this later application were approved, the application of Reuben Aaron's brother and his family – who were all of "Jewish of Middle East origin" – would no doubt be revived. Moreover, "It is not considered that the family is desirable immigrants."[30]

Nevertheless, despite their applications being turned down, the two Aaron sisters arrived on 20 August 1950, informing the Boarding Officer that their parents were Spanish nationals of the Jewish race. On 18 October 1950, immigration officer L. Guest wrote that the Boarding Officer said: "Miss E. Aaron shows very little trace of colour and in my opinion is quarter caste or less. Her sister appears dark but in my opinion is less than half caste." On this basis, he recommended allowing them to remain in Australia. At the same time, however, he expressed concern that this would again raise the question of Reuben's elder brother Aaron and his wife. On 21 November 1950, the sisters were granted permanent residence in Australia, and they were subsequently employed as typists in the civil service.[31]

By 1950, Jews whose relatives had entered Australia but who had been refused visas themselves began to arrive on tourist visas and to plead their cases from within the country. This disturbed a number of government officials, like the Hon. E. J. Harrison MP, Vice-President of the Executive Council and Minister for Defense Production. Harrison wrote to the Minister for Immigration Harold Holt, conveying his concern that people "ineligible for permanent entry to Australia are seeking to gain admission by coming to Australia as visitors and pressing their claims whilst here. This method of entry has reached disturbing proportions." Undoubtedly, he had in mind the two Aaron sisters, and their brother, who also gained permanent residence in Australia after arriving on a tourist visa in 1951, albeit not before several prominent Australians – including Chamber of Commerce President Withall, Liberal member for North Sydney W. Jack and General Manager of Manufacturers' Insurance H. Adam – had intervened on his behalf.[32]

Not all government officials were ill-disposed to Sephardic Jews. On 31 July 1950, A. G. Clark, Consul General for Australia in Shanghai, advocated that a group of Sephardim then living in China be granted entry visas. He emphasized that the Sephardim of Shanghai "have been British for two or three generations and consider themselves (as they are indeed universally regarded) as loyal British subjects" and played a "prominent role in the development of British interests in China". Clark expressed strong dissatisfaction with the way visa applications of Sephardic leaders like a certain Mr. Ezra and his wife were being handled. Mentioning other prominent Shanghai families like the Hayims, the Sassoons and the various branches of the Kadourie family, he pointed out that the Canadians did not consider "persons of the Hebrew race, although born in Asiatic countries or possessing the citizenship of another country . . . as Asiatics". Clark concluded that potential immigrants who were well known and respected, not only by the Jews but throughout the Commonwealth, should be "treated with every consideration if they should make applications".[33]

A minute of the Immigration Advisory Council, dated 15 October 1951, admitted that the treatment of Sephardim might be too rigid. However it expressed fear that, "If their close relatives were allowed unlimited entry there was always the possibility that the applications might quickly 'snowball' and get out of hand, and if this occurred there was a risk of our migration schemes being brought into disrepute".[34]

The vast proportion of the Department of Immigration correspondence dealing with the immigration of Sephardim clearly indicates the hysteria and paranoia engendered by the prospect of widespread Sephardic immigration. Indeed, increasing official resistance resulted in most of the applications presented in 1951 being turned down. The refusal of several applications for residence status made through the Jewish Welfare Board of Singapore provoked the Board to seek clarification on Australian immigration policy.[35]

While the Immigration Department's reply was that they were merely maintaining that each case was dealt with "on its own merits", T. H. Heyes wrote another "Confidential" letter to all consular offices in the East. He explained that while until 1948 Jews of Middle Eastern origin were eligible for the grant of entry permission, "subject to the usual conditions . . . in that year the Australian Authorities in India reported that large numbers of Middle East Jews were looking to Australia for their future home. The view was expressed that, they were not desirable migrants, also that many of them were non-European in appearance." It was then decided that no more Jews of Middle Eastern origin were to be admitted.[36]

Subsequently, when Jews originally from Egypt requested permission to bring their relatives to Australia, their applications were refused along with those of non-Jews from India, Singapore, China and the Middle East. These applicants were not usually rejected immediately. First, they (or their sponsors) were informed that the applications were under consideration. Then, after a year or two (or more), the applicant or sponsor would receive a letter informing them that the request had been turned down, usually adding that the applicant's profession was not needed in Australia. However, the real reasons for rejecting Sephardim were restricted to "Top Secret" and "Confidential" letters between the departments dealing with immigration.

Australian immigration authorities dealt differently with wealthy Sephardic businessmen whose export–import activity with other Eastern countries had an economic interest for Australia. Thus, E. Isaac (born in Penang but of Iraqi origin) was allowed entry by Immigration Minister Harold Holt in a very short time. His letter of visa approval, however, stated that he was being accepted to reside in Australia as a representative of his firm, and on the understanding that he would continue to conduct trade between Australia and Malaya.[37]

In 1952, the Executive Council of Australian Jewry formally requested that the question, "Are you Jewish", on Form 40 for persons sponsored by relatives and form 47 for these sponsored by the AJWS be deleted from the applications for entry visa because there was no similar question for non-Jews. If this were not done, the ECAJ said it would view the question as discrimination against Jews. The immigration authorities were faced with a dilemma: If the question was withdrawn, how would they be able to select prospective Asian applicants? Mr. Trelore, a senior officer in the Department of Immigration, was concerned that, "The Department will no longer be in a position to know whether the person seeking entry is Jewish and consequently existing policy in regard to the entry of Middle East Jews will be difficult to operate". Not wishing to offend the Australian Jewish community, but also feeling it necessary to know whether an applicant was a Jew, immigration authorities directed their officers to discreetly try to establish every applicant's religion. However, this was not until a year later, after additional complaints by the ECAJ.[38]

Similarly, in 1954, H. McGinness wrote to a Mr. Nutt of the Department of Immigration, expressing Mr. Holt's wish "to find another phrase less likely to be offensive to the Jewish organizations . . . one that does not infer [sic] that a person's Jewish faith plays any part in his eligibility". McGinness also suggested that "Jews of Middle Eastern origin" or "Middle East Jews" be changed to, "He/she claim to be of European descent, but are unable to submit evidence which would establish that claim, and therefore is ineligible for entry according to the Immigration Policy".[39]

The Israeli Law of Return encouraged all Jews to come to Israel, regardless of country of origin or color. In addition, between 1949 and 1952, over half a million Jews fleeing Arab lands poured into the new Jewish state. Once there, however, many of them found conditions intolerable and looked for other solutions, including Australia. When this increased the number of Middle Eastern Jews seeking to relocate to Australia, the Department of Immigration stipulated that any person wishing to enter Australia had to be sponsored by a relative already residing in the country, a condition that not many of these immigrants could satisfy.[40] Another directive instructed that, "Where application is made by a resident of Australia for the admission of a relative born in Palestine, it would be reasonable to accept that the person nominated was of European origin".[41]

In July 1954 another "Confidential" letter was circulated to all consulates to the effect that the Department of Immigration feared that an "influx of Jews" from the Middle East would attempt to enter Australia and that entry and tourist visas should be severely restricted, even to immediate relatives of those already in the country. Thus, Mrs. Reuben who wished to visit her daughter was refused a short-term tourist visa on the grounds, that "As a Middle East Jew, Mrs. Reuben was not eligible for entry under immigration policy".[42]

Such racial criteria were often explicit in government directives. In a letter to the chief Migration Officer in London, dated September 1953, Mr. Heyes outlined the conditions under which persons from the Middle East could immigrate to Australia: They "must be not less than 75 percent European in descent and furnish evidence of such. They must be predominantly European in appearance and they must be European in upbringing and mode of life and the type who would become readily assimilated in Australia".[43]

Thus, although geographically situated in the Asian region, the Australians made it clear that they meant to keep their society as white as if they were in the middle of Europe, if not Great Britain itself. As Stannard (1987:76) has pointed out: "What we were telling all the people who live in our region was that they were not as good as us, that we were really a superior race down here."

Sephardic Jewish applicants, of mixed European and Asian backgrounds, continued to pose difficulties for Australian bureaucrats. In addition, they or the Australian relatives who sponsored them were sometimes extremely persistent in resubmitting applications repeatedly after being turned down. Some Sephardic applicants went to Australia on tourist visas and sought to gain permanent residence once there. But, once there, they found that, although they had been told they could come to Australia under Commonwealth regulations, permission to travel on British Subject passports did not automatically imply right of residence.

When government policies began to evoke criticism even within Australia, Mr. Heyes responded by sending the Minister of Immigration a memorandum headed "Admission of Middle East Jews and Other Persons Born in Asia Who Claim to be of European Origin but Show Traces of Colour".[44] In his broadside, Heyes expressed annoyance at Sephardic persistence, and dismissed their claim to pure European descent, as "the great majority of cases showed unmistakable signs of an admixture of coloured blood". Nonetheless, he continued, the Immigration Advisory Council meeting of 27 August 1953 decided that the 75 percent European blood rule "need not be insisted upon", and that the wife and children of an applicant could be admitted with him.[45] In the second half of the 1950s the discriminatory policy toward the potential Jewish migrants eased gradually when in October 1957, 1,000 of the 5,000 Hungarian refugees – following the 1956 Hungarian Revolution – were Jewish. However, discriminatory government policy toward Sephardic migrants did not change until the late 1960s.

The Executive Council of Australian Jewry

Beginning with its establishment in 1937, the AJWS assisted Jews from Europe to find a home in Australia. Moreover the Executive Council of Australian Jewry (ECAJ), which had been established in January 1945 as the umbrella organization representing all Jews of Australia, informed Prime Minister John Curtin that it endorsed the AJWS's role in its function, stressing "the readiness and the determination of the Jewish community of Australia to welcome, encourage and assist with all means at its disposal all Jewish migrants admitted by the Commonwealth into this country".[46] However, while the ECAJ statement went on to specifically mention potential immigrants from Britain, the United States and central and northern Europe, it failed to include Jews from Arab countries in the Middle East, who were being increasingly persecuted as agents of Zionism.[47] The fact is that neither the AJWS nor the ECAJ displayed much enthusiasm for the arrival of Sephardim in Australia, in many cases refusing to represent prospective Sephardic immigrants. In addition, those who did manage to enter the country without their help quickly discovered that they could not rely on the AJWS for assistance in settling into their new lives.

In May 1956, Association of Sephardim President Aaron Aaron sent a letter to the president of the New South Wales Board of Jewish Deputies, expressing the anguish and disappointment of the Sephardim at this lack of assistance. Mr. Aaron made specific reference to an article in the *Sydney Jewish News*, dated 27 April 1956, entitled "Why Sephardis May Not Come Here." This article quoted a spokesman of the Department of Immigration in Canberra as saying, "Sephardis were not excluded as such, but that there was a government policy governing 'mixed races' specifying that applicants had to show that they were at least 75 percent European by descent, predominantly European in appearance, and European in education and mode of living." The Sephardim, Mr. Aaron went on, were shocked to learn of a policy of such importance from a newspaper article rather than from the ECAJ itself, which was purportedly looking out for the interests of all Jews. Moreover, he charged, not one Sephardic application for residence in Australia had been attained through the offices of ECAJ, although friendly non-Jews, including parliamentarians like William J. Aston, had helped many Sephardim, particularly in family reunification.[48]

Among the Ashkenazim, individuals like A. Landa and S. Einfeld did help some Sephardim referred to them through friends (Aaron 1979:126). Nevertheless, the Sephardim were provided no assistance by the Ashkenazi establishment. The Sephardic Jews felt humiliated, intimidated and degraded by this treatment – or lack of it – by the Ashkenazim. More than thirty years later, many members of that community still feel resentment and bitterness at their treatment by the official leaders of Australian Jewry, especially in view of the help they received from non-Jews.

Among those helped by Landa were the Rassaby brothers and their young sister. Hugh Rassaby gained an entry visa "because of his fair complexion, his English accent and his record serving in the British Indian Army stationed in Singapore", as communicated by his niece.

However, his younger brother, Maurice, who had graduated with a B.Sc. from the University of Calcutta, experienced many problems and was repeatedly refused because "he spoke English with an Indian accent". Mr. Landa, the member of Parliament who had succeeded in gaining an entry visa for Maurice (and several other Sephardim), told him that, "part of his problem was his dark complexion". The Rassabys' sister, Musel, was forced to leave Australia for New Zealand after her application for permanent residence was turned down. Musel only received her entry visa a year later, with Landa's persistence and her brothers' determination.

In contrast, when David a Sephardic Jew from India applied for a residence visa, the Department of Immigration turned to the ECAJ Chairman to find out about the Iraqi-Indian Jews living in Sydney. "The ECAJ Chairman told the immigration officers that these Jews have lived in India for a long time and 'claimed to be Jews' . . . but that he was not sure whether or not they were Jews."

When Mr. A. Solomon arrived in Australia in the early 1950s from Singapore, seeking help from the AJWS, "they did not recognize him as a Jew. They did not recognize that there was another type of Jew except the Ashkenazim." The person who related Mr. Solomon's story to me went on to describe how he was forced to move to Yagoona (far from any Jewish communal center), because the only way he could support himself was to work for the railway there. By cutting himself off from the Jewish community, he ended up marrying out of the faith. My informant claims that Solomon's family placed at least part of the blame for this on the AJWS. "If they had helped him find a job and a place to live here in Bondi, he would not have been cut off and might have married a Jewish girl. After all, he was a religious man and wanted very much to be among other Jews."

After the 1956 Sinai War the majority of Jews were expelled from Egypt, and several traveled to Australia. Upon arrival, an immigration officer boarded the ship accompanied by a member of the AJWS, who was there to "assist" the immigration officer as "an authority on the Jewish people". When the AJWS representative asked if there were any Jews on the ship, one Egyptian Jew recalled feeling flattered. Thinking that the Jews would receive preferential treatment, she rose and declared her Jewishness. Nevertheless, when the AJWS representative then asked her to prove this by speaking Yiddish, she was devastated. Then, she recovered enough to ask whether *he* could speak Ladino (the Judeo-Spanish language), and, when he said he could not, she told him that, to her, he was not a Jew.

Egyptian Jews were especially bitter at their treatment by the AJWS, since they arrived at the same time that many Jews fleeing Hungary were being welcomed by the Society with open arms. Sephardim who immigrated to Australia during the late 1960s and early 1970s had the same experience, since the Russian Jews then arriving in Australia were also more warmly received than they were.[49]

Many factors determine the direction and results of the immigration process. In the case of the Sephardim in Sydney, contemporary events – including the upheaval in the Middle East and the creation of Israel, the independence of India and the Chinese Revolution – all conspired toward their displacement. In contrast to these "push" factors the peace, prosperity and socio-economic opportunities in Australia exerted a strong "pull".

Overall, however, the would-be host community was hostile to prospective Sephardic immigrants, and there were strong anti-Jewish feelings among the wider population. This resulted in the Sephardim being labeled "undesirable" by the immigration authorities, and those who did succeed in gaining entry often found it extremely difficult to obtain immigrant visas for their families.[50]

More importantly, their fellow Jews, the Ashkenazim, at best displayed little interest in their co-religionists. Indeed, many seemed unwilling to recognize them as Jews (Aaron 1979:174–82). Although there is little excuse for the AJWS representatives' ongoing ignorance of their Sephardic brethren, a look at the Ashkenazi community's own position in Australia allows us to at least understand their fear and avoidance of the Sephardic immigrants. Raised in Australia, a majority of the Ashkenazim themselves wished to "pass" as "Australians". This led many to downplay or minimize their Jewish identity when inter-acting with non-Jews. Since Australian anti-Semitism was no secret, why invite ostracism and unpleasantness by identifying themselves too closely with the highly visible Sephardic Jews? In this, the Ashkenazim were responding to white Australian insecurities derived partly from the sense that Australia was an under-populated cultural/ethnic enclave in an overpopulated and threatening Asian world.

Summary and Conclusions: Facing up to the Wider Australian Society

The wider Australian society, as represented by the immigration authorities, was very much against the immigration of all Asians and did its best to prevent them from entering Australia, even as tourists. Their fear of "an influx of undesirable Jews beyond all proportions" may have communicated itself to the Australian Jewish community.[51] The Australians' division of the world into black and white, Asian and European, was deeply etched in almost everyone's thinking, reflecting the wider racism in Western society that had not exhausted itself in

World War II. Affected by these ideas as much as anyone else – and undoubtedly more painfully than the perpetrators – the Ashkenazi victims now desired to see themselves as white Europeans and full members of Australian society. Attempting to attain this status for themselves, they joined non-Jewish Australians in classifying the Sephardim as "half or at most three-quarter caste", and colluded in treating them as Asians.

In general, the treatment of Sephardic Jews seeking to settle in Australia provides a vivid instance of the workings of the White Australia policy, and illustrates how the ramifications of this policy led Ashkenazi and Sephardic Jews to assume opposing roles in the Australian context, since they were on opposite sides of the "color bar".

4

The Sephardic Family

Scholars of the modern urban family tend to reach one of two quite different conclusions: (1) that the modern family is based on the conjugal unit, and that kinship has lost many of its functions and some of its importance in the urban setting; or (2) that there is a strong persistence of extended kinship ties.[1]

Parsons (1943:178) calls the "isolated conjugal family" the basic unit of modern urban societies. In his view, the extended family has become decreasingly important in modern states, where adults are economically independent of both their families of orientation and their extended families. Parsons places crucial import on the dyadic relationship between husband and wife, based on a freedom of choice of partner in which the family of orientation has very little influence. He also stresses that choice of occupation in modern societies is a function of individual achievement rather than recruitment based on such ascribed institutions as kinship. He belongs to the group of researchers who place emphasis on individual ability to perform and equality of opportunity. In this, others who concluded that the Industrial Revolution and consequent technological advancement acted to reduce the socio-economic cohesiveness of the family join him.

Parsons and Bales (1956) and Young and Willmont (1973) concentrate on the change from traditional to modern structure, where the Industrial Revolution contributed to turn the family into a specialization agency. Basham (1978:91) and others base their studies on the shift from rural to urban structure and the migration process and its dramatic influence on the family and kinship ties. In contrast, studies of working-class families in East London point out the importance of kinship – especially of the mother–daughter tie – based on a high degree of mutual aid and support as well as on sentiment and sociability.

Litwak (1965) falls somewhere between the Parson–Wirth–Smelser and the Bott–Young–Wilmott–Firth groups. He believes the dominant type in the Western world is the modified extended family, consisting of a network of nuclear families who maintain their freedom while to some extent depending on each other economically.

Although Parsons' (1965) "isolated nuclear family" has found some expression in American society, many studies contradict his findings, for example, S. Benson (1981). For, the modified extended family is found in all sections of urban and rural modern society, manifesting itself differently in all classes. Indeed, the relatively impersonal nature of urban society may even encourage people to turn to kin for aid and social contact. However, this modern relationship is unlike that of the extended family in traditional society, in that the modern family can more easily choose to associate with those of their kin whom they prefer.

In this context, Litwak's "modified extended family" seems the best categorization of the modern family. This family may not live in close geographical proximity, and does not perform as a socio-economic unit, but it does provide its constituent units with an important, ongoing basis of support.

Centralized modern governments – with institutions such as formal education, welfare, old-age retirement, unemployment benefits and pensions – have usurped many traditional functions of the family. Thus, whereas the extended family or the restricted community to which they belonged fulfilled most needs of individuals in traditional societies, migrants to the West from these societies sought at least initial support from their extended kin and coethnics.

In immigrating to the Western world, the Sephardic family moved from a traditional, relatively closed social system with an autocratic regime – where the community fulfilled most of its own needs and the necessity of interacting with outsiders was limited – to a relatively open and democratic social system, in which there is a high level of interaction among diverse ethnic groups. The Sephardim come from societies based either on caste hierarchies where the individual is tied irrevocably to a traditionally endogamous occupational group, or on rigidly delineated ethnic groups.[2] The transition from the traditional to the Western society therefore brought about many changes in the structure and functions of the Sephardic family, including a decline in the birth rate and a rise in women's age of marriage. This resulted in smaller families, a narrowing of the average age difference between husbands and wives, and a dramatic decrease in the number of kin marriages.[3]

The introduction of compulsory education for girls as well as boys also created a fundamental change in the Sephardic family. In traditional society, girls received only enough education to enable them, once married, to manage their homes smoothly and carry out their domestic duties. In Australia today, however, Sephardic girls, like all other Australian females, partake of the education system and are in turn influenced by it in myriad ways.[4]

Increased education has also brought more women into the work force, which has resulted in an increase in their rights. In traditional society, few women were permitted to work outside of the home environment, and were under the complete control of their fathers or husbands. In modern society, where most women work and contribute financially to the household income at one stage or another of their lives, they have more to say about household decisions and more equality in marriage. This has also led to a rise in the divorce rate.[5]

With regard to sex, whereas marriages used to be arranged and girls not permitted to see their prospective husbands until their engagement, the modern young not only choose their own partners but are also free to spend time alone with their fiancés. In addition, the father's decreased control over family members and Western family laws have improved women's lives both within and outside of the family. Finally, whereas the dowry system was an important factor in traditional marriage this factor has been replaced by exchanges on both sides.[6]

Today's young Sephardic Australians tend to make their own decisions and take jobs that allow them to establish their own households. For them, achieved status has become more important than ascribed status. This contrasts with their elders, who were brought up in a society in which position was mostly determined by ascription.

The transition from one place to another, even within the same society, generally results in a certain degree of strain on the family. However, in the case of Sephardim, the impact of immigration to another society, with a new social system, caused nothing less than cultural shock. When crucial customs and values lose their meanings and, in time, disappear, the result is a cultural vacuum and confusion, especially for the younger generation. Their elders cling to their history and nostalgic memories, but younger people seek values and customs appropriate to their new environment, often borrowing these from the host society. Thus begins their process of acculturation.

In discussing the Sephardic family in order to assess the impact of immigration to Australia, it should again be stressed that the Sephardic community is viewed herein not as a cultural group, but as a social group comprised of people from diverse ethnic groups who were brought together through both external and internal pressures. A. L. Epstein (1981:6) argues that culture is manifest in the institutionalized behavior and in the customs acknowledged within a particular society or group. Thus, culture conveniently can be regarded as representing the accumulated stock of solutions, sometimes worked out over countless generations. The post-war non-Ashkenazi Jewish migrants who have come to constitute the elders in today's Sephardic community were brought together by religious needs and their desire to establish networks and organizations for socializing and mutual aid. Actually, however, the negative forces of distance from, and perceived rejection by, both the wider Australian community and their Ashkenazi co-religionists are the principal factors behind the formation of a discrete Sephardic community in Sydney.

The family was the focus of Sephardic interpersonal life in their countries of origin, just as Judaism provided the core of communal life; Smooha (1978:379) has remarked that, "Although the family plays a central role in the life of both Orientals and Ashkenazim, it has declined as a source of personal contacts."

Similarly, when Sephardic immigrants in Sydney found themselves under strong pressure to conform to a new society, they too were forced to redefine many traditional aspects of family life. Relationships among family members, as well as kinship structure, softened in a society that placed less emphasis on kinship. Moreover, the separation of families in immigration meant that many of them began life in Australia with a greatly attenuated web of kin. In order to adapt to this new social situation, they endeavored to alter traditional cultural elements to fit the new social order. Part of this adaptation was the establishment of Sephardic social groups to provide a reference group that would enhance their confidence and well-being.

The Social Structure

The traditional family was characterized by an endogamous, patrilineal, patriarchal, patrilocal and polygamous system.[7] Among the Sephardic communities of the Middle East, marriage between kin was a common, even preferred, practice. Marriage with outsiders was considered unwelcome until the middle of the twentieth century. It was believed it interrupted the functioning of the family as a socio-economic unit and tended to dissipate family property. Thus, kin marriage was viewed as contributing to the strength of kinship ties of the extended family. In addition, traditional Sephardic families were patrilineal in their countries of origin, a person belonging to his or her father's family. It was also patriarchal in that the father was the master of his family and decided the destiny of its members. Tradition legitimized his actions and his control over his wife and children.[8]

As in most traditional Middle Eastern families, as well as most traditional Jewish families in general, sons were preferred to daughters. It was indicated to me in many interviews that boys perpetuated the line of the family, gave it more socio-political power and perpetuated the honor of the family by advancing themselves educationally and working at more prestigious jobs than that of their fathers. Sons were often seen as an extension of their fathers' personalities, as someone through whom the fathers could vicariously achieve what they had not themselves been able to accomplish. This is demonstrated even in the congratulations that parents receive on the birth of a child: "When a son was born, the well wishers said 'Besiman Tov' [good fortune] and 'Tesewihum Sab-a' [may there be seven; seven in Jewish tradition being a lucky number]. If the newborn was a girl, they merely said 'Mazal Tov' [good luck], sometimes adding what were in effect words of sympathy, 'Al-Hamd Lilah Ala Salamitha' [thank God the mother is well] or 'Ala Rasa Libnin' [may boys follow her]". Stahl (1993) quoted an elderly Afghanistani Jewess stating, "when a boy is born, the sky rejoices for another male added to the Torah and prayers. When a daughter is born, the earth screams, 'another one was born to sweep me'". The same types of congratulations are still bestowed today, particularly among Iraqi and Indian Jews, and Singaporean Jews of Iraqi origin. The following instances illustrate how my interviewees and their families acted and reacted upon the birth of boy and girl children.

When Sophie's first grandchild turned out to be a girl, she remarked: "Oh, well. Next time it will be a boy. No harm done; In any event, a daughter always helps the mother while a son expects everything to be done for him, so that is at least one good thing about having a daughter first." Thus, Sophie attempted to persuade herself that it was better to have a girl first, although her disappointment was obvious.

When Rahma gave birth to her first child, a girl, her parents-in-law, who had planned to visit the young couple upon the birth, decided to cancel the visit. Rahma's comment to me showed her obvious hurt: "My in-laws may consider themselves very advanced and modern [they were born in America], but they behave as if they were still living in Iraq or in India even though they have never been there. But, really, I am not surprised at their behavior, because all of them, deep in their hearts, still prefer to have more boys than girls." When Rahma was pregnant for the second time, her in-laws could not decide whether to plan a trip. However, within a week of her having a boy, they arrived and stayed for three months, "to help her". As she put it: "My mother-in-law said that they must help me. After all, giving birth is not easy." Then she continued, "As if giving birth to a boy is more strenuous than giving birth to a girl!"

Paulette, an Egyptian woman with six sons, told me jokingly that her husband (of Iraqi origin) is called Abu-l'bnin (the father of the sons) by close Iraqi friends, and that this name is one to be proud of. Moreover, many members of the community have indicated to Paulette that she must have been blessed by God to give birth to six sons, that he must have favored her.

On the other hand, after Mabel had four sons, her mother was very worried that Mabel would fall victim to the evil eye. Mabel explained that she herself was not superstitious, but just the same she wanted a daughter too. Then she continued telling me how proud her husband is of his sons, particularly when they accompany him to synagogue each morning and evening. This, according to Mabel, has given him a sense of strength. (Later she gave birth to a daughter.)

Divorce: Past and Present

Polygamy was permitted in the traditional Jewish societies from which the Sydney Sephardim emigrated, although it was exercised on a very small scale in the hundred years prior to 1950. It has been abandoned since immigration to Israel and other Western societies. According to the Jewish religion, a man who has been married for ten years without producing children can divorce his wife and remarry in order to fulfill the commandment to "Be fruitful and multiply." But a woman who was divorced for not conceiving had little chance of remarrying (no one ever daring to suggest that the husband might be the infertile one).[9] Such women were much better off if they remained with their husbands, who would take a second wife. Furthermore, as women in Islamic societies were not allowed to work outside of the home and the Jewish community assumed this cultural pattern, cast-off wives would not be able to survive financially on their own. Girls were brought up to love children and big families, "even if it be at the price of a second wife".[10]

Thus, divorce was almost unheard of in the countries of origin – and was considered a family tragedy and condemned by the community when it did occur. In the few cases where a husband became dissatisfied with his wife, he could divorce her and she had little to say in her defense. But the rabbis made divorce difficult, advocating and facilitating polygamy instead – which was permitted by both Jewish and Iraqi Muslim law.[11] Nonetheless, such plural marriages were relatively rare. Thus, of the 27,042 Iraqi women who immigrated to Israel in 1950–51, only 226 or 0.8 percent were divorced.[12] And the Iraqis and other Asian immigrants to Sydney were not forthcoming on the frequency of polygamy among them as they were ashamed of this practice and tended to exclude it when discussing their family history. What was clearly evident was that the divorce rate has increased dramatically among Sephardim in Australia, where compatibility is given more weight than it was in the countries of origin, where the rabbis and the community did not consider it a sufficient reason to divorce.

The case of a divorce among an Asian of Iraqi descent illustrates that married women had fewer rights in their countries of origin than in Australia. This man divorced his wife and took their two children away from her because she was not fit to care for them – a decision supported by the rabbinical court even though it was widely known that he had betrayed her with a non-Jewish woman (whom he later married after she had converted to Judaism). The man's first wife wanted to stay with him even in a polygamous marriage, so she could care for her own children. Nevertheless, the woman he wished to marry adamantly refused strongly to enter a polygamous marriage.

Although the new wife did not raise the children from his first marriage, their father placing them in the care of his aunt, he still forbade the children's mother to see them. Visitation rights became possible only some twenty years after they had all immigrated to Australia.

It is not surprising, therefore, that women preferred to stay married rather than suffer the stigma of divorce, with its loss of financial support and possibly of their children as well. On the other hand, a wife could decide to leave her husband and move back with her parents or live in a brother's home; but this, too, was rare. In such situations, the rabbinical authorities would dissolve the marriage if the husband were unable to persuade her to return to him.

Table 4.1   Marriages and Divorces among the Sydney Jewish Community between 1968 and 1985

Period	Marriage	Divorces	Percent of Divorces
1968–1972	429	98	22.8
1973–1977	368	144	39.1
1978–1982*	345	200	58.0
1983–1985**	221	113	51.1

* Following new divorce legislation
** Three-year period

The data made available to me by the *Beth Din* of Sydney points to an increase in the number of divorces among Sephardim in Australia, especially since 1977 when new Australian divorce legislation made divorce easier. Thus, the divorce rate rose from 22.8 percent of all Jewish marriages in 1972, to almost 40 percent in 1977, and jumped to 58 percent in 1982, after the new legislation went into effect, settling back to 51.1 percent by 1985 (see table 4.1).

During the same period (1968–85), about 80 marriages a year (or 1,363 marriages in total) were recorded as having been performed at Sydney's largest Ashkenazi synagogues and the Sephardic synagogue. The number of marriages a year ranged from a high of 92 in 1973–77 to a low of 69 in 1978–82, with the figure rising to 74 in the period 1983–85. Based on my interviews I estimate that a further 200 marriages took place during the same period in other congregations. But Jews who chose civil marriage over a religiously sanctioned one are not counted here.

With the above figure in mind, it may appear that the number of divorces within the Jewish community will continue to increase, mostly due to the redress of previous imbalances in acknowledging women's rights, including rights in respect to their children and their property, by both the civil and religious systems. As to the sharp decline in the number of marriages recorded, this may be attributable to many people choosing to marry in civil ceremonies. Most of the divorces recorded by the Sydney *Beth Din* were due to incompatibility, several involving mixed Sephardic–Ashkenazi marriages. The experiences of some of these couples, a majority of whom comprised Sephardic men married to Ashkenazi women, are detailed below.

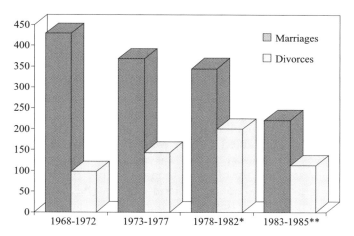

* Following new divorce legislation
** Three-year period

Figure 4.1   Marriage and Divorce in the Sydney Jewish Community

Ben, a successful thirty-seven-year-old Sephardic lawyer, divorced his wife after seven years. Although he felt that his wife was a difficult person, he stated that he would still be married had it not been for the interference of his parents, particularly his mother, "a very demanding woman". Although he had expected some difficulties since he and his wife "come from different worlds . . . but at least we were both brought up in Australia", his parents did not like his wife because they felt she was "too spoiled" and her parents did not like his family. Neither set of parents-in-law made much of an effort to get on with each other. He felt that this, together with his parents' interference, had a damaging effect on his marriage. After fighting his wife to gain custody of the two children, and losing, they did not speak to each other for years, communicating only through lawyers. But, at the time of the interview, he said they were very good friends and had an amicable relationship. As he put it, "It took us years to get over the poisonous atmosphere created between us by our backgrounds and our parents." He reckoned that if they had lived far away from both sets of parents their marriage would have survived. In order to understand this situation, one must remember that Ben's parents were brought up in a traditional society in which sons and their wives are expected to submit to the sons' parents' authority.

Another Sephardic man, an accountant, married to an Ashkenazi woman, decided to divorce his wife after a year. The couple had dated for four years while she was studying medicine, during which time he was very helpful, supportive and understanding. He waited patiently for her to graduate, and they were married a few months later. Their families and friends had high expectations for this marriage because he was – or seemed to be – so proud of her achievements. As one woman put it, "She spent so much time studying, and worked so hard to succeed, and he never pressured her. If he was willing to go through all those difficult years they should be right for each other." But once she began working, he told the rabbis, he hardly saw her because she was at the hospital most of the time. And, when not working, she was so tired that they had no life together. He could not see himself continuing in this fashion. He complained that her work meant that she did not cook, the house was not attended to and she certainly did not exemplify the "typical" housewife. Another woman familiar with the couple commented that she did not understand what had happened to him. "It could be that it suddenly dawned on him that she earned more money than he could ever hope to earn, and he feels degraded. Otherwise, he surely knew that she would have to spend much time in hospital pursuing her career, particularly during the first few years."

The Katari family, too, consisted of a Sephardic father and an Ashkenazi mother. However, two of their three daughters, all of whom were born and raised in Sydney and were in their early twenties during my research, married Ashkenazi men. The parents were happily married for twenty-five years. The mother assumed an active role in the Sephardic community early on and learned "all the secrets of Indian cooking" from her mother-in-law, who lived with them for a few years. Indeed, she often said that had it not been for her blond hair and blue eyes, others would have taken her as Indian. The two daughters who married Ashkenazi partners chose men born in Sydney. One was divorced after three years of marriage, and the other was happily married and expecting her first child. The third daughter married a non-

Jewish Australian of English ancestry, who claimed that he did not believe in any religion, and divorced him after two years. She said that one of the reasons for the divorce was that he had said he did not object to her raising their children Jewish, but after the marriage he changed his mind. The daughter objected to this and began to focus on other problems that had resulted in their not getting on as well as she had expected. She later married a man of Sephardic origin who was born in Sydney.

Sabina, sixty years old at the time of my research, was born in Iraq and immigrated to Sydney in the early 1950s. Her marriage, too, lasted less than a year. She met "a Jewish man" after living in Sydney for several years, and was engaged to him after dating him for eight months. The wedding was planned for a year later, when she was twenty-nine, but she became pregnant a month before it was to take place. Her husband left her when she was about seven months pregnant, and "did not even come to the hospital to see his son" when the baby was born. Then he left Australia and divorced her several years later. She "did not mind about the divorce, because I was not going to get married again anyway . . . but I was deeply hurt that he did not care about his own son, whom he never saw until the child was almost two. And he never supported either of us. It was my fault for not realizing that he had no heart before we were married." I learned from Sabina's family that if it had not been for their support, she and the child would not have had "food on the table". They, however, blame her for getting pregnant before the wedding.

According to the restricted data available from the *Beth Din*, despite the increasing trend toward Ashkenazi–Sephardic marriages among the Australian-born generation, the divorce rate among these couples does not seem to deviate significantly from that of the Australian Jewish community as a whole. It does, however, deviate considerably from marriages within the Sephardic community (see table 4.1). If this is correct, it is probably due to the young generation of Sephardim and Ashkenazim who were equally exposed to the cultural and social conditions of Australian society, and the lessening influence of family tradition on their lives. In other words, by living in the same area, Sydney's Eastern Suburbs, and attending the same schools, the young Sephardim became more Ashkenized and more familiar culturally to the Ashkenazim. In addition, the small size of the Sephardic community, particularly those of marriageable age, means that Sephardim have to marry Ashkenazim if they wish to remain within the Jewish community in Australia.

Nonetheless, Dan, a single twenty-eight-year-old with university degrees, who was brought up in Australia, stated that, "I will never marry an Ashkenazi girl. There is nothing like having an unspoiled

Sephardic wife, who does not demand that things be done for her. On the other hand, she must at least have completed high school and be from a good family." Dan's wish to benefit from both worlds by marrying an educated Sephardic woman from a good family, who at the same time would submit to him in accordance with Sephardic tradition, may be traced to the marriages of his three brothers to Ashkenazi women, all of which ended in divorce. It seems that the children in this family underwent a too-rapid acculturation into the Australianized Ashkenazi culture, abandoning their tradition before they had a chance to adjust to the new society, but expecting others to adjust to them. (Three years later, Dan married a non-Jew, had a daughter and cut himself off completely from Jewish life and the Jewish community.)

Table 4.2 Marriages and Divorces Registered in the Sydney Sephardi Synagogue between 1963 and 1987

	Number of Marriages	%	Number of Divorces	%	Total Divorces	%
Sephardi/Sephardi	66	64.3	2	3.0	2	18.2
Sephardi/Ashkenazi	29	28.0	8	27.6	8	72.7
Sephardi Males/ Converts to Judaism	8	7.7	1	12.5	1	9
Total	103		11		11	100

While divorce is almost unheard of among the over 55 generation, regardless of the ethnic origin of the spouse, and the younger generation is gravitating toward more successful marriages with Ashkenazim – the generation in between remains problematic. Members of this generation were raised to adhere to the traditional patterns of their communities in their countries of origin and came to Australia in their late teens. However, as several of them conveyed to me, once in Australia they felt they were expected to shed this way of life and to adapt to an alien new cultural and social system in which divorce was not considered a cause for ostracism. Among this generation, divorce seems to be more acute, particularly if they married Ashkenazim brought up in the Western tradition. After studying the community for a number of years, it seems that this group accounts for the largest numbers of divorces.

Of the 103 marriages performed in the Sydney Sephardic synagogue between August 1963 and July 1987, 10.7 percent ended in divorce. Of the 11 cases of divorce, 72.7 percent were between Sephardic and Ashkenazi partners. This list, of course, does not include divorces between Sephardim and Ashkenazim who were not married in the Sephardic synagogue; I know of at least 14 of these cases.

One of my informants commented that when an Ashkenazi man marries a Sephardic woman, he expects her to be subservient and she expects to have more freedom. Moreover, while she is subservient for a few years because of her upbringing, she gradually becomes more independent, because of her new environment. When this happens, the marriage begins to break down. This informant added that Sephardic men usually marry Ashkenazi women to raise their social status, but do not expect their wives to differ from their mothers in the home or in domestic life. Thus, in both cases, the wives do not live up to the husband's conscious or unconscious expectations; he does not relish her challenge to his authority, but is unable to turn the clock back in the case of an Ashkenazi wife, or to stop it from ticking on in the case of a Sephardic wife. In this context, it seems that marriages between those of different backgrounds usually sustain more friction than in-marriages.

Studies conducted in these areas show clearly that the divorce rate among interracial and inter-ethnic marriages is significantly higher than that among in-marriages. In the 1950s and 1960s, Sephardic–Ashkenazi unions were looked upon with great disapproval. Those who entered such marriages were not given much chance for success for several reasons, not the least the Jewish community's attitude, which stigmatized such unions.

If a man initiates the divorce, he finds it relatively easy to do so under Jewish law. Nevertheless, even today, Jewish women must obtain a divorce from their husbands. Since the woman's freedom depends on her husband's willingness to grant the divorce, this can lead to virtual blackmail (although there are also women who withhold divorces to the same end). Rabbi Israel Porush (1977:193), head of Sydney's Beth Din, outlined the Australian situation as follows:

> The Rabbinate has been seriously concerned about problems relating to Jewish divorce, or the *get* . . . When one of the parties refuses to cooperate and the *get* is withheld, the parties are regarded as still married in Jewish Law. Untold hardship has been caused thereby, particularly to Jewish women, who may have received a civil divorce but cannot remarry because their vindictive husbands refuse to give a *get*.

In 1975, the rabbinical courts of Sydney and Melbourne asked the Attorney-General of Australia and the Senate Committee on Divorce to include appropriate legislation as part of the new Family Law Bill that was submitted to Parliament. They suggested following Israeli legislation under which men can be imprisoned through court order if they appear to be behaving unreasonably in refusing to grant their wives a *get*. The Committee on Divorce refused to implement this suggestion on the grounds that in Australia, where religious communities conduct their own religious affairs, the government cannot impose civil restrictions that interfere with the religious conduct of any ethnic or religious group. Rabbi Porush commented: "These efforts failed on the grounds that the Court had no power to enforce the religious requirements of any section of the community."

Among the instances in which Sephardic men in Australia have blackmailed their wives with unrealistic demands, mostly financial, is the case of Elsie. Elsie married Sam, a divorced man, in 1973. They seemed to be living happily for four years, except that she was unable to become pregnant. According to Elsie, they worked hard, bought a nice house and were getting on well with each other until the day she came home from work to find that her husband had changed the locks to keep her out. Stunned that he would prevent her from entering her own home, she asked her brother for help. But he refused to become involved. When Elsie was finally able to confront her husband, he only said that he did not want to see her anymore. She felt that the reason for his rejection of her was that she could not conceive. When she came to grips with the idea of having to divorce him, and asked him to give her a *get*, Sam refused until she paid him for "the four years he lost". When Elsie sought help from the Sephardic rabbi, his reaction was that she should not have gotten involved with Sam in the first place. "You knew that he had been married before, and that it would be putting your healthy head into a sick bed." Shocked by this reaction, Elsie resigned her membership in the synagogue. But this did not stop the same rabbi from later approaching her and proposing that she pay her husband several thousand dollars in order to gain her freedom. Again disgusted by the rabbi's suggestion, she refused. "I didn't have the money even though I wanted my freedom very badly." Ten years later, in 1987, she was still unable to remarry because he had not yet granted her a *get*, and the rabbinical court was unable to force him to do so.

According to Dalia, who was born in Singapore and came to Australia at the age of eighteen, she and Tony – a Jew born in Australia to parents of Polish origin – had a very bad marriage from the beginning. They kept on having children, until there were six, after which they kept on trying to "work things out". After twelve years, however, she "had had enough" and moved to her mother's with the children. Tony took her to Family Court, which awarded him custody of the four older children on the basis that it was she who had left the home. According to Dalia, the court therefore ruled that she also had no right to financial support, except to cover the expenses of the two children left in her custody. In addition, since Tony held full title to their house, she was not entitled to any part of that. I learned Tony's side of the story from a member of his family, who warned me not to ask him any questions because "he was a bitter man". My source told me that, "He loved her very much. They had their ups and downs, but don't we all?" He was outgoing and she was quiet. She did not tell him that she was not happy with him, and he was deeply hurt when she took the children and left without ever saying anything to him. Tony had complained to my informant that Dalia had neglected the children during the last few years of their marriage and that it was on this basis that the court had granted him custody of four of the children. Tony remained bitter for many years after their separation, getting the court to rule that Dalia could not see the children in his custody because she had allegedly incited them to run away from him twice. Not even when one of the boys was *Bar-Mitzvah* did he allow her to take part. This case was in the *Beth Din* during the years of my field-work in Sydney during which Tony refused to give Dalia a *get*. It was not until eight years after their separation that he did so, because he wanted to remarry. (The *Beth Din* also failed to persuade Tony to allow Dalia to see their children.)

Although these cases are relatively rare, they illustrate how Jewish husbands can utilize their strong position *vis-à-vis* their wives to undermine the rights of women under Australian civil law.[13]

The following is an extreme case that can best illustrate the inferior position of women in Jewish law: Orah and Yehieh Abrahams were married in Yemen when she was fourteen, and came to Israel. By 22 she had five children but was unhappy because her husband was brutal and used to batter and imprisoned her. At 24 she left him, asking for a divorce. When he refused the rabbinical court imprisoned him. He remained in prison for thirty years rather than comply with the court's ruling. She, of course, had been unable to remarry until his death in prison in December 1994.

Choosing a Partner

Among traditional Sephardim, negotiating a suitable match and marriage was considered a father's obligation. In the majority of cases girls themselves played a completely passive role. Not only did men alone formally regulate marriages, but the father controlled all the property and paid the bride price, the *mohar*; thus sons could rarely afford to choose brides of whom their fathers disapproved. As to the consent of the daughter, in some cases this was "obtained" beforehand, in others it was completely disregarded.

Several clauses in the *Ketubah*, the Jewish marriage contract, deal specifically with sanctioned formulae, such as "the declaration that the *mohar* was paid and received and the enumeration of the dowry received by the husband", concerning what is constituted to be the legal framework of marriage according to *halakhic* ethics.[14]

Until the end of the nineteenth century, girls were married at the age of twelve or thirteen, and sometimes even at eleven. By about 1913, the age was raised and the majority were marrying at fifteen.[15] The general pattern was that the father would arrange for a husband for his daughter when she reached eleven or twelve, after which he would bring the prospective husband to the house to show him to her. In most cases, she submitted to her father's will. Several women told me: "I was just a child and did not know about marriage", or "My mother always told me to say yes", or "My parents loved me . . . it was obvious that they would make the right choice for me."

The same patterns of choosing a wife existed among the Iraqi Jewish communities of China and India. However, in Asia, where age as well as wealth and power tend to give a man sexual privilege, there was a tendency for older men to marry young women or girls.

The examples cited below show clearly that girls were rarely an active party in the choice of their prospective husbands.

Mrs. Abraham, from Iraq, told me proudly that her father was a learned man. Unlike most fathers, he asked for her consent before contracting her marriage. He brought the prospective husband home when she was about fourteen years old, and said to her, "Well, daughter, look at him and tell me if you like him." Nevertheless, embarrassed and proud that "my father actually asked me, I could not dream of refusing his choice for me. After all, he was a learned man and he loved me. I of course married that man because he was chosen for me by my father."

Mrs. Moses was married in India at the age of thirteen. When she was eleven, her parents betrothed her to a man twenty-five years her senior. She recalled that she would take her engagement ring off her finger and hide it in her pocket every morning before she went to school because she was so embarrassed at her early engagement to a man twenty-five years older than she was. When her nine-year-old sister told the girls at school that she was engaged Mrs. Moses kicked her, pulled her hair and made her tell them that she had lied. Once married, Mrs. Moses bore eleven children in rapid succession. She recalls "My husband, may his soul rest in peace, had a very strong hand over me and the children. I had to do all the household work, take care of the children and help him in the shop. He never let me have any money for myself, buying everything for the house himself." On their arrival in Australia, her children, who were by then married, urged her to leave him, but she would not do so. As she put it, "It is all from God, and I never spoke one bad word about him. After all, he was my husband and I learned to love him and to do as he told me."

Mrs. Erena, also from India, was married at thirteen to a man thirty-seven years her senior. By the age of twenty-two, she had given birth to five children. She said that her brother, who was four years older than she was, used to accompany her whenever she left the house. She always introduced him as her husband, "because I was ashamed to say that my husband was so old. But, I did love him. He must have been the best husband for me because my parents chose him for me, and after all they loved me very much so how could they have done otherwise?"

Other testimonies given to me highlight the plight of many young boys, who also had little choice of partner. Mr. Avner from Iraq was in his early fifties when I interviewed him. He stated that he was forced by his uncle to marry a woman he did not like. After thirteen years of marriage and three children, they ended their marriage with a messy divorce. As the eldest boy in his family, Mr. Avner had to take responsibility for the household when his father died, becoming the breadwinner. In those days, his family was very poor even though he had a good profession and employment. His uncle, who was quite rich, told him that if he married the girl in question he would help the family financially. However, after the marriage, the uncle "washed his hands of the family". He "felt as though he had been in prison for thirteen years". This man and his sister conveyed to me that they knew many other young men in similar situations who were forced into marriages they clearly did not want by their family's financial situation.

While both men/boys and girls were often forced into unwanted marriages in their countries of origin, women seem to have been more heavily disadvantaged. In both cases, the wishes and desires of the larger family seem to have been more important than those of the individuals concerned. For the focus when contracting a marriage was on the family, its honor and status, and its welfare, rather than on the compatibility of the spouses.[16]

Love was regarded as an unnecessary precondition to marriage in these Sephardic communities. The notion was that the partners would eventually learn to love one another. Since the young were socialized into reliance on and submission to parental judgment and authority, particularly that of the father, it was not unusual for young Sephardic men to marry women that they would not have chosen for themselves and to be unable to rebel because of these strict socializing processes. Not only did they not want to hurt their parents' feelings, but also they were usually dependent on their father's support in establishing their own family. Finally yet importantly, they were unsure about their own limited experience and felt that their parents' long experience must work to their benefit in the end.

Thus, environment exerts a great influence on the preparation of children for marriage. Nevertheless, the social order of the Sephardic communities did break down with the mass migration after World War II to the extent that many engagement promises were dissolved.

However, I encountered several cases in which contracts between families were kept even when this meant that one prospective partner had to immigrate to another country in order to fulfill the contract. In one case, the prospective partners did not see each other for a number of years. In two other cases, they were first cousins.

Selecting one's own partner is a function of Western society, which concerns itself with individual rights. Parsons and Bales (1956) and Schrieft (1989) point out that choice of partner and marriage are defined as an achieved status in the West. However, although the emphasis is on individual choice, one cannot disregard the influence of that individual's position in society, that is, the community to which he or she belongs, his status and occupational position. Not to speak of the grip that tradition still exerts.[17] This means that men in the Sephardic community of Sydney still prefer their wives to be either inferior or equal to them socially (educational and professional background), as was the case when the community was more rigidly divided into classes in the countries of origin. Thus, among the replies to my questionnaire, there was only one case where a woman had a profession that is classified as higher on the social scale than that of her husband – who, probably not coincidently, is not of Sephardic origin.

Love seems to be "the basis for mate selection and that this emphasis is functional for that system in that this society demands relative freedom of movement".[18] However, even in modern societies, ethnicity, religion, social class, locality, etc. usually circumscribe love. Every child is socialized into a specific reference group or into several reference groups at the same time, during his or her lifetime.

The following examples illustrate that, even after thirty years in Australia and Israel, many Sephardim still do not regard love as a necessary component of marriage.

Jacob Shoshan, a 55-year-old businessman, described his marriage in the following words: "We lived in Israel for about ten years. I was still young and did not want to marry, but my father was nagging me so much that almost every week he told me he had found a girl for me from a good home and that I should see her. I myself did not feel like it, but I did not want to displease him. So I took out many girls once, and I never really got to know them because I always had to bring them home no later than eight o'clock. When my father told me about the woman who is now my wife, he said, 'She is a good girl from a respected family.' I was so tired of his nagging that I agreed to marry her. Two weeks after we met, we were engaged. Two months later, we were married. Then I brought her to Australia. I must say that I have always told my wife that I do not love her, and that I did not marry her out of love. But, I have a great deal of respect and affection for her. She has been a good wife and a marvelous mother."

Abraham, who is one of the more affluent members of the Sydney Jewish community, and who has been living in Australia for twenty-eight years, talked about his daughter and her marriage. "I gave her a good education. She did very well at university, and she is very successful in her profession. When she decided to get married it was to a man who is, firstly, not Jewish and, secondly, has not got the brain she has. She said she wanted to marry him because she loves him. Such a stupid excuse!" As to his daughter's relationship with her husband: "She says she loves him, but how can a woman in her right mind love a man who behaves as if he is a slave? My daughter can ask him in front of others to do the most humiliating jobs such as washing dishes or hanging out the wash, and he will do them. Now you tell me, what woman would want to marry a man who has no pride in himself and lets her dictate to him?"

The Iraqi Shalom and Hadar families met in Sydney about thirty years ago and became very close. Both came from affluent backgrounds. The Shalom family's sons both graduated from university, as did their father, and the mother graduated from high school in Iraq at a time when very few girls studied or worked. Over the past few centuries, the Hadar family had produced many religious leaders in Iraq, although the family in Australia observes few of the customs and traditions. The Hadars have four daughters, all of whom graduated from high school and work as secretaries. The Shaloms' eldest son, Rudy, married a non-Jewish Australian, which led to estrangement with his family for a number of years. However, after his first daughter was born, he was forgiven and again accepted in his parents' home.[19] Solomon, the Shaloms' second son, sought out Miriam, the Hadars' eldest daughter, when he was in his twenties. Miriam recalls that, "Solomon kept asking me out, but I did not like him in that way. It was more a case of sisterly affection. Then his mother telephoned mine and asked her to exert her influence in getting me to go out with Solomon, in the hope that we would eventually marry. He is really a nice charming man, but I was madly in love with John [an Ashkenazi Jew]. My mother begged me to go out with Solomon in order to please her friend, Mrs. Shalom." It seems that Solomon's mother spoke persistently to Miriam's mother about the possibility of the two young people getting together and making a family.

However, Miriam married John and the couple had three daughters. Miriam recalls that, "When the Hadars finally realized that I was really going to marry John, Mrs. Hadar called my mother and told her off: 'How can you allow your daughter to marry an Ashkenazi boy? They are like the *goyim* [non-Jews]; not like us. My son comes from a good family with a good upbringing. He has a good education, and your daughter is marrying a man with no education and no profession, who is not even an Iraqi like us.'" Miriam's marriage and that conversation caused a rift between the two families that lasted for a number of years. Solomon, in his mid-forties, was still unmarried in 1994. Miriam relates that Solomon's mother and other relatives view her giving birth to three girls and no boys as an indication that she should have married Solomon – for he would no doubt have had many sons instead of daughters!

Many Sephardic children, particularly males from lower-class families who have a university education and a good profession, find it easier to marry Ashkenazi spouses or even non-Jews. This is partly because, when they marry "out", they are free of the obligation to marry someone whose family background and social standing will be approved by the Sephardic community.

David started out by wanting to marry only a Sephardic girl, or not marrying at all. Nevertheless, one of the two Sephardic girls he dated was "too primitive," and the other "too conservative and backward". He met an Ashkenazi girl to whom he was engaged for four years. Then he left her and met a non-Jewish Australian woman, whom he married. The couple had a daughter. David's sister-in-law told me, however, that he is very unhappy because he finds his wife too "advanced". She does not like being at home and leaves the house messy, never having dinner ready, etc. In an informal interview, David's former Ashkenazi fiancé told me that he was like a little boy who expected her to do everything for him – and she did. She cared for him in all possible ways, but he took her for granted and never reciprocated, as if she were his mother. According to her, their relationship deteriorated after she decided "to liberate him" by ceasing to respond to his demands.

Rachamim came to Australia from Singapore at the age of thirteen. From a very religious Sephardic family, he married an Ashkenazi teacher, with whom he has three daughters and two sons. Although he is a regular participant in religious services, Rachamim does not participate in the social affairs of the community. His wife said at first that she was very happy to remain at home, especially since this is what her husband wanted. But a little while afterward, she said: "I admit that I miss the school. I miss teaching very much, and I do get fed up at times." Nevertheless, she, like most Ashkenazi women who marry traditional Sephardic men, said that her husband, the children and the home are the most important things in her life.

These cases demonstrate that people able to take advantage of the mobility offered to them by a new society, but who cannot utilize this new mobility to increase their status within the traditional world that still exists to a certain degree in Sydney, become dissatisfied with the traditional Sephardic community. They feel held back by the elders striving to maintain the hierarchy that existed in another world – which many of them view as irrelevant, backward and boring. More mobile within Australian society, they reject their ethnicity. This phenomenon is more vivid among community members who marry Ashkenazim or non-Jews. Those who marry Ashkenazi spouses gain higher status in the eyes of the Sephardic community. What they are really saying and there is a sociological message behind it – is that people cannot always "make it" if they remain in their own community. Moreover, the community reinforces this idea by assigning full acceptance and higher status to its members only after they have "proven themselves in the world". Thus, Sephardim who marry Ashkenazim adopt the Ashkenazi manner and use Ashkenazi modes of behavior to signal that they are of a higher status than the rest of their community. In short, Ashkenazi means a higher status in the eyes of many Sephardim. As one woman told me, "I would give part of my life to have been born an Ashkenazi." In fact, many Sephardim, particularly among the young, would like to be "Ashkenized".

Most Sephardic women who marry Ashkenazi men adopt their husband's way of life and become part of their family although not always a fully accepted member. These women usually affiliate with the Ashkenazi congregation and social system. However, when Sephardic men who marry Ashkenazi women find that they have not thereby achieved a high standing within the Ashkenazi community, and are not accepted by their in-laws' social circle, they often return to the Sephardic community. What seems to be happening, then, is that some of those who leave the community through marriage or otherwise, come back when they realize that they can now be respected within the community. Many of the Sydney Sephardim who left, returned because the outside world did not fulfill all their expectations and they were still not fully accepted by the Ashkenazi community or by Australian society. They felt as being at the periphery of both groups. Those who choose to remain out rarely become involved in either Ashkenazi or Sephardic social life, and are lost to both communities.

It is important to stress the role that marriage between members of different ethnic groups plays in the process of assimilating to a new host society, or, in the case of the Sephardim, to the majority Ashkenazi culture. Intermarriage not only increases the frequency of interaction between immigrants and the host society but together with such factors as socio-economic status and intergroup contact, also increases the level of assimilation into the host culture. All other factors notwithstanding, intermarriage rates are the most useful indicators of full assimilation. At the same time, however, intermarriage enhances the potential for friction and tension. Glazer and Moynihan (1963) found that intermarriages between different religious groups usually strengthened the religious identity of one and weakened the other. The intermarriage rate of any ethnic group is largely a function of the importance that group assigns to the family as a social institution within the group, after all intermarriage is a fundamental step away from the primary group and its social and cultural network.

As we have seen, the family was an extremely important institution in the life of Sephardim in traditional society, but it has been edging closer to the more "Australianized" – and less centralized – Ashkenazi family. This is illustrated particularly in the changing position of Sephardic women, who have increased chances for higher education and for participation in the work force, even after they marry.[20]

Because different ethnic groups attach different values to various aspects of their culture, it is difficult to determine the dimension in which assimilation occurs first. Intermarriage is both the result and the cause of assimilation. Considerable intermarriage cannot be expected without a certain degree of integration. However, once intermarriage does occur, the rate of assimilation is accelerated. The relationship between intermarriage and assimilation and acculturation in the case of Sephardim marrying Ashkenazim, depends greatly on the size of the group and its cohesiveness. The Sephardic group in Sydney is small and lacks cohesiveness, and therefore depends to a large degree on the Ashkenazi social institutions. Data of this research indicate that as the Sephardic family in Sydney continues to move toward increased freedom of the individual from parental control, the intermarriage rate will continue to climb.

Relationships between Family Members

The family in traditional society was viewed as a corporate entity; most responsibility was collective rather than individual. The individual's personal standing, ability, compatibility – and, most important, character – were given little consideration. A family member's actions were viewed as the actions of that person's family. In choosing marital partners for its members, families usually focused on the social standing and the wealth of the family of the prospective spouse, and the beauty of the prospective wife. These factors chiefly determined the dowry size.

In these societies, particularly in the Sephardic communities of the Middle East and Asia, the individual subordinated his or her interests to those of the organic unit of the family. Household heads held ultimate power over their wives and children. They were the decision-makers in most matters, representing the family in the community and being the sole breadwinners. The wives' personal property was for their use and control, as were the children, whose education and care they determined. Children were expected to treat their fathers with respect and to acknowledge and accept their authority. Strict obedience was an essential component of the father–child relationship. A wife could rarely challenge his authority at home.[21]

After immigration to Australia, several women who described their marital situation as miserable did not leave their husbands despite encouragement from their children, because they were under the control of their authoritarian spouses and afraid of arousing the wrath of the community.

One woman told me: "We were born for each other, and this is from God. If I left him, I would bring shame on my family because I would be defying God's ruling. Also, he must be a good man because he came from a good family that was highly respected by the community. So you see he cannot be so bad."

Another woman, whose husband was fourteen years older than she was, said that her husband was patient with her, "even though he sometimes hit me". She justified this behavior by saying that she was very young and "he had to teach me a lesson when I did not do as he instructed". He had enough on his mind, she said, because they were very poor and had eight children. Therefore, he "let his worries out on me". But, in most cases he apologized later and asked for her forgiveness. This woman concluded by saying, "You see, he is not so bad after all. He really has a heart of gold."

Another middle-aged woman told me about her parents' relationship. Several years after emigrating from Iraq to Israel, her father decided to move the family to Australia. She recalled, "As far as I can remember, when I was young my father was the nicest person in the world. He always treated us with patience and love. He gave us whatever we wanted if it was in his power. But he was always very mean to our mother, telling her off all the time. Even now that he is on pension, he is very generous to me and to my children, and buys us anything we ask for. But he rarely gave my mother money, and when he did she had to account to him for how she spent every penny." This couple were in their early sixties at the time of the interview, and the wife had left her husband three times. However, she went back to him every time, the third time to care for him after he had a massive heart attack. According to their daughter, they seemed to be happier than before.

In the eyes of many fathers and grandfathers within the Sydney Sephardic community, their position in the country of origin entailed more responsibilities than privileges. They had to represent the honor of the family in all spheres. Not only were they responsible for the behavior of their families, but they believed that if they misbehaved in any way, they would not be the only ones held to account: in the eyes of God, the family members were part of this misconduct. They were therefore under heavy pressure to do nothing that might be misconstrued by the community in order to protect the names of their wives and children as well as their own. The following examples illustrate the position of these fathers on the one hand, and that of their wives and children on the other.

In response to a question about his father, a middle-aged member of the Sephardic community confessed that his father, "may his soul rest in peace, was a hard, uncompromising person and very authoritarian when it came to the honor and dignity of the family. When he decided to punish you, God help you. You remembered it for the rest of your life. However, I cannot deny that it made a man out of me and my brothers. I, of course, do not exercise the same power over my children. For example, if I want them to come to synagogue with me on the Sabbath and they refuse, I simply bribe them. I don't claim that my way is better than that of my father, but I do not have the heart to hurt my children as he did. I love them too much."

Another middle-aged Sydney Sephardic spoke of his father a month after his death. "My father, may his soul rest in peace, was a very good father. He never laid a hand on us. He taught us respect and brought us up well." When I asked him about his and his brothers' relationship with their father, he replied proudly: "In most instances, we listened to him. We rarely talked back to him for there was no need to do so. We simply told our mother and she usually told him. He did not like to be interrupted. When we behaved in a silly manner as children, our mother threatened to tell him and that was usually enough to make us behave, even though she rarely did tell him. That was a much better way to bring up children. I slaved for my children, to give them a good education. But I sometimes doubt that they appreciate all the hard work that I and my wife have put into raising them."

In contrast, fathers described how family responsibility affected their lives in their countries of origin. Thus, one father of several sons, whose children complained endlessly and bitterly about his treatment of them in the homeland, answered my question about paternal authority as follows: "I saw my position as one of honor, and I carried it out with dignity. I taught my sons, to the best of my knowledge and ability, how to become honorable members of their families and the community. I, of course, did not always like my position. When one of my sons misbehaved and I had to punish him with a spanking, every blow was a blow to my own heart. I did not like doing it at all, but this was the only way that I knew. I was afraid that if I just talked reason to them, they might see it as a sign of weakness and not respect me. They surely would not understand it as an act of love. We, the fathers of our generation, were not allowed to demonstrate feelings of love and affection; that was the job of the mother. But, I ask you, do you think that I did not love my children? I would give my life for them without any hesitation."

A grandmother complaining about her grandchildren's "lack of discipline" agreed that an authoritative father is necessary. She underlined this by quoting the biblical phrase which translates from Hebrew as, "He who spares the rod *hates* his son." "The problem with children today," she continued, "is that they have no respect for their parents or the elderly. Do you know why my grandchildren are like that? Always answering back and hardly ever listening? It is because their father was always away and their mother could not discipline them properly. It is the father's job to discipline his children, and when he is not around, they grow wild. In Singapore this would never have happened." After a few minutes of silence, the grandmother said, "Do you think that we did not love our children? We, like others in the community, wanted to bring up our children properly, to be proud Jews. My husband, may his soul rest in peace, was a great disciplinarian, and he knew what he was doing. But do you really think for a moment that he did not love his children? Let me tell you, he loved them very much, but he did not think it was necessary to show it to them."

Disobedience to parents, particularly to fathers, was considered a serious error in Islamic countries. Although this situation had been undergoing a gradual change in the fifty years before mass immigration, the role formation and authority structure of the Sephardic family underwent a further drastic change when Middle Eastern Jews moved to Western-oriented countries. In Australia, for example, the laws give women a share in the property and also it is much more common for the court to give custody of the children to the mother. This is a status that women could have never dreamed of in the countries of origin. While the father is still considered head of the family, his actions are open to question by his wife and children. Now his status and that of his family is mainly determined by his occupation and earning capacity, as well as his ability to perform the role of family leader. Moreover, this, in turn, helps to determine his relationship with both his wife and his children.

In the old country, a Sephardic wife had few rights in the event of her husband's death. In accordance with *halakhah*, the eldest son usually inherited his father's position as the head of the family, becoming the main breadwinner and decision-maker. Property was divided among the sons; the daughters did not inherit anything. As head of the family, the eldest son was obliged to support his mother and provide dowries for his sisters. If the deceased man's children were still young, the husband's family supported the widow and the children. In a majority of these cases, the husband's family also managed the deceased's property.

In 1924, this halakhic ruling came under criticism from Iraqi Jews, who submitted a proposal to the Baghdadi Jewish community to the effect that daughters receive half the inheritance that sons received, as

was the case among Muslims in Iraq. However, the heads of the community who viewed rabbinical law as supreme rejected this.

When a husband died childless, Jewish law demanded that his widow
marry his brother, in a *levirate* marriage, in order to produce a son who
would carry the name of the deceased. If the brother-in-law did not want
her, or if she could convince him that such a marriage would not be
beneficial to either party, a *halizah* ceremony was performed, releasing
her from the levirate tie and freeing her to marry someone else. The
custom of levirate marriage, as prescribed in Deuteronomy 25:5–6, was
practiced by Sephardic communities long after it had been replaced by
halizah in the Ashkenazi communities, where the rabbis usually pressured the deceased's brother to free his sister-in-law.[22] In 1950, the Chief
Rabbinate of Israel made *halizah* obligatory.

Familial Authority Today

The trend among Sephardim in Sydney is toward increasing freedom
from parental control and responsibility for one's own actions rather
than group responsibility under the aegis of the father. Thus, children
may continue to respect their parents, especially their father's views,
without feeling constrained to act upon them. Smooha (1978:114) argues
that there has been a similar "decline of parental authority" within the
Sephardic family in Israel because of the "growing democratization in
respect to sex and age differentiation which took place among Orientals
during the last two decades". But Layish and Shaham (1991) comment
that, while the distribution of authority is legitimized on a different
basis in the democratic family than in the traditional one, the father is
still the primary executive member or head of the family. Thus, among
Sydney Sephardim, the father's authority has become limited, and it is
now shared by other members of the family as well as by communal
socialization agencies. On the other hand, he still retains theoretical
sovereignty over his family. For no matter their position in the modern
social structure of Australian society, most Sephardic women still relate
to their husbands and fathers as "the boss"; even though their husbands
may leave many matters, including some outside the domestic sphere,
in their hands.[23] There is, for example, still a clear-cut division of labor
with husbands in charge of family finances and wives assuming full
responsibility for the domestic sphere.

Wives in Australia have greater autonomy than their mothers had in
their countries of origin. They receive more respect from their husbands,
who often seek their advice. But in general, the husband remains the
major authority on social and communal matters, and wives who earn
more than their husbands may have problems. Moreover, many of the
women I interviewed indicated a reluctance to exchange their role as

homemakers and child-rearers with that of breadwinner. One striking response, from young married women raised in Australia, was that they did not desire to work outside the home, even when their children were grown up. This view was succinctly expressed by one respondent, who "would not like to be in the place of any man, because men have to work and worry about making money. It must be terrible for a man to have all the responsibilities and worries." This woman concluded: "We women are free of all these worries, and thank God for that!"

Sephardic husbands in Sydney seem to spend more time in the home than their fathers and grandfathers did in their countries of origin. Among the reasons for this are the steady decrease in working hours and the advent of television, as well as changes in values. This means that young husbands tend to participate in caring for children and other members of the family, more than their fathers did, although the wives are still the chief contributors. It may therefore be that, like the modern urban family in general, there is an increasing tendency toward equal "allocation of power".[24]

The Socialization of Children

In traditional society, the family was almost the sole socialization agent in a child's life. Like many other ethnic groups who immigrated to Australia, the Sephardic family has lost many crucial functions in the socialization of its children to such civic institutions as childcare, education and welfare agencies.

As community and other institutions adopt increased responsibility and provide an ever-growing basket of services for children, Australian society has an increasing influence on the structure of the Sephardic family. Children are no longer considered the "property" of their fathers. Both the state and the community protect them (and their mothers) from the arbitrary use of power by family heads. Even education and health, which had heretofore been left entirely to the father's discretion, are increasingly falling under the jurisdiction of schools and public-health authorities. On the other hand, there is no doubt that the transition from traditional society to the modern state has given more power to wives and children. Although children are still brought up to respect their parents, there has been a shift from blind obedience to compromise and sometimes conflict. This is natural in the pluralistic situation of Australian society, where the element of isolation from outsiders does not exist as it did in the countries of origin, and family members are exposed to, and participate in, the cultural system of the society.[25]

While the traditional Sephardic communities were divided into classes, all tended to adhere to a similar adult-centered pattern in which almost every activity centered on and was directed by adults, for (especially male) adults, and the children had to adapt to this pattern of life. Young Sephardic families in Sydney are placing increasing emphasis on the perceived interests of the child, centering family activities and functions around them and their needs rather than on those of the nuclear and extended families or the community.

It has been suggested that, despite differences in family lifestyle among the various ethnic groups in Australian society, there is "a more generalized hegemony" of beliefs about what constitutes 'normal' family life, and that this cuts across class and ethnic boundaries. Nevertheless, it is still the family which introduces the children into their class and ethnic groups. Moreover, the family reproduces the class structure to which its members belong. As Cass (1977:168) puts it: "Children inherit a set of life chances as surely as they inherit property or poverty: life chances in education, occupation and the acquisition of property that constitute the basis of their future opportunities."

The decline in birth rate of the Sephardic family has also played a major role in improving both the welfare of children and the relationship between parents and children. Due to the spread of family planning, the average family today has three to four children, as opposed to about seven to ten in the old country.

A greater demonstration of affection between parents (particularly the father) and children is one of the results of the more casual relationship between them. Many of the children in the families I interviewed were not afraid to speak their minds in the presence of their fathers, although they felt more relaxed when only their mothers were present.

The position of the Sephardic daughter has also changed drastically. In the countries of origin, daughters received their education at home, from their mothers and grandmothers. They were trained to submit to their husbands and to put him and their children's needs first, giving little consideration to their own needs. After marriage, they moved from subordination to the father to subordination and obedience to the husband – and to his mother. For here, as in traditional China, we find women dominating other women. Rabbis and other leaders of Jewish communities in the Middle East and Asia encouraged the seclusion of Sephardic women from public religious life, under the assumption that danger abounded outside the home. As in many immigrant groups in Australia, Sephardic men and women regard women's careers as secondary to those of men.

Although today's Sephardic woman enjoys a secular education, at least until the age of sixteen, her Ashkenazi sisters are afforded much more opportunity for a career and social mobility. This may be because the Sephardim have had a shorter period of exposure to the modernized host society.

Occupation and Socialization

As mentioned previously, despite the extensive changes in family dynamics, there is still a very explicit division between the two sexes regarding work – the professional occupational role is still viewed mainly as a masculine prerogative. The young boy must begin to think about what he is going to do. He cannot be content with his ascribed statuses but must take responsibility for his future. In the modern state, girls experience problems *vis-à-vis* occupation that only boys experienced in the traditional society. In Western society, "the pattern seems to have shifted to the point where she plans at least for education beyond early adolescence and very often, if not generally, for a job beyond that".[26]

Among Sephardic women born in Israel or Western countries such as Australia, a woman's success in kinship, friendship and career depends on the extent to which she is able to define these roles as important to her – as distinct from the role of wife and mother. This depends mainly on her level of education and type of socialization. Young Sephardic women are able to cope with the different roles more successfully than older women are because they have not been as rigidly socialized.[27]

The following cases illustrate that lower-middle, middle and upper-middle-class professionals all exhibit a similar pattern, although there has been some change in the attitude of upper-middle-class professionals toward wives and the domestic role. These case histories have been streamlined drastically to protect the privacy of informants, particularly of those in the upper and middle classes, so that they are not identifiable within the Sephardic community.

Caroline, a thirty-two year-old Ashkenazi woman married to a Sephardic accountant, is a high school teacher who worked for several years before she was married. At the time of the interview, she was awaiting the birth of her fourth child. Caroline adopted Orthodoxy when she married and found this way of life difficult to adjust to. After the birth of her first child, she was determined to go back to teaching, but her husband objected strongly, arguing that he was able to provide for his family adequately. He could not accept Caroline's satisfaction with her work as a reason for her leaving the home and not caring for her children. She only began to enjoy being at home after the birth of her second child, mainly, she recalled, because she had learned to accept it by then. Thus, as Caroline began to acquiesce to her husband's expectations, she internalized them to the point where she began to enjoy being a housewife (or so she says).

Rachel, another Ashkenazi teacher married to a Sephardic man, was thirty-five years old. She worked for a couple of years after her marriage, and then had two boys, two years and eleven months old at the time of our interview. Rachel repeatedly stressed that she was unhappy at home and would like to return to work; however, she acknowledged that her duty as a housewife and mother made this impossible at the time. It would have been much easier for her to accept her role as a housewife, she said, if her parents lived in Sydney and were able to help her occasionally by minding the children. She thought she might eventually go back to teaching, to "get out of the house a little". Thus, it seems that Rachel had not yet accepted her husband's views of the division of roles, and that her inability to internalize her husband's expectation left her unhappy and unfulfilled in her marriage. Six years after the interview, she divorced her husband and went back to her parents. Shocked, her husband could not understand "what had come over her".

Forty-three year-old Stella was one of six children born in Singapore to Egyptian parents. She married a Singaporean man of Iraqi origin who is one of eleven children. They have seven sons. Stella's parents objected to her marriage because her husband was not from a "good" family. A secretary and receptionist by profession, Stella was out of the work force for eighteen years. At the time of our interview, her eldest son was twenty-two and married with a child, her youngest was eleven, and she had just returned to work. She enjoyed her job and said she met very interesting people. She only wished that she had gone back to work earlier. Her mother, on the other hand, was not at all happy. Upon the mother complaining that, "He was never any good. I knew from the beginning that he was no good for her. Why should she go out to work after so many years at home? Shouldn't he be able to provide for her and the children?" Stella turned to me and said, "She will never understand that I want to work and that I love it. She is very old-fashioned." Stella later divorced her husband of twenty-eight years because "he did not approve of the new 'me'. My financial independence killed him. So he gave me a hard time."

Dana, from Iraq, is forty-four years old. She is a secretary and bookkeeper, and her Iraqi husband is in the clothing business. They have two sons, aged eighteen and fourteen at the time of our interview. Dana remained at home for eight years after marriage. When we spoke she had been working again for two years at a part-time job and was planning to work full-time. She said she would have liked to have gone back to work earlier, particularly because she and her husband had to pay off a mortgage. And although her husband, "unlike other Sephardic husbands", did not object strongly, he pointed out that he would rather she stay at home than leave the children in the care of others. Dana felt that he was more "modern" than most other Sephardic men were because he "let her choose" and did not pressure her. She completely internalized her position.

Ruth, thirty-two years old, was born in Sydney to parents of Iraqi origin and married an Ashkenazi chemist. She is a doctor with one child, and she was expecting a second at the time of the interview. She remained at home for six months after the birth of the first and then returned to part-time work in a local clinic. Her mother, who was taking care of the child almost full-time, occasionally complained that she had no free time. While she felt obliged to help her daughter out, she told me that even though her daughter is lucky because her Ashkenazi husband is open-minded and helps with the housework, she thought Ruth should take a few years off from work to raise her children. Ruth, on the other hand, argued that she could not be away from her profession for too long, and that she loved it even though the work is demanding and she was often tired. She knows that she is very lucky to have an understanding and supportive husband, but was sorry that her career has strained her relationship with her mother. In terms of socialization, this case is unusual. Ruth, who was born and brought up in Australia, married to a man who supports her in every possible way, felt "liberated" from the "Sephardic framework". Her mother, who was socialized in Iraq and had internalized the Sephardic traditional pattern of rigid division of labor, clearly did not approve of her daughter's behavior. Ruth was also criticized for her devotion to her work by her contemporaries but did not bend to their pressure either.

All under the age of forty-five, these women represent a cross-section of young Sephardic women and Ashkenazi women married to Sephardic men. With the exception of the medical doctor, all conform to Sephardic expectations of women. Several women like them told me they were forced by their financial situation to go back to work when their children were one or two, and their mothers looked after the children. And they are the exception. It seems that Sephardic wives accept or conform to the rigid division of labor, whether or not they really want to. Ashkenazi wives initially try to please their husbands, fulfilling the roles that their husbands feel they should play, but not generally with much success.

When young Sephardic women work, they are usually secretaries, receptionists or sales assistants. Several are teachers. When families own businesses, the wives usually work with their husbands. When the mothers of young children begin to work, it is mostly part-time so they can still perform most domestic chores. However, when the wives begin full-time jobs, husbands usually are asked to help with household duties. Most men I interviewed indicated distaste for cleaning the house, washing dishes, bathing the children or changing nappies, although they do not mind outside chores such as shopping, fetching the children from school or minding them for a few hours when their wives worked. As the partners in a marriage gain a higher education, the division of labor tends to become increasingly blurred, but this process is gradual. However, in most cases, even though a wife has a full-time job and spends the same number of hours outside the home as her husband, she is expected to perform most of the domestic duties. Even among the most liberal husbands, who help in the home, only one said they "share" the housework; the others all said they "help" their wives, thereby making it clear that such duties "belong to the wife". Working women are forced to work "a second shift" at home, where little has been required of their husband.[28]

In the open and democratic Australian system, girls and boys go through a more liberal process of socialization in which there is very little differentiation between the sexes, at least in the early years. Even with the increased consideration given to the socio-psychological need of girls and wives, there is still a long road ahead before the cognitive and affective craving for stability and inner security of Sephardic women is satisfied.

Kinship Relationships

It is clear that the problems of socialization in Western society become much more complicated than they were in the countries of origin. In countries like Australia, industrialization led to a reorganization of the family as a 'more specialized agency' than it had been in the past.[29] The process of modernization has also brought about changes in values and in kinship relationships, which have caused rifts within the kinship system. Whereas in the country of origin few institutions were independent of kinship status, there are many modern non-kinship structures, such as states, the church, large business firms, universities and professional associations, which further reduce the importance of kinship units in our society. However, although the family has become a more specialized agency, it is no less important, because the society is dependent exclusively on it for the performance of certain of its essential functions.

The interaction between family members may be examined along two dimensions: generation and class. On the generational level, it can be said that the kinship relationship is still an important and integral part of the lives of elders in the Sydney Sephardic community, but younger people who were born in Australia or who came there as children tend to function on the basis of dyadic relationships. Thus, people no longer seek aid from a relative merely because that individual is kin; it would have to be a person with whom the help-seeker had a friendly relationship with as well. And this becomes more difficult as relatives increasingly come together only once or twice a year, during the Jewish New Year and Passover, instead of having daily interaction and assuming the mutual obligations of the Sephardic family in the homeland. Another cause of weakened relatives' obligations outside the nuclear family is marriage outside the family and the community. Where marriage occurs between Sephardim and Ashkenazim or Sephardim and non-Jews, the Sephardic partners generally alienate themselves from their relatives. Alienation also occurs in marriages within the community when the spouses are from different classes or religious backgrounds.

Although it is becoming increasingly nuclear, the Sephardic family still maintains some presence of relatives outside the nuclear family, albeit in a weakened form. Grandparents usually care for the young when parents work, but this is no longer a given. It would be appropriate to label today's Sephardic extended family "modified extended" because it generally includes parents, children and grandchildren, but no peripheral kin. Coult and Habenstein (1965:2–4) distinguish between "the isolated nuclear family" of Parsons and non-nuclear kin. They argue that if one views the nuclear family as a corporate group, then Parsons' hypothesis of the isolated nuclear family would be correct. But if one accepts non-nuclear kin relationships as the basis of the family, as is the case in America, it should be labeled "modified extended".

One of the major reasons for the continuing decline of intense cooperation between members of the extended family lies in the realization that the Sephardic community lives in an open, urban, multicultural society, where interaction between members of different ethnic and cultural groups brings members of these groups into close contact through the education system and the work place. As Basham (1978:91) puts it:

> Progress in modern society 'does' seem to emphasize the importance of non-familial socialization . . . and to place a premium on friends rather than kin in meeting our needs for companionship.

The relationship between personality, culture and social structure could be highlighted in the socialization of Sephardic family members into the new social system in modern states. The most complicated issue seems to be the adults' socialization to new and different cultural and social structures. The "reeducation" of these adults leads to changes in both lifestyle and family formation, which forces a redefinition of the relationship between family members and a shift in power and authority.

One can draw an analogy between Zelditch's (1956:377–78) description of the socialization of the individual in American society and Bell and Newby's (1975:159) mobility and resocialization of Italian families to modern systems, and socialization among the members of the Sydney Sephardic community. Zelditch,[30] who speak in terms of ego experience, suggests that the interactions within which the socialization process operates can be compared to a man climbing a ladder. Members of the modern Sephardic family who internalized cultural mores and behaviors in the country of origin, and who are still unsure of the socialization process in the new country, cling to the first rung of the ladder even when they have taken a tentative step toward the second. Older members of the community, who have lost authority over their families, often remain on the ground, not even attempting to ascend to the first rung, but preferring to live on nostalgic memories. Young adults take the first step up when they endeavor to enter the acculturation process.

Sephardic families in Sydney are increasingly apathetic toward their communal institutions. These have lost some of their functions and vitality as a driving force for the community in the new setting. For Sephardim, as with many ethnic groups the family, which was the essence of the community, has become too strained to serve even as a significant source of sociability among its members.

It appears, then, that the solidarity of the Sephardic family is no longer identified by a uniformity of behavior among its members or by strong adherence to tradition. It has drastically weakened in Sydney. Even religion, which was the center of social life and which seems to be more resistant to acculturation than ethnicity, has lost some of its vitality.

Summary and Conclusions: **Changes in Kinship Ties**

Whereas in the countries of origin the traditional extended family, with its strong kinship ties, fulfilled many social, religious and economic functions, in the Western world the family has become an agency that specializes in the rearing of and caring for children. Whereas kinship relations were the most important form of relation, an institution of rights and obligations, the independence from parents and individualism encouraged in modern society means that relations between members of the nuclear family have changed dramatically. Thus, the type of relationship that exists between parents and children largely determines the intensity of relationships individuals will have with the rest of their kin. Osterreich (1965:131–65) speaks of "kin orientation", "degree of obligation" and "ideological commitments" in kinship systems in traditional and Western societies, concerning many factors, among them geographical movements.

In the homeland, the Sephardic family and kinship relations were among the most fundamental institutions of the community, socializing members, particularly the young, into their various family, kinship and community roles. The transition to the modern state has undermined this institution and dramatically curtailed its functions. As ties between family members, particularly between husband and wife and father and children, underwent changes, the position of the husband has been severely weakened. One elderly member of the community, who came from Singapore, said jokingly: "I have always been both in Singapore and here, the minister for foreign affairs, and my wife, minister of the interior." While women have adopted a much more active role in the community, very few pursue careers. And, while their position, status and rights in the areas of marriage, divorce, child custody and property settlement have been improving, Jewish law still dictates that they cannot initiate divorce, although the *Beth Din* is far more sympathetic to them today, particularly in the areas of child custody and property settlements.

Kinship ties suffered greatly upon emigration from traditional to modern societies. The traditional extended and semi-extended household units have now become modified nuclear families. As families no longer live together in compounds, the degree of interaction and social contact they obtained in the countries of origin rarely exists today. The relationship of rights and obligations between relatives is not as committed as it was, but that between parents, children and grandchildren is still relatively strong.

In short, the Sephardic family in Sydney has undergone many changes, some extensive, and others gradual. In this, it is following the pattern of acculturation of the Ashkenazi family into the Australian family type.

5

Residence, Social Mobility and Ethnic Identity

Ethnicity, race and socio-economic background have spatial components that may be readily identified as indicative of settlement and adjustment of the group.[1] The residential variable is one of many factors that determine a person's societal status.[2]

The Sephardic community in Sydney has two reference groups: the Anglo-Celtic Australian community and the Ashkenazi Jewish community. The influence of the Ashkenazim on Sephardic Jewish identity is, however, much stronger than that of the general Anglo-Celtic community. Because the Sephardim are a complicated minority within a minority, their general pattern of acculturation and assimilation is not into the culture of the larger society but into that of the Australianized Ashkenazi minority. The marginality of the Sephardim *vis-à-vis* the Ashkenazim and the larger Australian society can be seen, among other things, in their pattern of residential changes within Sydney. Much of the research on ethnic groups and ethnic identity implies a relationship between residential patterns of a particular group and that group's social interactions with the wider community, which in turn influences the manifestation of ethnic identity of members of the group in question.

The immigrant's place of residence plays an important part in his or her adaptation and adjustment. Residential clustering of migrant groups is one of the most distinctive features of their settlements. On arrival in a new country, individuals usually seek to live among members of their own ethnic groups for familiarity and emotional support. When assimilation does take place, the immigrant groups tend to lose their social and spatial identity with the ethnic enclave.[3]

Children of immigrants often aspire to move away from the core ethnic residential areas, while their parents remain in segregated communities. Ethnic ties may initially be stronger than social ties. Thus, while there is a positive relationship between assimilation and residence, this relationship does not generally disrupt the pattern of spatial differentiation among ethnic groups.[4]

In the wider perspective of social structure and its relationship to spatial structure, one must distinguish between voluntary and involuntary segregation. Voluntary segregation derives from cultural, linguistic and religious differences between the host society and the ethnic group, and generally applies to the original immigrants and their first-generation children. In these cases, the emergence of culturally distinct ethnic communities bound by common ties of race, culture, nationality and religion, which render them culturally distinct and assign them a separate identity, has the positive element of voluntary association. However, when following generations desire to leave the ethnic residential areas and cannot do so due to low socio-economic status or place in society, their segregation becomes involuntary and therefore viewed by them as negative.[5]

Johnston (1971:239) emphasizes the "push-and-pull" factors in residential mobility, highlighting four sets of forces that are central to the decision to move: family life-cycle; social mobility and social mobility aspirations; residential environment; and social and neighborhood participation. Evidently, the greater a person's involvement in his or her locality the less the desire to move. Other factors that may facilitate or impede movement are individual resources and the availability of affordable housing.

The issue of residential mobility and ethnic identity is viewed herein from a psychodynamic perspective. For, status anxiety is an important factor underlying the behavior of individuals and groups who undergo socio-economic change during immigration to modern Western societies. Research has shown that, in modern societies where emphasis is placed on individualism and the individual's rights, the home and environment are intimately bound to one's self-concept, reflecting on personality, social status, accomplishments and identity.[6]

Anxiety has generally been defined as the individual's emotional response to perceived danger.[7] In terms of psychodynamic analysis, anxiety may stem from several sources and is usually greatest when the situation is unclear and the nature of the threat uncertain. In the lower class, it is largely a subsistence anxiety, whereas in the middle and upper classes, it is mainly status anxiety, stemming from the individual's awareness of his or her own status in relation to that of the neighbors.[8] Members of any group who have improved their socio-economic status (usually associated with residential movement) therefore attempt to avoid contact with individuals who are racially or ethnically similar to them but of much lower status in the host society. In this sense, anxiety is applied to residential status and social mobility. Furthermore the status is ambiguous in two respects: in terms of uncertainty as to where one belongs and uncertainty about one's expected role performance.[9] This is strongly tied to the anxiety of the group regarding the type of behavior that is expected of them by a higher status group. Thus, problems of adaptation or lack of them, derive mainly from the emotional conditions and marginal position of individuals or their group.[10]

In a socio-psychological sense, group marginality generally implies values and attitudes generated from interaction between groups, awareness of differences between them and value judgments concerning the significance of the differences.[11] In the case of the Sephardim, this relationship is characterized by an undesired separation from two groups: the Ashkenazim and "white" Australians. Marginality and alienation can be further characterized as ultimately relating to the "subjective state of an individual at a given moment" when alienated individuals become aware of their marginal status. Furthermore, such interactive aspects of personality development work in tandem with alienation caused by unhealthy states of anxiety based on defense mechanisms.[12]

Status anxiety can be understood in terms of the interaction between social, ethnic and residential variables. In this respect, the social life of the nuclear family, as well as the modified extended family, provides clues to the position of the individual in the host society. Moreover, relations within the family, between members of differential status, may shed light on the relationship between members of the ethnic community.

This chapter examines residential change in relation to class, mobility, social change and kinship, as well as their influences on the Sephardic ethnic identity, within the theoretical context of status anxiety and marginality.

Socio-Geographical Distance and Patterns of Kin Contact

In their countries of origin, Sephardic family members usually lived in close proximity to the household of the husband's parents and maintained an extended socio-economic network with their relatives. The parents' household united all siblings and instilled in them a sense of responsibility toward one another, regardless of wealth or individual personality traits. For instance, after the death of the father, the elder brother usually assumed responsibility for his mother and younger siblings, particularly younger sisters. This family cohesiveness was enhanced by the tendency of the Jewish community to segregate itself geographically and socially from the broader society. In contrast, while the children of immigrants to Australia may still live close to their parents, they are no longer so isolated from the host society, interacting regularly with individuals from different ethnic groups in the course of their daily lives. Consequently, there is less family cohesiveness. Moreover, while the older immigrants continue to emphasize ethnic factors, young couples tend to shift their focus to class and status.[13]

Socio-geographical distance tends to influence contact between kin in terms of its intensity, frequency, quality and type (e.g., face-to-face, mail, telephone, meeting on ceremonial occasions), which in turn affects the strength or weakness of the kinship network. With movement to a new area, kinship ties tend to weaken or break down. Moreover, varying degrees of upward mobility tend to increase social distances between family members, irrespective of geographical distances. Hence, there is a decline in the frequency of face-to-face interaction between members of the extended family, which is accompanied by a loosening of social and economic obligations to one another. This process is often related to acculturation to Ashkenazi culture and Australian society, which tends to accompany the geographical move-ment.[14]

Changes in place of residence, accompanied by weaker kinship ties, also tend to blur the division of labor between husband and wife, which tends to be less clearly defined or more flexible, with the husband taking on more domestic and childcare chores and the wife working outside the home. This is largely due to the move away from the family of orien-tation, so that most young wives no longer receive the help and support they used to enjoy from their female relatives. Moreover, there is a need for the wife to supplement her husband's income in order to afford their more expensive home.[15] Many Sephardic families no longer adhere to the pattern of family obligations and commitments characteristic of the homelands, a shift that goes beyond the "natural" estrangement of time, death of parents and the establishment of new families of procreation. It should be noted that, while the move to a higher status suburb within the Eastern Suburbs often entailed quite small geographical distances, interviewees frequently cited geographical separation as the main reason for infrequent contact.

The geographical distances involved may be small, but social distances are large. Varying degrees of upward mobility tend to increase social distances between members of these families. Thus, although most Sephardim remain within Bondi, the area of the suburb in which they choose to live reflects different social and/or economic statuses. Although older people tend to cling to their original neighborhoods, young couples usually wish to move to neighborhoods where they will be among those of their improved class and/or status. The situation of

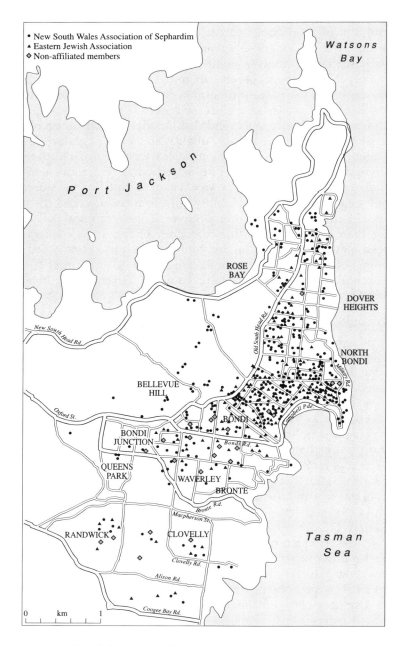

Map 5.1   Sephardi Residence in the Eastern Suburbs

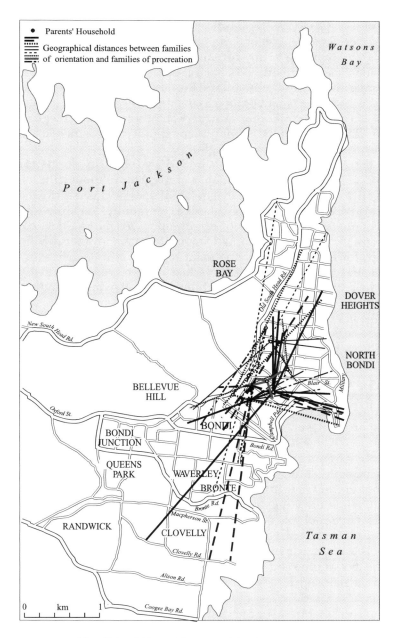

Map 5.2 A Typical Pattern of Family Dispersion

the younger working class is similar to that of older members of the community. Gans (1962) and Gale (1999) suggest that familial closeness and cohesiveness in general is a general working-class phenomenon that is not exclusive to any community. They attribute the stability of working-class neighborhoods, in large measure, to the strong emphasis on family and kinship cohesion and the desire of working-class children to live in the same neighborhood as their parents.[16] Initially ethnic identity was a stronger force than class in promoting residential segregation. This is largely true of the Sephardic community in Australia today and was true in their countries of origin.

In the case of the Sephardim in Sydney, ethnicity seems to have played a role in promoting residential segregation although the fact that a majority of Sephardim still live in Bondi does not necessarily indicate a strong Sephardic identity or cohesive community. Regardless of their class status in the countries of origin, upon arrival in a new country immigrants usually seek to live among members of their own ethnic groups for familiarity and emotional support. In time, however, such residential segregation (and the social matrix brought with it) may become a hindrance to social mobility. The following examples illustrate the frequency and quality of contact between members of families, and the new pattern of kin relation among Sephardim in Sydney.[17]

The **Sadik family** comprises three siblings, two brothers and a sister. Family members arrived in Sydney, from China, between 1948 and 1956. Initially, they lived together with their parents. As children married, they established a first residence within walking distance of their parents. They celebrated all holidays together and relied on each other for much of their social interaction and financial aid. In time, the oldest brother, Sam, established his own factory and moved to Double Bay, an exclusive harbor-side district about five kilometers away from his parents. Sam and his Ashkenazi wife identify themselves and their children as Australians. Sister Sarah and her Sephardic husband were successful enough to purchase a large house in the more up-scale North Bondi, while the youngest brother, Ron, an artist with a low income, remains in Bondi Junction with his Sephardic wife and children. Sam's children went to private schools, while Ron's attended government schools. Although interaction between each sibling and his or her family lessened over time and with the differences in income, greater interaction was maintained between Sam and Sarah, and Sarah and Ron, than between Sam and the less affluent brother Ron.

Sam and Ron rarely see each other or have telephone contact. Sam and Sarah see each other somewhat more frequently, although only about three to four times each year, and talk occasionally by telephone. Sarah sees Ron at least once a month, and speaks to him even more often. She helps Ron financially whenever possible, whereas Sam does not. This pattern would rarely occur in the country of origin, where the parents' influence united all siblings and instilled a sense of responsibility toward each other, regardless of wealth or individual personality traits.

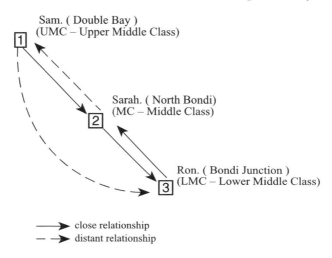

Figure 5.1   The Sadik Family – Pattern of Interaction

The Iraqi **Shasha family** comprises five brothers and a sister. They arrived in Sydney in the mid-1950s and early 1960s, after spending some time in Israel. The first to arrive in Sydney was Isaac, who established a food business. Isaac then brought his siblings – Aaron, Abraham, Jacob, Moses and Sharon – to Australia. A few years later, he brought over his parents so that they could be near their children and grandchildren. Isaac helped all his brothers set up businesses. When they arrived in Sydney, all members of the family lived in Bondi and North Bondi and were close, visiting each other during the week and socializing with each other on weekends. However, as Aaron and Moses joined Isaac in the middle class, they moved to North Ryde, South Sydney and North Shore, respectively. Once this happened, their social contacts and economic responsibility toward the others gradually diminished. Today, they "see each other on happy and sad occasions" but not always on the high holidays, because they are not observant. Abraham and Jacob still live in lower-class Bondi and Sharon lives in middle-class Rose Bay.

Isaac maintains good relations with Sharon and all of his brothers except Moses, with whom he is not on speaking terms due to a financial misunderstanding. Isaac telephones his brothers and sisters occasionally, but says he is too involved in his business to see them. They all seem to maintain telephone links, but rarely see each other. Abraham and

Jacob live in the same area, mix within the same social circle and have the most intense contact of all the siblings; but even they see each other much less frequently than in the past. Aaron seldom sees other members of the family. Although Isaac continues to maintain links with most of his siblings, most of his social circle comprises upper middle-class business people, most of whom are Jewish. As he puts it, "We all came here and I helped my family get work. They worked very hard and they are doing very well. Our children have achieved high academic standards; we have lawyers, doctors and other university graduates in our family. However, we lost the most important thing – our family unity. We used to be much more concerned about each other. Our wives used to phone each other every day, even though we did not live far from each other. Now we really have to make a great effort to see one another. We have all gotten a little too busy and carried away with business, and somehow we don't see eye to eye anymore. I miss the days when we were close and helped one another."

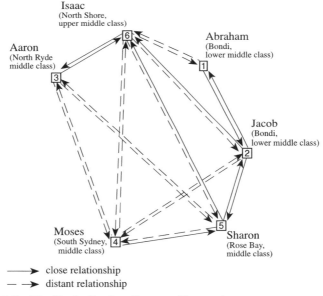

Figure 5.2   The Shasha Family – Pattern of Interaction

Nine of the eleven **Zamir** children immigrated to Australia (the other two going to Israel and America) from Bombay in the mid-1950s. The family was very poor in India. After migration to Sydney, the family maintained close ties, and there was a strong commitment to help one another. The four siblings who were married in India lived close to their parents in Bondi, and three of the remaining five siblings lived with their parents for a considerable length of time after their marriage.

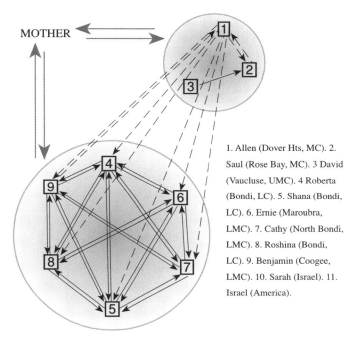

1. Allen (Dover Hts, MC). 2. Saul (Rose Bay, MC). 3 David (Vaucluse, UMC). 4 Roberta (Bondi, LC). 5. Shana (Bondi, LC). 6. Ernie (Maroubra, LMC). 7. Cathy (North Bondi, LMC). 8. Roshina (Bondi, LC). 9. Benjamin (Coogee, LMC). 10. Sarah (Israel). 11. Israel (America).

Figure 5.3   The Zamir Family – Pattern of Interaction

Allen, Saul and David Zamir loosened their ties with their siblings after becoming financially successful and moving to the middle-class Eastern Suburbs of Dover Heights, Rose Bay and Vaucluse, respectively, suburbs with the highest concentration of Jews in Sydney. The father of the family sees "two types of people" among his children: those who wish to remain Jewish and stay with the family, and those who want to become "Australians". While he is pleased that his children have become financially successful, particularly after their poverty in India, he finds it "heart-rending" that they have become geographically (and socially) distant from one another. Those family members who continue to live in lower-class Bondi and lower-middle-class North Bondi, who are relatively close to each other, particularly the four sisters, see their mother very often and each other at least once a week. The more successful brothers – Allen, Saul and David – tend to see each other less frequently, even rarely. Allen, an accountant, who married an Ashkenazi, lives in middle-class Dover Heights with her and their three children. He maintains strong links with his mother, but rarely sees his other siblings except in synagogue. Although he and Saul mix with the same circle of friends, they do not get on very well. David, the third successful brother, is divorced and lives in upper middle-class Vaucluse. He is not on speaking terms with many of his brothers and sisters, who feel that success has destroyed him. All siblings maintain a very strong link with their mother, who appears to hold them together; when those who no longer live in Bondi do meet, it is usually when visiting her. This family demonstrates a clear case of a family divided along class lines.

It is obvious from the above that the relationship between distance and frequency of contact is not always inverted, i.e., that distance is not necessarily the cause of infrequent contact. Indeed, my findings are evidence that many of the people I interviewed had reasons for not wanting to maintain close ties with their kin. This kinship phenomenon is similar to that found among many members of the Sephardic community, quite a few of whom clearly feel that remaining within their own ethnic group impedes their social mobility and that of their families. As one of them put it: "There are some Sephardim who do not know how to behave in public, and they bring shame to the good name of our group." Still, there seems to be much more contact between members of the nuclear family than among modified-extended family networks, geographical distance apparently exerting a stronger influence where the desire to remain in touch has already been weakened.

However, while geographical distance is not the only or even main cause of infrequent contact, it is often utilized to rationalize the lack of contact between upwardly mobile Sephardim and their relatives. This in itself is of sociological importance *vis-à-vis* identity, especially when there is a short distance between first homes in the lower-class neighborhoods and the new homes in the higher-class suburbs. In the context of my fieldwork, it is clear that there is a general trend among Sephardic families in Sydney to break away from the traditional patterns of family obligation and commitment. This is associated with absorption of Western values, where economic success and social mobility play far greater roles than kinship and communal relationships dictated by tradition.

Upward Mobility and "Ashkenization"

When Sephardim began to arrive in Australia in the late 1940s and early 1950s, Australians saw the world in terms of "blacks" and "whites", Asian and European.[18] This reflected the racism in Australian society that had not exhausted itself in World War II and in its aftermath. In keeping with an explicit White Australia Policy, the immigration authorities labeled the Sephardim as an "undesirable class of Jews".[19]

These attitudes continued to manifest themselves in the 1980s, despite official abolishment of that policy. Thus, a migrant attitudes survey conducted by the Australian government in the mid-1980s disclosed that 27 percent of Australians in Sydney felt there were too many Asians and Middle Easterners in their neighborhood.[20]

More important to the Sephardim, however, is acceptance by their fellow Jews.[21] The Ashkenazim are far more assimilated into the host society, and generally they have obtained higher levels of education, associated with higher societal positions. This is mainly due to their length of stay in the host country and their place in the Australian class system. Indeed, many Sephardim rank themselves lower than they do Ashkenazim and aspire to reach the higher status they attribute to them. Additionally, racial background is important: Ashkenazim are closer to the Australian prototype than Sephardim, who are clearly Middle Eastern or Oriental in appearance. Racial and ethnic differences are evident in the relationship between these two Jewish groups, and there is considerable pressure on a Sephardic married to an Ashkenazi to acculturate into an Australianized version of Ashkenazi culture.[22]

The Ashkenazim have displayed little positive interest in their co-religionists, many even unwilling to recognize the Sephardim as Jews.[23] Examination of the position of the Ashkenazim and Sephardim in Australia provides some explanation for this state of affairs.

The White Australia Policy had deep ramifications that were felt not only by Jews in general but even between them. The Ashkenazim, most of whom today have been raised in Australia, desire to see themselves as white Europeans and fully part of Australian society, whereas the Sephardim were classified and treated as part of the undesirable Asian groups seeking entry into Australia. Moreover, the Ashkenazim often displayed a tendency to underplay their Jewish identity or to minimize it in interaction with non-Jews. They thus viewed close identification with Sephardim – who emphasized their Jewishness to minimize their Asian identity – as an invitation to unpleasantness and ostracism.

Social mix based on ethnic background has a significant effect on relations with neighbors and on neighborhood satisfaction, particularly when an entire neighborhood is composed of relative newcomers. Newcomers tend to move to neighborhoods that will help ease cultural shock, those that are ethnically and culturally familiar to them. For immigrants arriving in a new country, friendship and neighbors are crucial factors in their social life, particularly friends with whom they had long-lasting relationships in the country of origin. While homogeneous ethnic background becomes less significant the longer immigrants remain in a host society, the ethnic neighborhood remains a component of the identity of the immigrant generation itself, which usually adjusts to the host society much more slowly than the younger generation. Even when they become financially and socially successful, first-generation immigrants are less prone to move to more up-scale areas.[24]

Sephardim in Sydney have experienced reasonably high levels of mutual assistance between neighbors and friends during their first years in Australia. Ginsburg and Marans (1980:106–7) report a similar trend in Israel: "[I]rrespective of the type of micro-neighborhood in which they lived, Asian-African (Oriental) Jews tended to report higher levels of mutual assistance among neighbors than Europeans." However, as time passed, and people became involved in a wider network of contacts, there was a natural decline in the level of these local contacts, particularly in the case of the younger generation.

Most Sydney Sephardim, particularly the young, tend to measure their success, first *vis-à-vis* the Ashkenazim, and only then *vis-à-vis* wider Australian society. During their early years in Australia, their principal measure of success is economic status; other factors, such as level of education, have little bearing on their sense of status. Education, however, does exert a great influence on ethnic identity. For, as they become better educated, the Sephardim tend to become more secular and to place less importance on their ethnic identity. Nonetheless, the economic factor is most significant to the Sephardic sense of how well and to what degree they have adjusted to life in Australia.

The lower middle-class suburbs of Bondi or North Bondi, where most Sephardim live, have a high concentration of flats and a very high population density. In Bondi, the density of the overseas-born population varies substantially from one neighborhood to another. Although there is a wide range of socio-economic levels, and the majority of its inhabitants are of European origin, it is a lower-class area with some lower middle-class pockets.[25] Most Ashkenazim live in more up-scale middle and upper middle-class areas within the Eastern Suburbs, such as Vaucluse, Rose Bay, Dover Heights, Double Bay or Darling Point, where they have white Anglo-Australian non-Jewish neighbors who do not view them as "ethnics".

During the years of my research, I witnessed the upwardly mobile moves of at least twenty Sephardic families, three of whom moved to houses that were no "better", newer, or larger, but were in more prestigious middle-class areas. While their moves did not seem to affect their identity as Jews, there was a significant change in their sense of Sephardic Jewish identity: Whereas in the old area of residence they identified themselves as Sephardim among Sephardim, in the new areas they viewed themselves as Australian Jews. And as their Sephardic identity weakened, the emphasis on their newly acquired Australian Jewish identity became increasingly stronger.

When Lulu, originally from Iraq, lived in a lower-class area of Bondi, she complained of her treatment by Ashkenazim. Identifying herself as "one-hundred percent Sephardic", she nonetheless sent her children to Yeshiva College (the ultra-Orthodox Hasidic day school), but said that she would send them to a government high school rather than to Moriah College (an Orthodox school), which the Sephardim claimed was run by Ashkenazi policy-makers who gave Sephardic culture short shrift. "I don't want my children to be looked down on. Because we live in Australia, my husband and I feel that our children should not be isolated within the Jewish community. We would like them to learn about Australia and grow up to be good Australians." Commenting on her brother's marriage to an Ashkenazi woman, Lulu complained, "He thinks too much of himself. He has become snobbish, and you know why? Because he married an Ashkenazi girl he looks down on us. Now he thinks we are savages." However, when Lulu's family moved to a better area, she did send one of her children to Moriah College. Three years later, she said. "My husband and I are happy with the school, and I don't understand why there should be a division between us. It should not be Ashkenazim and Sephardim. We should unite and be one group, with one culture. After all, we are all Jews."

The Carkuk family, of Iraqi origin, initially lived in Bondi and defined their identity as Sephardic. The husband, in particular, was very forceful in proclaiming his pride in his Sephardic origin and identity. To emphasize this he told me stories about the "glorious past" of Sephardim in the homeland. "I have nothing to be ashamed of. Our heritage and culture are beautiful. I cannot understand many Sephardim who behave in a manner that brings shame and disgrace to our people." But this man's resentment of Sephardim who did not act in accordance with his idea of proper behavior evinced his ambivalence toward his identity. Three years later, after his family had moved to a higher status Ashkenazi neighborhood only a few streets away from their previous house in Bondi, he had changed ideas of Sephardic superiority: "What is this garbage all about? We are all Jews, and we should stick with each other. In any case, we are Australians first. We live here, not in Israel." Now deeply disturbed by the schism between Sephardim and Ashkenazim, he sought – somewhat unsuccessfully – to convince himself that this schism did not exist.

While preparing a seminar for Ashkenazim and non-Jewish Australians about the history of the Sephardim, the organizers approached Gilla, of Indian origin, to speak on various aspects of Sephardic culture. She refused, despite her parents being prominent members of the Sephardic community, because she felt remote from Sephardic culture and refused to participate in Sephardic-oriented activities. Indeed, Gilla did not wish to perpetuate either Sephardic identity or culture. This separation from her ethnic group occurred after she married an Ashkenazi. A regular participant in Sephardic communal activities before her marriage, once married, Gilla abruptly terminated her involvement in the community's social and religious life. She and her husband moved to a higher status area, albeit with the aid of a very high mortgage. Their children were being raised as Ashkenazim, and were not exposed to Oriental food, languages or to the Sephardic community in Sydney. Thus, "marital mobility" must be added to the list of factors that lead to residential change and increasing detachment from the Sephardic community.

In many other instances, residential change was associated with a marked lessening of Sephardic identity within as short a time as three years. With upward residential mobility, these families become Ashkenized, viewing their move as an "improvement of identity" as well as of residence. Although they do not "forget" their Sephardic backgrounds, their expressed identity becomes more "flexible" and they begin to view identity as an individual choice. Thus, whereas in the past their expressed and internalized identities tended to be identical (i.e. Sephardic), and varied little through interaction with people of other backgrounds, today they are far more inclined to harbor more flexible identities (both openly expressed and internalized) and to tailor their expressed identity to a specific instrumental context. For example, for a number of years the United Israel Appeal (UIA) meetings of the Sephardic congregation were poorly attended and it raised minimal contributions. However, when Sephardim attended UIA meetings organized by Ashkenazi congregations, they donated generously. One Sephardic family, which refused all requests to help establish a new Sephardic community center, contributed substantially to the support of a Hasidic organization's newly established and Hasidic-run high school, thereby attempting to be accepted by the Ashkenazim.

It is important to note that many of those who move to areas in which the majority of the Jews are of Ashkenazi origin aspire to successful incorporation into Ashkenazi society. Those who do maintain their Sephardic identity despite such moves are proof that Ashkenazi culture is not forced upon them in their new neighborhoods.

For example, as happened with many Singaporean Jews, Adam arrived in Australia from Iraq via Singapore – he was virtually penniless and moved to a Western suburb. He expected members of the Sydney Jewish community to help him adjust find a suitable job and welcome his three children into the Jewish youth groups, so that they would remain Jewish. But he was disillusioned by his treatment on the part of Jewish institutions run by Ashkenazi policy-makers, which made him "feel small and inferior". In response, he vowed to maintain his Sephardic identity with pride. Adam eventually became quite affluent, and moved his family to Rose Bay. Nevertheless, he always consciously retained his Sephardic identity: "It is a pity that so many Sephardim want to shed their beautiful culture and tradition to adopt the Ashkenazi way of life." Two of his three children married Ashkenazi spouses, and yet he claims that his family are still proud members of the Sephardic community. While he does not think that Ashkenazim and Sephardim should amalgamate, because they are still quite different from one another, he does think that they should live side by side, mingle and respect each other. His daughters who married Ashkenazim, on the other hand, dismissed their father's desire to preserve the differences between Ashkenazim and Sephardim as stubborn and old-fashioned.

Change of Reference Groups

Sephardim who make an effort to become "Australianized" usually do so after their efforts to become "Ashkenized" failed and they are not accepted by Ashkenazim. This is especially true of the younger generation, who have been disappointed when their professional and/or economic success have not earned them acceptance by the Ashkenazi elite. Rather than becoming marginal to that group, they change their group of reference to Australian Anglo-Saxons. They refer to the Sephardic group only occasionally, as they no longer feel an integral part of it.

  This group is composed mostly of successful businessmen, like Danny, who was born in Iraq, raised in Israel and immigrated to Australia with his family when he was sixteen. Although he and his family truly wanted to be part of the Jewish community, they quickly found that the Jews of Sydney were strictly divided into two groups, and that the Ashkenazim "looked down on" him both socially and in business. Consequently, he decided early on to treat non-Jewish Australians as his reference group. As Danny began to do well in his own business, his three children became very active in Jewish youth movements. Although he and his wife still have many non-Jewish friends, they "made a conscious decision to try to be more involved in the Jewish community" and the Jewish Ashkenazi establishment, in order to keep their children within the Jewish world. However, his wife said that they were made to feel inferior and felt inadequate and out of place most of the time. As Danny puts it: "This type of attitude is what made us escape from Israel." Gradually Danny and his family stopped keeping kosher, they are not members of any Jewish organization and rarely celebrate Jewish holidays. They reexamined their failure to provide an adequate Jewish upbringing for their children when their son married a non-Jew. However, they were still adamant that, given the same conditions, they saw very little possibility of behaving in any other manner.

Shalom, too, came to Australia with his family after having spent some time in Israel. Originally from a poor family in India, he graduated from the Law School of New South Wales University and established his own law firm, which is highly successful. Shalom married an Ashkenazi woman but divorced her on the grounds of incompatibility after five years and having two children. Although he maintains a kosher home and attends synagogue several times a year, "for the sake of the children", he does not want anything to do with the Jewish community – either Sephardic or Ashkenazi – because "the Ashkenazim think very highly of themselves and treat the Sephardim as though they were backward, inferior and stupid. And the Sephardim don't help the situation by allowing the Ashkenazim to behave toward them in such a manner." Indeed, he sees one of the reasons for the breakdown of his marriage in the lack of cordiality between his Ashkenazi parents-in-law and his Sephardic parents. He also stated that his parents-in-law objected to his relationship with their daughter from the outset. As his wife told him without mincing words, they objected to his Sephardic origin.

Shalom concluded our interview, saying that he did not want to adhere to either group, and that he was proud to be an Australian. He hoped, however, that his children would somehow become proud "Australian Jews"; members of a united Jewish community, in Australia, in which there would no longer be an inferior–superior relationship between Sephardim and Ashkenazim. In the meantime, he prefers to associate with non-Jews while remaining an observant Jew himself.

While many Sephardim (both in Sydney and in Israel) seek upward mobility through Ashkenization or acculturation into the host culture, the crucial question is, "To what degree are individuals free to pursue social mobility?" Many Sephardim who have done well financially may not wish to go through the process of becoming Ashkenized. Sephardim in Israel are forced to accept Ashkenazi idioms in expressing their socio-economic mobility. Outside Israel there is a certain outlet for these individuals who can attain a higher status and move upward socially within the host society by avoiding the Ashkenazi community and Ashkenazi social scale. Even there, however, they are subject to exclusion by Australians who harbor racial discrimination against Asians.

Summary and Conclusion: Becoming a Minority within a Minority

The initial establishment of the Sephardic community in the mainly Ashkenazi Eastern suburbs of Sydney in the 1950s and 1960s was an attempt to replicate a traditional Sephardic community in a modern Western city. They desired to maintain spatial proximity to the synagogue, which would allow Sephardim to interact with each other on a regular basis and to forge a mutually supportive moral community.[26] Really, being a Sephardic in Sydney has involved a kind of "self-ghettoization" within the Bondi neighborhood. Thus, an important part of Sephardic identity has been based on localization in the lower-class Eastern suburbs.[27]

Movement away from the Sephardic area has inevitably involved some degree of estrangement from the community. As the higher-status neighborhoods to which Sephardim aspire are centers of Ashkenazi residence, and as higher social status for Jews in Sydney is associated with being Ashkenazi, it is not surprising that upwardly mobile Sephardim are drawn to identify with Ashkenazim, whether or not they are accepted as such.

It is of utmost importance to highlight the situation of Sephardim as a minority within a minority. The Ashkenazi minority provides a buffer between the Sephardic community and Australian society. While Sephardim attempt to emulate Ashkenazi culture, they also adopt many of the minority characteristics of the Ashkenazim in Australia. This situation makes the position of Sephardim precarious and confusing.

Social mobility, however, implies the downplaying of Sephardic identity and the adoption of a pan-Jewish identification that is seen as an Australianized "Ashkenized" Jewish identity. Indeed, the process of acculturation into the larger Jewish community and Australian society has tended to create a "negative" ingredient in the ethnic Sephardic identity. This is apparent especially within the younger generation, where we witness the disintegration of the modified extended family and the breakdown of nuclear familial ties. Individual Sephardim who "move up" seek acceptance by Ashkenazim. They feel that the less they are affiliated to the Sephardim, and the more they are involved in Ashkenazi Jewish affairs, the more quickly they will be accepted by the Ashkenazi community. Yet, they are not always accepted by their co-religionists. Instead, some find acceptance within the non-Jewish business community, which affords them a better status in the general community. Those that do so generally do not belong to any Jewish organization or synagogue.

There is a crucial question regarding the degree of freedom that the individual has in regard to his or her social mobility. Many Sephardim who have done well financially may not wish to be Ashkenized. In countries in which there is a wide non-Jewish population, there is a certain outlet for these individuals. In Australia they can achieve upward social and class mobility within the host society while avoiding the Ashkenazi social scale and community, although they are subject to some exclusion, as there is still racial discrimination against Asians within the Australian society.

It is an interesting universal phenomenon that any kind of mobility, geographic or social, often tends to separate individuals from their ethnic group. This occurs for a number of reasons, one of them status anxiety. People are usually conscious of their own status and of that of their neighborhood. Sephardim who have worked hard, achieved a higher socio-economic status and moved into higher status neighborhoods, do not usually wish to associate with people from a lower-class area. They fear that this will halt their upward progress, as they might be classed with people from Bondi instead of those from Vaucluse, Darling Point or other upper middle-class areas.

Status anxiety stems from problems of marginality and identity crisis. This is particularly true of immigrants who arrive in the host society from lower classes, with little wealth, and who are channeled into low status positions upon arrival.[28] The Sephardim were marginal in their countries of origin, too, but unlike most immigrants to the West, they cannot return to their homelands. Moreover, they come from a different and somewhat marginal religious background. In Australia, as long as they live near each other in Bondi, they can buffer themselves somewhat, escaping into an ethnic sanctuary. However, many feel that in order to be socially mobile they must minimize their participation in the Sephardic community by extending their participation outside the Sephardic group, mainly within the larger Jewish community. Peterson-Royce (1982:5–6) has labeled the behavior of "individuals or groups who feel that they are in an inferior position seek to improve their situation" as "long-term identity switching". Such individuals begin to use the Australian or the Ashkenazi evaluation scale, depending on who they choose as their reference group. They may claim to have participated in, and be accepted by, that particular group. However, when they "pass out"[29] to the larger society they have difficulty in operating on the regional, occupational, religious, educational, ethnic and generational level, due to their imperfect command of the appropriate idioms. Their initial residential and cultural isolation has prevented them from gaining the necessary knowledge to function in these domains.[30]

Once they acquire this knowledge and learn how to operate outside of their world, particularly if they are successful and upwardly mobile, they do not wish to return to the world they left behind. Consequently,

Double Bay and Rose Bay Sephardim tend not to associate with Sephardim from Bondi, particularly on the social level. It seems that status anxiety is a continual factor. Not surprisingly, the small groups of Sephardim who manage to achieve socio-geographical mobility reduce their association to their localized group, as well as their identification with the customs and lifestyle of the group.

The situation is similar in Israel, where Ashkenazim tend to live in better-class areas, while the Sephardim live in lower-class neighborhoods.[31] An attitudinal study of an ethnically mixed housing project in Israel found that Ashkenazim were ranked highest and the Moroccan group (a sub-group of the Sephardim) lowest. More significant were the findings that Moroccans rated themselves lower than they do European Jews: "[In] their attempt to gain more complete acceptance, it is suggested that North Africans are conforming to norms of the dominant groups in the social system, even when these include certain forms of prejudice toward them".[32]

I argue that people must achieve a firm, clear sense of identification with the heritage and culture of their in-group before they can achieve a secure "ground" for a sense of well-being. Many researchers assume that a minority culture functions best within a territorial enclave, where its members can build their own ethnic institutions. However, in-group solidarity undoubtedly isolates people from other groups in the society.[33] In its Australian version the Ashkenazi Jewish culture in Sydney is perpetuated through an extensive use of ethnic institutions. The only formal institution of Sydney's Sephardic Jewish community, however, is a synagogue, which is less than thriving.

Some researchers have contended that social class is a more important factor than ethnic origin in the assessment of upward social mobility. Many argue that lower-class individuals are judged by middle-class individuals, and by themselves, in accordance with middle-class idioms, cultural notions and rationality. In a sense, they become victims of the hegemony of the middle class.[34] Connell (1977), too, argues that the working class has been institutionally and ideologically incorporated into the middle class by the middle class. It is my contention, however, that the ethnic factor plays an important part in class and status categorization. As Weingrod (1965:39) argues in his study of Israeli society: "Europeans, or to use the more common designation, Ashkenazim, are ranked higher than Middle Easterners, or Sephardim. To come from Poland or Britain is, ipso facto, to be more prestigious than to have one's origins in Egypt or Iraq. This rift is fundamental, and it runs throughout the society."[35]

When Sephardim attempt to become more Ashkenized and still maintain their religion, they lose their culture, and even their religion becomes increasingly Ashkenized. For Pan-Judaism relates to class mobility, and in most cases class mobility leads to religious modification.[36] In other words, the Sephardim become not Australians, but more like the Ashkenazim. Current indications point strongly to the continuing of Sephardic acculturation to the Ashkenazi variant of Australian culture and to structural and residential assimilation into the Ashkenazi community.

The residential factor plays an important part in the ethnic stratification of groups, although on a much smaller scale. Whereas Ashkenazim are characterized by high institutional and residential concentrations, the Sephardim are increasingly moving toward residential dispersion. The socio-economic factors of education, income and occupation influence the segregation and dispersion of Sephardim, particularly their pattern of residential movement. One may conclude that the vertical mobility of the Sephardim in the Eastern suburbs tends to weaken their ties with their relatives and kin as well as with their Sephardic friends. This vertical and social mobility involves a concurrent attempt to establish closer relationships with Ashkenazim. By moving to the same neighborhood, they hope that the relationship will become one of Jew to Jewish neighbor. This move, even when it involves the very small geographical distance of even a mile or two, places the Sephardim in another world. The desire to be accepted by the Ashkenazi world accelerates isolation from other Sephardim, which in turn tends to encourage the development of negative elements of Sephardic identity.

There is an implicit message here: that social mobility requires residential and ethnic mobility. Those who become socially mobile yet desire to remain within the Sephardic community in an ethnic rather than a residential sense, find themselves experiencing status anxiety, marginality and alienation. They feel pressured to shed their ethnic identity as part of the process of social mobility.

6

Religious Organization and Secular Power

When ethnic groups immigrate to societies different from their own in values, culture and institutions, they often feel considerable pressure to assimilate into the host culture. This may affect their traditional institutions and their bases of power. As religion is one of the cornerstones of ethnic identity and way of life, it is interesting to see how religious individuals strive to maintain their status and power in an assimilating community.

In choosing their original places of residence in Australia, Sephardic immigrants considered the Jewishness of an area as well as the ethnic Sephardic factor. When they moved to Bondi, Jews already lived there. By establishing a distinct Sephardic community in Bondi, the Sephardim were attempting to replicate a traditional Sephardic community in which they could not only interact with each other on a regular basis but also maintain a mutually supportive moral community with proximity to the synagogue. This self-ghettoization, in an environment of modernization and secularization, seems to have clarified the different sources of social power, leading to conflict in making decisions concerning religious organization and ritual. In studying the importance of religion for the Sydney Sephardim, in the past and the present as well as in the traditional and the modern society, these conflicts are examined and analyzed in terms of the immigrant situation and acculturation, thereby illuminating the problems of ethno-religious identity for Sephardim in general and for the Sydney Sephardim in particular.

When I arrived in Sydney in 1979, I was struck by the small number of elderly men and women who attended Sabbath services. By 1989, this number had shrunk even further. And even fewer youth and young adults attended religious or social functions. Daily services that are supposed to be held three times a day, with a *minyan* (or quorum) of ten men, were held only a few times a week due to lack of a *minyan*. This relative isolation of the elders of the Sephardic community from mainstream Australian Jewish life is indicative of the breakdown of Sephardic ethnic identity. Although the Sephardic community considers itself Orthodox, not even many of the elder generation observe all Jewish laws and practices. Those who continue to participate in religious services do so out of religiosity and the need to perpetuate the tradition, as it was practiced in the homeland.

The meeting of the faithful in a place of worship has important social functions. The synagogue is the arena for transmitting the reinterpreted symbols and myths that foster accommodation to changing circumstance.[1] Yet, religious attendance is shrinking, and the running of the synagogue has become increasingly problematic. This is due in part to the office of the rabbi in Sephardic history and in part to conflicts over religious policy resulting from the social cleavages and secular interests found in an acculturating community.

The Rabbi: A Socio-Political Figure

In Iraq, India and Egypt the rabbi received his authority and legitimacy as spiritual and social leader from the governments of those countries. The *hakham* or "wise man" was one of the chief decision-makers for both the internal and external affairs of the community.[2]

In the Ottoman Empire the Chief Rabbi, or *Hakham Bashi*, was "the supreme authority in all religious matters and in charge of all *hakhamim* and heads of the community". As a representative of the government, he also had political power over the community and was responsible for collecting government taxes in the Jewish communities under his jurisdiction.[3]

The religious and secular duties, as well as privileges of the *Hakhamim Bashi*, were intertwined to such a degree that it was difficult to distinguish between their religious and secular functions. Indeed, their considerable obligations to the government and preoccupation with the community's external affairs left them little time for religious affairs, which they usually assigned to schoolteachers. "The powers vested in the *Hakham Bashi* show that the Ottoman authorities regarded him as their representative *vis-à-vis* the Jewish population, who performed official functions on behalf of the Jews, and so he was regarded by the Jews themselves."[4]

In 1862, there was growing unrest among members of the Jewish community, who bitterly resented the rabbinate's control over institutions established by Ottoman law. A new constitution in 1865 allowed the laity to play a role, limited the domination of the *Hakham Bashi* and the rest of the rabbinate to the point where they were sometimes forced to consult with a council of laymen prior to their rulings.[5]

In the Western world, the roles and functions of the rabbi have decreased and there is a clear-cut division between the rabbi's religious and social functions.[6] In Sydney, the Sephardic rabbi is engaged mostly with religious rituals, and he has lost his traditional role as the highest authority on socio-religious issues. Since its establishment, all the spiritual leaders of the Sephardic community have complained that interference by the Board of Management and the Religious Committee of the NSW Association of Sephardim prevented them from carrying out their religious duties. Even decisions regarding social functions have required approval by the Ladies Auxiliary or the Board of Management.

Any discussion on the religious authority of the rabbi must, of necessity, take up the issue of rituals, rites and sacred symbols. The rabbi derives his power from his knowledge, his conduct and his performance of rituals. The forces of a religion in supporting social values rest "on the ability of its symbols to formulate a world in which these values, as well as the forces opposing their realization, are fundamental ingredients".[7]

From a sociological point of view, rituals are essentially concerned with preservation of the social order. Thus, every ritual, including religious rituals, involves some struggle for power, in which those holding power attempt to maintain their hegemony over the meaning that influences and expresses the world views of the people and their understanding of the world.[8] As Geertz (1973:109) puts it, "Religious belief involves a prior acceptance of authority."

In a world of increasing secularization and status competition between groups, particularly in situations of acculturation, the power to control the meaning of symbolic rituals and the ability of religious authorities to structure worlds views is called into question. The representatives of that authority, in this case the rabbis, can retain power only if they are able to inject new meanings into old symbols as well as help reconstruct an adjusted ethnic identity. There have been several areas of conflict between the Sephardic congregation of Sydney and their rabbi.

Control of Liturgy

The first rabbi of the community, who took up his position in 1962, resigned in 1979, claiming that the constant interference in the performance of his rabbinical duties on the part of community leaders made his job impossible. Although many members of the religious and executive committees complained about the rabbi, he claimed that the community as a whole respected him. Of the three Sephardic rabbis who were interviewed to replace him, one turned down the position and two others were deemed "overly dogmatic" by some members of the religious committee. As one community leader said, "We are a small Sephardic community attempting to live among the Ashkenazim. If we are going to employ a rabbi who from the outset upsets our equilibrium with the Ashkenazim and destroys our ties with them, we will be left alone. And let's face it, we cannot afford this. We want our prospective rabbi to bring back Sephardim who are no longer affiliated with our congregation."

What the congregation wanted, in other words, was a rabbi who would "adjust" his religious beliefs to suit the social needs of the community by integrating the Sephardim with the higher-status Ashkenazi community. Thus, the leaders in effect told prospective rabbis: "Don't be too Orthodox and you'll be accepted. Otherwise you will be ignored and we will be left behind." In stating that their secular community needs would determine their choice of religious office-holder the laity made it clear that any rabbi they chose would have little to say about community decision-making – in sharp contrast to the situation in their countries of origin.

Another instance where the religious arena was used as a stage for the power struggle to gain status in the social and secular world occurred at the beginning of 1984, when the community hired a rabbi from Israel, after a three-year period in which nobody filled the office. From the beginning, the rabbi's role was viewed differently by him and the laity, and he faced constant criticism, the religious committee even questioning his knowledge of Torah and *Halachah*. The rabbi felt that he was being dictated to by the committee, who in turn were distressed that he avoided them and had little respect for their ideas. In the end he was asked to resign, the executive finding it impossible to accept his socio-religious authority. The conflict generated ill feeling – politicizing and polarizing the entire fragile community. Centered on the manner in which his resignation was requested, the rabbi's performance became a secondary issue. The rabbi's supporters organized a petition signed by eighty members of the community, most of whom rarely participated in its social or religious activities. The congregation's constitution calls for an extraordinary meeting of its members in the event of a dispute over the resignation of a rabbi and it requires twenty-five signatories to support the rabbi. Since the executive wanted to avoid an action that would call their authority and power into question, they agreed to let the rabbi stay on if he would "improve" his performance (in order to save face in the eyes of the Ashkenazi community).

It later became clear that those who had supported the rabbi had done so as a political tactic to "get back at" the most influential individuals in the community, who they felt dominated the executive and religious committees. (Indeed, they indicated quite openly that they felt the rabbi was "a dud".) Here, the synagogue, which had been the pillar and one of the primary centers for religious authority in the traditional society, was used as a platform for a purely social and political struggle.

This rabbi returned to Israel in the late 1980s. The next one faced similar problems. Most members agreed that he demonstrated vast knowledge and had a good command of his duties, that he had leadership qualities and charisma. He was an avid speaker, and they liked him. Nonetheless, he was asked to resign in early 1993; plans to fire him began early in 1992, due to another power struggle between him and the executive and religious committees. A senior member of the executive described him as being "too powerful, obstinate and with no control over his mouth". However, the rabbi claims that he was too religious for the community, in particular for the executive, which wanted him to "modify" religion to suit their life-style, and to turn a blind eye when they failed to adhere to religious laws. It was when he refused to do so that he was forced to leave.

It appears, then, that the Sephardic community has forcefully exhibited the painful process of acculturation and adjustment through its continued struggle over the position of the rabbi in the community, and that his qualities and personality play a relatively minor role *vis-à-vis* the desire of its powerful senior members to run the community in accordance with their own wishes. The only rabbi who could succeed in this situation would be one who "fitted" their ideas of ritual observance. The three rabbis in question were under tremendous pressure to "perform the miracle" of reviving the community by "delivering the goods" quickly.

The Clash between Religious Law and Social Norms

Segregation of the Sexes in the Synagogue

The Orthodox Sephardic like the Orthodox Ashkenazi synagogue maintains strict physical division between men and women: men seated on the ground floor and women in "the gallery", in the traditional manner. Women must follow the service and view the Torah ark from afar.[9] In the period between 1962 and 1982, however, older women were allowed to sit in the back rows downstairs during the High Holidays, with no partition to screen them off from the men. In early 1985, the rabbi advised the religious committee that this went against *halachic* law and suggested the use of a partition.

The Religious Committee agreed with the rabbi and brought the matter up at the next monthly board meeting. It resulted in one of the stormiest meetings held for several years. Those who were against it pointed out that the situation had prevailed for twenty years and that placing a partition would degrade and humiliate those women who attended services, and would cause many of them to cease attending. Those in favor maintained that the Sephardic synagogue must follow the example of the Orthodox Ashkenazi congregations. A majority voted in favor of the partition.

But the matter was far from closed. During a social gathering at the synagogue the following week, a petition against the partition was circulated by a congregation member not on the executive, who was not supposed to know what had been discussed at the meeting. Evidently, the matter had been leaked by a member of the executive to "right" the situation – obviously with some success. Another member of the executive pointed out that "the whole argument is the use of a partition for only three days a year. What a waste! The energy of the community should be put to a better use". When the rabbi asked how a supposedly Orthodox community could even think of acting contrary to the ruling of *Halachah*, he found little support among the members, who obviously had second thoughts about the partition. Indeed, it was not until late 1988, three years after the controversy broke out, that a symbolic see-through silk partition was installed.

This rabbi could not accommodate himself to the community's desire to give more weight to acculturation than to strict religious law. When it came to *Halachah*, he was unable to "sell" religion to his "consumers" by allowing them a say in how it should be conducted. Indeed, all three Sephardic rabbis failed to understand that they would have to inculcate new meanings into the old symbols in order to survive in an acculturating group. The third rabbi exacerbated the situation when he attempted to rectify past lapses, which was taken as a direct – and extreme – affront by those who had been responsible for the lapse in the first place, and who derived legitimacy for their influence through their unsubstantiated claim of ritual knowledge.

One community leader explained the rabbi's desire to increase the degree of Orthodox observance as follows: "This rabbi turned religious only ten years ago. He does not come from a religious family, nor does he have a religious history or background. So he goes by the book and adheres strictly to *Halachah*. But we brought our *minhagim* [customs], which have been in operation for the last three or four hundred years, from our homeland. He cannot come and tell us we are wrong, because if the rabbis of three hundred years ago made amendments or additions to certain rules, they must have had very good reasons to accommodate to environmental or other changes."

This conflict highlights a fundamental problem not unique to the Sydney Sephardic community. Orthodox rabbis the world over must face the increasing influence of the secular, modern world. In many cases, religious codes have been manipulated by political and religious leaders, to the point where they become unimportant symbols. In other instances, like that of Sydney, control of the performance of religious ritual becomes the central battleground on which the struggle for political dominance of a community is conducted.[10]

One cannot end this section without referring to the status of women in the Jewish world. As Gale (1997:326) stated, this conflict "reflected a far more fundamental issue involving contrary definitions of the status of women by a religious system and by contemporary modern social system". Solomon (1994:120) asked "can one any longer accept as divine or authoritative a Torah which discriminates against women?"

Dominance by the Laity: The Sunday School Curriculum

The importance of a Sunday School curriculum lies in its socialization function, its inculcation of ethno-religious and group identity into the younger generation. As such, its content is a legitimate focus for attention. However, the Sunday School curriculum is prone to the same struggle for power over religious institutions exhibited in other areas, this time channeled into different interpretations of the Jewish identity that were intended to be preserved.

At the end of 1984, when the relatively new rabbi was asked to prepare a Sunday School's curriculum for 1985, he agreed reluctantly because he knew that he would not be able to open the next year of the school if the congregation's president and Sunday School headmaster did not see and approve it. As he feared, the president criticized his curriculum for being too heavily religious. After a vitriolic discussion, in which the president insulted his professional ability, the rabbi carried the day. But, in the end, the president was triumphant – albeit tragically so. For, out of fifty children enrolled at the beginning of the year, only eleven were still attending Sunday School by the end of the year – most of them only because they were forced to do so by their fathers. The president charged that the curriculum was "too religious" and above the children's heads. But the rabbi staunchly maintained, "You cannot compromise religion."

The conflict here is a triple one: the fundamental one between the rabbi as religious leader and the president as social leader; between two personalities; and between the religious and secular leaderships. The conflict spread to the laity, where it became a generational issue. Although the president had been a hard-working member of the religious committee for twenty years, and had volunteered to serve the community in many capacities before assuming its presidency, many members of the community, particularly young adults, felt that he had exploited his position to carry out autocratic decisions made largely on his own. In this respect, his behavior was similar to most previous presidents, most of whom were elderly and believed that their office gave them the right to rule the community as they saw fit, even in religious matters about which they knew little or nothing. When the new rabbi arrived with hard-line ideas of his own, the president was threatened by the newcomer's expertise.

After several clashes, the president began to criticize or correct the rabbi in the presence of the congregation, where such public criticism by the congregation's "elder statesman" created friction among both the board and the members. The power struggle here, between the president who wanted the rabbi to submit to his authority, and the rabbi who did not, paralleled the conflict between the rabbi and the religious committee, whose members saw their traditional standing as "experts" threatened. The situation had not altered by the time I left Sydney in late 1991. The last rabbi left the congregation after similar occurrences in 1993. It seems that the Sephardic need to acculturate to the modern host society is at constant war with their traditional backgrounds. Whether tradition will lose out before the Sephardim feel enough at home in Sydney to return to their traditional Orthodoxy – as have the Orthodox Ashkenazim – remains to be seen.

The Naming Ceremony for a Baby Girl

This ceremony is unique to Sephardim and derives from custom rather than *Halachic* ruling. Held on the Sabbath, it begins with the father being called up to the altar to read a special passage about *"Yonati be'hagve hasela"* (O my dove, who art in the clefts of the rock) to honor the birth of his daughter. Then he names the baby girl and proceeds to read a part of the *parasha* (portion of the Bible) for that week.[11] This is followed by a party at home for family and friends. However, according to *halachic* law, Jews are not permitted to carry children outside the vicinity of their home on the Sabbath. Thus, when one father wanted to bring his baby girl to synagogue for her naming ceremony, the rabbi told him he could not do so. But the rabbi promised him he would be called up to read from the Torah on that *Shabbat*, at which time his daughter would be named. During the service the *shamash* (caretaker who allocates duties to the Torah readers) shouted out that a baby could not be named in her absence. Both the rabbi and the father were mortified in public. Later, the president denied responsibility for what had happened because he was not in charge of Torah readings. The *shamash* – who has been in this capacity for over twenty years – said that neither the president nor the rabbi could tell him what to do *vis-à-vis* allocation of readings around the altar.

The religious committee blamed the unfortunate occurrence on the rabbi: "The law forbidding Jews to carry children outside the vicinity of their home on the Sabbath and High Holidays is not a Torah law, but a *halachic* ruling, made by a rabbi. And, although *halachic* rulings apply to all Jews, we Sephardim have a *minhag* [custom] of carrying our children to synagogue on this day. In fact, it is considered an honor to bring the child to the synagogue to be named. We Sephardim have had this *minhag* for many generations, and we do not intend to change our tradition. Not only would that offend many members of our community, but it would be giving up our traditions." The baby's father was not bothered by the question of whether or not he could bring his daughter to the synagogue; what offended him was being prevented from being called up to the Torah and naming his daughter.

This father had fallen victim to a power struggle between the major participants, the rabbi, the president and the *shamash*. Every Jew is allowed to read from the Torah, whether he is celebrating a special occasion or not. Furthermore, it is true that only the *shamash* and only he allocates the Torah readings, since he is responsible for generating donations to the synagogue. People who are called up to the altar usually donate substantial amounts of money. Consequently, the smooth running of the synagogue dictates there be cooperation and communication between the rabbi and the *shamash*. In this instance, the *shamash* saw himself as superior to the rabbi. With regard to the most important issue here, the *halachic* rule that a Jew cannot carry his child outside the vicinity of his home, it is true that most traditional Jews kept this to the letter. Nevertheless, it is also true that Jews in Iraq did carry their children to synagogue, and they did not defy *halacha* by so doing. For, in areas heavily populated by Jews, rabbis could construct an *"Eruv"*, that is, extending the home vicinity to the whole area. This allowed men to carry their prayer books and shawls to synagogue, and for mothers and children to attend services. It is evident that the religious committee's members were ignorant of this fact and reasons for it.

The struggle for power in the synagogue resulted in a complete breakdown of communication between the rabbi and the religious committee. For the rabbi attempted to bring rapid changes to the community with no period of adjustment, and the committee stopped him from doing so without consultation with the membership. In this incident, the rabbi did not inform the *shamash* of the procedure agreed upon after he had spoken to the father. He claimed that the synagogue was his domain and that the *shamash* should have submitted to his rabbinical authority, no matter what.

Religious Rituals for the Birth of a Boy

When a boy is born to a Jewish family, the father is called up on the Sabbath to read a section of that week's Torah portion. In Sephardic synagogues all men present also sing the ode *Yehi Shalom Behechalecha* ("there will be peace within thy palaces").[12] In the case of a man who had married out of the faith, the rabbi objected to calling him up to read the Torah portion, even though the mother was in the process of converting. The president said that every Jewish man has the right to be called up to read from the Bible, and instructed the *shamash* to call the father to the altar in defiance of the rabbi's ruling. The whole argument took place during the service and in front of the congregation, demonstrating the congregation's lack of respect for religious authority. One member put it: "The rabbi is like the head and the congregation is the body, and when we mistreat the head we are actually mistreating and affecting our body badly." Here the rabbi prevented the father from reading the Torah portion concerning the birth of his son – who was not a Jew according to the *halachah*.

Intergroup Conflict – Intergenerational Power Struggle within the Executive and the Religious Committee

Many members of the Sephardic community felt that the president "always ran to his big brothers in the Ashkenazi community" rather than consult with them, in an attempt to be like the Ashkenazim and gain their respect as a sign of acceptance and acculturation into the Westernized Ashkenazi community. In the minds of these members, the president exemplified their "negative identity" and used his position to legitimize his undemocratic style of decision-making.[13]

It turns out that this president wanted to be the only one who had official contact with the rabbi; he did not look favorably upon members who attempted to do the same. At a meeting of the executive committee at which the president presented a long list demonstrating the rabbi's incompetence, the board moved to invite the rabbi to the next meeting to relate his view of his duties and his difficulties in carrying them out. The motion was passed unanimously after a three-and-a-half-hour debate. However, the president called an emergency board meeting the following week, which he opened with a statement threatening to resign if the board insisted on the meeting with the rabbi. He said that he had consulted with "important people in the Ashkenazi community", including rabbis, and "they all told me that this would not only humiliate the rabbi but also put my authority in question – as a vote of no confidence in me". This caused great agitation among the board members, since the synagogue's constitution stipulates that a motion passed by a majority must be implemented, and even an autocratic president cannot change the constitution unilaterally. Even more disturbing was the board's feeling that the confidentiality of the meeting had been compromised by seeking advice from outsiders. Needless to say, the meeting with the rabbi never took place.

The feeling in the community was that the problem stemmed from the absolute freedom in social and religious matters the president enjoyed during the three years when there was no rabbi. This issue can also be seen as the behavior of a "past-oriented" elite within a "future-oriented" community.[14] For, despite an executive of seventeen members, elders on the board would have liked to rule the community as it was in the countries of origin, where one or several elderly made the decisions. As this incident highlights, the structure of the community has been organized by the president and powerful elders in a way that perpetuates the traditional structure. Their authority has been challenged, with little success, by younger acculturated members who attempted to introduce democratic decision-making – in this case through recourse to the constitution.

The Sephardic community's committee for religious affairs provides another example of the struggle for power between the generations; between those who wish to continue the traditions of the past and those who seek a new way, more in line with organizational procedure in modern, Western society. The religious committee was supposed to help the rabbi carry out his religious duties and to mediate between him and the executive. This committee, however, has never functioned effectively.

A major reason for this failure is the generation gap among its members. Two of its five or six members, between 26–40 years of age, represent the younger generation. But, despite the size of the population they represent, they are rarely consulted on such crucial matters as the choice of a new rabbi. These decisions were made by the committee's older members, in conjunction with the executive. One young member summed it up by stating: "What are we elected for? I have just about had it. We are the young who are supposed to take over from the old and who are elected by the executive to be on the religious committee. Yet, whenever we open our mouths to voice our opinions or objections, we are shut up by elders, who tell us, 'You must be patient. You have no experience and you don't understand. When you reach our age, you'll understand what we mean.'"

Thus, the younger generation's attempts to separate secular and religious matters – in line with the way they have done so in their professional and social lives – have never been able to withstand the elders' desire to continue running the community as a traditional Orthodox group. The younger generation wanted the elders to use traditional symbols to create a new manifestation of Judaism, "an identity that can adapt to present social conditions in the modern changing world".[15]

The Generation Gap and Acculturation

The Youth Organization

In 1980, the executive decided to deal with the urgent problem of Sephardic youth who were seeking friends and activities in the larger Jewish community, and which they viewed as threatening the continuation of the Sephardim as a unique group. A young member of the executive who was well known among the teenagers was appointed to establish a youth club under the auspices of the synagogue. By concentrating on social activities – although some religious activities were to be included – it was hoped that there would be a gradual return of Sephardic young people from the Ashkenazi youth clubs.

This young man, who was himself active in Ashkenazi youth groups, knew many others whom he felt would prefer a Sephardic-based group if it was organized and run in an interesting way. He called a meeting, which was attended by thirty youth. During the meeting he asked the young people to fill out a questionnaire so he could take it back to the executive. Most respondents remarked that the elders who run the community gave them little opportunity to participate; that they ruled the community with "iron hands" and gave little preference to youth. They claimed that they felt more at home in other Jewish organizations, where they were treated more like adults. They wanted to be given a chance to prove that they could contribute something to the community. When the young member of the executive brought his findings to the attention of the board at its next meeting, he was severely criticized, the elders claiming that this was a wrong kind of inquiry. The findings of the questionnaire generated considerable tension between the two generations on the board; the old felt that it negated their contribution to the community; and the young fully supported the young man's findings. Hurt by the reaction of the elders, the young man stayed away from board meetings for several months, and the issue of a youth club was dropped until a new rabbi arrived four years later. When this young man stood for another position the following year, he was isolated and given the impression that he was not needed by the executive. As a result, he ceased being active in the running of the community for several years.

His reaction was not atypical. Several other young members elected to the board soon became disillusioned when the elders refused to share authority. One of them told me angrily: "We all feel that we are denied freedom of participation on important issues. When we do achieve some success, elders on the executive congratulate us, but somehow manage to imply that we could have done a better job if we had paid more attention to their ideas. They like to indulge themselves by telling stories about their achievements in the old country, and I am tired of wasting my time listening to them".

The inability of the older generation to let go was also demonstrated when Dan, another younger man, agreed to stand for the position of community president. Although he was backed strongly by other young members, an older member publicly told him that he would be better off as vice-president, "until you gain experience and learn the ropes". Another elder, who valued the connection with the Ashkenazi community, asked Dan whether he knew "important members of the Jewish community because it is important to know who to approach when we need them. If they don't know you they won't take much notice of you." Disgusted, Dan decided to withdraw although he had been on the executive for a number of years and was known to be a valuable member of the community. As one young board member put it, "What more does he have to do to prove he is worth it?"

The elders' response to involvement of the young epitomizes their loss of power in Western society, to which they have not – and cannot – acculturate, as the young have. The paradox here is that, in their attempt to maintain the traditional style and level of religious practice, presumably to pass it on to future generations, they are alienating the very group for whom they wish to preserve the tradition. For, when younger members of the board see that they are being disregarded or criticized, they often discontinue their membership and are lost as future carriers of the Sephardic tradition.

In an address to members of the Sephardic executive, the head of the Sydney *Beth Din* said:

> "You, now, in 1984, have one hundred and forty children born to Sephardic parents in a non-Jewish society. You have already lost these children, and even if you work hard, you will bring back only a fraction of them. In twelve to fifteen years time, this place [the synagogue] will be empty because you are not building up your youth. Now you are virtually a moshav zekenim [old people's home]. So work very hard to gear yourselves to the younger generation. Make them proud of their culture, tradition and their Sephardic identity. So far, you have done nothing to nurture this vineyard, which has the potential to be full of vitality, of youth who have not been touched by you leaders of the community. This vineyard will eventually die if you do not nurture it."

An inter-ethnic conflict

Aside from the undemocratic manner in which the Sephardic community was being run, an inter-ethnic conflict had been brewing since the late 1970s, when there was a clear ethno-political and ethno-religious shift in the community. From a near equilibrium between the Egyptians and the Iraqi-Indians in the early 1970s, the power shifted almost exclusively to the latter group. The final straw in this shift was the change from the Spanish–Portuguese Prayer-Book, which the Egyptians had used in Egypt, to the Iraqi version, which both Iraqis and Iraqi-Indians had used in the past.

The number of Egyptians on the board declined from five to one, and many Egyptians who had been religiously and socially active stopped attending services and social functions. Furthermore, several Egyptians joined Ashkenazi congregations, where they felt their children were more welcome. One person justified his resignation from the Sephardic community and his joining membership in an Ashkenazi congregation by claiming: "It is better to have lost your children to the Ashkenazi version of religion than to have lost them altogether."

Religious Observance

There are clear indications that, in the countries of origin, the Sephardic community found its solutions to organizational problems through the extensive use of religious idioms. As Goitein (1982:200) demonstrates, "The interweaving of the religious with the secular occurred in many aspects of life. All areas of existence could be adjudicated by a religious court or would be subjected to comment and censure by a preacher." Due to processes such as immigration, modernization and education, the Sephardic community of Australia has followed the Ashkenazi shift from religious principle to the use of symbolic actions and ethno-religious symbols.[16]

My survey questionnaire posed several questions aimed at shedding light on the religiosity and Sephardic Jewish identity of members of the Sydney Sephardim. The questionnaire was mailed to a random sample of 25 percent (n = 140) of the community, of whom 61.4 percent (n = 86) responded. Eight completed questionnaires were found unsuitable and not used in the final analysis, which left 78 (59.1 percent) counted.

The degree of religiosity found demonstrates that the group appears to be developing a symbolic identity, through a symbolic religion. Most members of the Sephardic congregation adapt their religious practices to suit their way of life rather than change their lifestyle to accommodate religion. They continue to signal their identity to other Jews by adhering to practices they find "convenient", and ignoring the rest.

Table 6.1 and figure 6.1 illustrate the frequency of synagogue attendance of Sephardim in Sydney, based on responses to the questionnaire; they demonstrate clearly that the highest synagogue attendance is among people who have been in Australia for sixteen to twenty years.

This group arrived in Australia in the 1960s as young married couples with small children, or married and had children in Australia. One can label them "problematic" because they have undergone a type of social-ization that left them not knowing how to bring up their children. By attending the synagogue, they attempted to continue the life they had been raised in, where religion was an important source of social life. However, religious life in Australia is largely separated from social life by Jews as well as by members of other religions.[17] As a result, while they attend synagogue in an effort to solve their problem of religious *vis-à-vis* social identity, they have ambivalent feelings about main-taining this symbolic link with their Sephardic traditions and identity. As one 52 year old, put it, "If I don't attend every now and then, I feel completely cut off. I don't know the dates of the holidays and feel out of place. Attending a synagogue, even though not on a regular basis, gives me a sense of belonging and makes me feel good. On the other hand, we must remember that we live in Australia and can't lead our life as we did in the old country. We mingle with people from all over the world and we have to live among them."

Table 6.1 Cross-Tabulation of Frequency of Synagogue Attendance by Length of Time in Australia

Frequency of Attendance	Number of Years in Australia								
	5	6–10	11–15	16–20	21–25	26–30	31–35	36+	n (%)
1. Once a week	0	0	2	7	3	2	1	1	16 (25)
2. At least once a month	0	0	3	3	2	0	3	0	11 (17.2)
3. High Holidays	4	6	4	10	2	2	1	3	32 (50.0)
4. Special Occasions	0	0	3	1	1	0	0	0	5 (7.8)
	4	6	12	21	8	4	5	4	64 (100)
	(6.3)	(9.4)	(18.8)	(32.8)	(12.5)	(6.3)	(7.8)	(6.3)	(100.0)

This substantiates Abramson's (1975:167) findings that, although reli-gious attendance is the most frequently used measure of religious involvement or attachment in America, it is only a symbolic link to reli-gion and does not indicate degree of religiosity or religious practice. For his findings revealed that while religious attendance fell from 69 percent among first-generation immigrants to 35 percent among the third gener-ation, synagogue membership rose dramatically among the American-born generations. He concluded that synagogue membership has become a social need to belong rather than a religious need to attend and observe.

Thus, I take frequency of attendance at religious services as one of many factors indicating religious identity, and not necessarily demonstrative of degree of religiosity. For the Sephardim in Sydney, this is a symbolic act that seems to facilitate maintenance of their ethnic identity and provides them with means of communicating this identity to the outside worlds of Ashkenazim and other Australians, when this seems desirable.

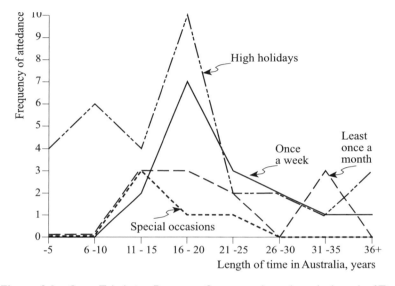

Figure 6.1   Cross Tabulation Frequency Synagogue Attendance by Length of Time in Australia

This finding explains the slight rise in the synagogue membership over the years and the concomitant decline in attendance. During the first three years of my research, regular synagogue membership fell only slightly, whereas attendance on the high holidays dropped sharply: In 1980, 370 people attended New Year and the Day of Atonement services. In 1981, attendance was only 250, and it dropped to about 200 in 1982. In a community of about 540 members (the Association of Sephardim) there was a drop from 71.1 percent to 38.46 percent attendance within three years (1980 = 370 or 71 percent; 1981 = 250 or 48.07 percent; 1982 = 200 or 38.46 percent).

The sharp decline in synagogue attendance, particularly on the high holidays, has more than one explanation. In addition to attrition through acculturation to the Ashkenazi world, as in the case of the Egyptians mentioned above, the congregation had no rabbi during these three years.

Tables 6.2 and 6.3 demonstrate that the Sephardim are following in the footsteps of the Ashkenazim. While their parent home in Sydney is more observant of Jewish ritual than that of the respondents', the latter are still far more observant than the home of the Ashkenazim. If the trend toward less observance continues, the gap between the Sephardic and Ashkenazi level of observance may eventually disappear.

Table 6.2 Jewish Ritual Observances (in percentages)

Practices	Sephardi Community		NSW Jewish Community	
	Respondents	Parents	Respondents	Parents
Pork and shellfish at home	12	6	46	24
Kosher meat in home	58	81	23	61
Separate utensils	36	55	22	57
Special dinner Friday night home	74	86	55	77
Candles lit on Friday night	83	95	63	82
Smoking allowed on Sabbath	46	29	64	44
Seder on Passover	86	92	82	90
Bread eaten on Passover	7	3	34	16
Fast on Yom Kippur	96	97	80	92
Candles lit on Hanukah	80	90	52	76

Note: The NSW Jewish Community Survey is taken from Encel and Buckley 1972.

Tables 6.2 and 6.3 demonstrate that the percentage of respondents who eat pork and shellfish at home is almost twice that of their parents; only about two-thirds of those whose parents keep separate utensils for meat and milk do so themselves. However, the percentage of those who make a special meal and light candles on the Sabbath and at Hanukah is much closer to that of their parents. But almost half of the younger generation smoke on the Sabbath.

The seemingly high level of observance indicated by the 85.5 percent of respondents who make a *Seder* at their homes on Passover is in reality attributable to the *Seder*'s expressive functions in fulfilling the social and familial need to gather together to celebrate an important Jewish holiday and custom as a group. Thus, whereas the *Seder* of past generations was mainly a religious celebration, its function today is mainly social for the majority of Western Jews.

This survey shows that four groups emerge in the parent–child comparison: (1) The relatively small and quite insignificant Orthodox

Table 6.3 Cross-Tabulation of Age and Ritual Observances

Age/Ritual Observance	18–29 (n=11)	30–39 (n=22)	40–49 (n=15)	50–59 (n=14)	60 & over (n=15)	Total (n=77)
Pork and shellfish at home	2 (18.18)	3 (13.64)	2 (13.33)	1 (7.14)	1 (6.66)	9 (11.68)
Kosher meat	7 (63.63)	12 (54.54)	9 (60.00)	8 (57.14)	8 (53.33)	44 (57.14)
Separate utensils	4 (36.36)	7 (31.81)	6 (40.00)	5 (35.71)	6 (40.00)	28 (36.36)
Special dinner Friday	9 (81.81)	14 (63.63)	12 (80.00)	11 (78.57)	10 (66.66)	56 (72.72)
Candles lit Friday	9 (81.81)	17 (77.27)	13 (86.66)	11 (78.57)	12 (80.00)	62 (80.51)
Smoking on Sabbath	10 (90.90)	8 (36.36)	9 (60.00)	7 (50.00)	3 (20.00)	37 (48.05)
Seder on Passover	10 (90.90)	19 (83.36)	11 (73.33)	12 (85.71)	13 (86.66)	65 (84.41)
No bread on Passover	11=100	20 (90.90)	14 (93.33)	13 (92.85)	14 (93.33)	72 (93.50)
Fast on Yom Kippur	11=100	21 (95.45)	14 (93.33)	14=100	14 (93.33)	74 (96.10)
Candles lit on Hanukah	7 (63.63)	19 (86.36)	12 (80.00)	11 (78.57)	12 (80.00)	61 (79.22)

Note: The first number indicates the number of cases; and the number in brackets indicates percentage.

group, where both parents and children are observant. (2) The non-Orthodox cluster whose parents maintain traditions but who are not at all observant themselves. (3) The newly traditional whose parents were not observant but who have adopted religious observance themselves.(4) The agnostics, who did not come from observant homes and are not observant themselves but who are still affiliated to the community. The questions that may be asked is what makes them Jews in their own eyes and how do they signal their identity to others.

The majority of the Sephardic community belong to the second group. They are in the process of secularization, as the secular aspects of life in Australia symbolize higher status in the socio-economic sphere in both the Australian and the Ashkenazi community.

Those in the third group, the newly observant, may have been influenced by their children having attended the *Yeshiva* ultra-Orthodox day school in which 50 percent of the pupils are of Sephardic origin: Several families became observant in order to prevent confusion in the minds of their children who attended the *Yeshiva* school. Or simply because that school generates a considerable amount of parental involvement. During the fieldwork years, I witnessed many Sephardim with children in the *Yeshiva* giving help to the school rather than to the Sephardic synagogue. In 1985, Sephardic women contributed many recipes for a cookbook published by the *Yeshiva*. Other Sephardim believe that acceptance into the religious enclaves of the Ashkenazi community will help them gain social acceptance among the Ashkenazim, or that giving their children the opportunity to socialize with religious Ashkenazi Jews broadens their Jewish acquaintance and increases their chances of marrying within the Jewish faith.

The agnostics are quite marginal to the community, participating in social activities such as parties or an evening of cards, but refusing to attend services except, possibly, on the high holidays. Their sense of Jewish identity may be based on their double rejection from Ashkenazim and Australians.

It is worth noting that these groups are not divided by explicit boundaries, and that many combinations may be found among them. For example, in one family where the parents are Orthodox two of the five children married ultra-Orthodox men and became comparatively more observant than their parents were – to the point where they will not even eat in their parents' home. One married out of the faith and lives in the Western suburbs, where very few Jews live. Although the other two married Jewish partners, they do not keep kosher homes, although they do sometimes participate in religious activities.

Aside from those who have come closer to the Ashkenazi community out of religious status considerations, many Sephardim adopted Ashkenazi religious ways because they were not taught about their

Sephardic religious customs and traditions at home. It is possible to predict that the majority of the children of this group will be lost to the Sephardic community in one generation.

Another reason why Sephardim are sending their children to Ashkenazi schools and social activities is that they feel the Sephardic congregation does not cater to their children. As one member who resigned from the Sephardic congregation put it: "I am proud to be Sephardic, but during all these years little has been done to encourage Sephardic children to be involved in the religious activities of the synagogue. We became members of another congregation for our children's sake, so they will have a future within the Jewish world." He concluded: "We better lose them to the Ashkenazi culture rather than lose them to Judaism altogether". Another member told me: "Let's face it, we are a small group and we are limited in the choice of marriage partners. I can tell you that in no time most of our children will be marrying non-Jewish partners."

Summary and Conclusions: **The Dilemma of Continuity, Identity and Power**

The situation of the organized Sephardic religious community in Sydney is paradoxical. After doing everything in its power to find a rabbi, and meanwhile maintaining a certain level of Orthodoxy in the synagogue, the secular leaders did not allow the rabbi that was finally hired to assume responsibility in the religious sphere – the reason for which he was ostensibly hired. The same thing occurred when the rabbi left and another was hired. This pattern is similar to the one that Lenski (1961:306) found among ethno-religious groups in America, where: "Older members of the group typically try to preserve the character of the organization which has satisfied their needs in the past so effectively. By virtue of the slow rate of turnover in mature social organizations, the 'command posts' (to use Mills' apt phrase) tend to be dominated by older persons who are psychologically the most committed to stability and continuity."

It seems that the elders want a rabbi for official purposes only. They want him to focus only on the technicalities of religious observance, while they maintain control and authority over the community through the lay committee. This reflects the decreased importance of religion – but not to those who attempt to replicate it in its traditional form – and the increased importance of social issues. The real issue, then, is the strength of religion as a unifying body, whether it has a stronger power base than secular institutions.

In his discussion of the importance of religion in the life of a group,

Lenski (1961:307) claims that, "[B]asic patterns of [religious] action are linked with the beliefs about the nature of the forces which ultimately control human destiny. These beliefs are not subject to empirical demonstration but are accepted on faith. Hence, patterns of action handed down from one's parents, and therefore associated with an important source of authority, persist for a long time even in hostile environments." While Lenski's argument can be applied to Sephardic communities in their countries of origin, it does not seem to suit the socio-religious situation of the Sephardic community in Sydney. For, while the older Sephardim accept belief on faith, the young neither share this notion nor feel that the actions of older members are conducive to stability or continuity. The young may want to believe, but are not convinced that the old beliefs are still valid. "We have blindly followed these beliefs," one young Sephardic told me "but our children will not follow us as we followed our parents, not in this country." Friction between the generations on this issue continues to alienate the young as the old attempt to regain the power they lost in a new world by clinging to it in the religious setting.

The elders want the past to continue to dominate the present, and religious traditions are the only thing they could bring relatively unchanged to the new country. As a consequence, they do not differentiate between religion and culture, which together constitute a way of life, an ethnic identity dominated by religion.[18]

The sub-ethnic division of the community also weakens the position of religion within the group. The attempt to promulgate a uniform official liturgy heightens cultural differences and sparks additional conflict, especially when it is used as a tool to appropriate secular community power. Religious differences persist to maintain ethnic differences, and these are used as coping mechanisms for survival. Thus, religious affiliation is a means of maintaining group identity, and ethnic divisions are expressed through and by religious division, which may provoke even greater interference into religious affairs by sub-ethnic factions.[19]

The preservation of identity through religion is a problem for Sephardim because their traditional and cultural communal base is gradually narrowing. The focus on Sephardic identity is consequently diminishing. The transformation, due to Sephardic migration from traditional societies to modern states, together with the diminution of the *Hakham Bashi*'s institutional power in religious and social matters, have undermined the whole socio-religious fabric of the Sephardic community.

The Sephardim in Sydney are doubly prone to insecurity in this regard. Since the Sephardim cannot find their place within either of their reference groups, the elders cling to their ethno-religious identity, in which the negative ingredients are increasing rapidly, while the young become Ashkenized or acculturate into Australian society. Herberg views religious identification and its application as the answer to the growing need for psychological stability and adjustment. [20]

The degree of loyalty or conformity to the group depends greatly on internal and external social pressures. Whereas Sephardim used to accept the rabbi's leadership and authority without question, in Australia a majority increasingly question the authority of the religious leadership and the value of their religious rituals. Even finding ten males to participate in the daily services has become difficult. Thus, their priorities and preferences have changed along with their environment. And like the rest of the modern world, the Sephardim place individual interests before community needs, and do not always see the common interests on which their group's continuity depends.

Internal forces,[21] the generation gap, the cultural division between the Iraqi-Indian and Egyptian groups and between the Iraqis and Indians, together with the social divisions created during the community's formative years because of disputes among influential families, have all obstructed community identity. The result is a fragile community that is divided into religious and secular Sephardim (the latter greatly outnumbering the former) and into sub-ethnic factions.

A minority of the members volunteer to help organize or participate in those religious and social activities and carry the burden of the entire community. The same group form the *minyan* on a daily basis hence the community can keep the doors of the synagogue open; the same group of women plan and carry out the entertainments for those religious celebrations and social functions that are held.

The external pressures on the group – the transition to Western society and the reduction of external threat – are the most important factors in the decline of the Sephardic group's identity and cohesion. In the homelands, particularly in Iraq and India, the Sephardim were more occupied with the survival of their community as a Jewish group and in perpetuating their culture and traditions. They functioned as an autonomous ethno-religious group, in which religion was the prime concern. This was accomplished mostly through religious idioms and the extensive use of religious symbols – as is still the case in Israel today.[22] They were happy to give priority to their ethnic group's interests. Today, in Sydney, the elders continue to run the community as a traditional Orthodox group, blurring the lines between secular and religious matters when it suits their purposes. For the new generation, however, individual rights and interests are increasingly important as they struggle to adjust to the host society. They do not perceive a unifying positive identity based on religion as relevant. Moreover, their disaffection from the community has been hastened and deepened by what they view as the elders' attempts to maintain authority when they have not been able to foster stability or continuity.

The diversification of the Sephardic community has weakened the position of religion within the group, and the generation gap is only one component of this diversification. The greater dilemma is that, today, the community comprises people with a far greater diversity of occupations, educational backgrounds and experiences than in the homeland, where many were poor and relied on the few rich members of the community to finance Jewish education and prayer. Nevertheless, here too the generation gap plays a role. For this is precisely where there is a split between the older generation, which wishes to retain control although it no longer comprises the wealthiest and most educated members, and the younger generation, for whom "getting ahead" is paramount. A similar situation prevails in Israel, where: "[T]he gulf separating the younger and the older generation of Middle Eastern immigrants has widened. The older generation has retained very little prestige and often pathetically lacks self-esteem".[23] In the synagogue, the old created a theatre for themselves that made them feel important and needed by the community.[24] The young saw the old make themselves ridiculous and so they opted out and moved away from the community.

Conflicts over institutional religious matters usually reflect greater issues of power in ethnic immigrant communities. In the Western world, religion has changed its function to suit the emotional and social needs of ethnic groups undergoing acculturation.[25] Thus, while it still plays a symbolic role in the lives of members of these groups, among the Sephardim of Sydney the Sephardic manifestations of religion have become an increasingly irrelevant, if not negative, force in the context of internal and external pressures. In the threatening situation of immigration and loss of status, the older generation attempts to replicate the religion and rituals of their homelands in Australia, to preserve their status and ethnic identity.[26] By excluding the young, they heighten, rather than reduce, the negative social ethnic identity that precludes the granting of respect.

In the traditional world, the rabbi was religious and social leader, teacher and judge. However, in Sydney his authority has been curtailed to the point where he is considered a "technician" of religious rituals and ceremonies, whose tasks are decided upon by lay leaders of the community. Although the community's rabbis were very different in personality, capability and drive, they were all treated much the same and pressured in a similar way. When these rabbis were not seen as "cooperating", the elders made them the focus of their own anxieties, pressured them to the point where they could hardly function and finally secured their resignations. This created a situation in which both the rabbi and the young were left in a double bind.

In the modern world, religion has "suffered a crushing blow",[27] its role becoming a symbolic one rather than a way of life as it was in the traditional world.[28] Today religion reflects problems of identity without being able to offer a serious alternative. When religion provided an all-encompassing basis for the group's traditional culture, it was impossible to divorce it from culture. However, in the new situation we see the emergence of "the synthetic Jew"[29] – or in my words, "the symbolic Jew" – who may affiliate with several congregations and synagogues and consider himself "religious" while he knows little about Jewish religious law and does not follow its teachings or precepts. In other words, religion functions symbolically to maintain a superficial ethnic identity, and survives because it satisfies the social and communal needs of the majority in a group. Only for a small minority does it satisfy real religious needs.

7

Conclusion: A Paradoxical Community

An examination of the Sephardic social and religious institutions in Sydney, Australia, suggests that the Sephardic experience is different from that of most other minority or ethnic groups: – whereas most groups usually acculturate to the host society's culture, the Sephardim tend to use another minority group – the Ashkenazim – as their major reference group.[1]

Although a majority of sociologists agree that ethnicity and ethnic group identity persist in modern Western societies, they disagree as to the persistence and significance of ethnic culture. Moreover, each author emphasizes different components of the same phenomenon. Thus, Glazer and Moynihan view ethnic groups as pressure groups and A. Cohen focuses on ethnicity as a basis for the mobilization of political power. Barth does not completely disregard culture, but insists that the most important factor in the preservation of ethnic groups is the maintenance of group boundaries. In contrast to Barth, G. J. Patterson and Gans (1979) claim that ethnics perpetuate their groups through ethnic symbols, and that this does not necessarily entail the revival of an ethnic way of life or ethnic customs, which have largely disappeared.

Researchers agree that ethnic groups tend to acculturate to the host society's culture, but point out that structurally separate institutions help preserve ethnic distinctiveness. The fact that cultural assimilation can take place in the absence of structural assimilation means that the sociological process of assimilation is relatively slow in comparison with the relatively more rapid cultural process, especially for groups like the Asians in Australia, who are largely rejected by their host society. This is the case with the Sephardic community in Sydney, which has acculturated to the Ashkenazi culture quite rapidly but whose assimilation into Ashkenazi and Australian societies has been retarded by rejection. By hindering the Sephardim from assimilating, the Ashkenazim and the Australians "help" Sephardim perpetuate their identity, but in a negative manner that strongly affects their self-esteem.

Status Anxiety and Marginality

Gist and Wright (1973:23) argue that, "[B]arriers tend to be divisive rather than integrative in inter-group relations, but the same barriers may be integrative rather than divisive for intra-group relations." From the time that the Sephardim began arriving in Sydney, barriers were established between them and the well-established Ashkenazi community. Many members of Sydney's Sephardic community claim that they were afforded little assistance by the Ashkenazim upon their arrival, although they expected their fellow Jews to welcome them warmly. At best, however, they were ignored by Australian Jews, who were preoccupied with absorbing World War II refugees with whom they had a greater affinity. Although the Sephardim were also victims of post-war political upheavals, their cultures, traditions and appearance set them apart.

The barriers of ethnicity between the two communities initially improved Sephardic intra-group relations, artificially narrowing the social and cultural distances within the sub-ethnic groups of Sephardim. Their awareness of their identity as Oriental Jews was strong enough to create a sense of community. As Gist and Wright (1973:23) note: "The emergence of a community solidarity and awareness may occur if it experiences deprivation over a considerable length of time as a result of discrimination, exploitation or physical attack." Thus, the sense of community that developed among the Sephardim of Sydney was largely a result of discrimination against them as Asians and their double rejection by the Ashkenazi community and Australian society. The barriers that worked as catalysts in the initial establishment of the Sephardic community did not, however, help foster either community consensus or organization, because the "spirit of optimism" for the future and the favorable "psychological climate" necessary for this to occur were lacking. The existing climate is one of despair, characterized by repeated unsuccessful attempts to establish the strong social institutions – such as schools, youth movements, etc. – that would ensure their survival.

In India, the barriers between the Bene-Israel and the Iraqi Jews were those of caste, class, power, wealth and life-style. Social and religious interaction between the two groups was limited, and marriage rejected by the Iraqis, the superordinate group. The Iraqi Jews viewed association with the Bene-Israel as posing a threat to their status among the

British and other Indians. Egyptian Jews, on the other hand, saw them-selves as part of "modern" Europe, rather than as part of traditional, "backward" Egypt, and considered themselves superior to indigenous Egyptians, treating the latter with contempt. Whereas the Sephardic Jews in India and Egypt were in a superordinate position, in Sydney they came to occupy a subordinate position *vis-à-vis* the dominant Ashkenazim. Given the White Australia immigration policy and anti-Semitic tendency within Australia, the Ashkenazim undoubtedly felt that their own status would suffer if they mingled very much with the Sephardim.[2]

The Ashkenazim had been in Australia for several generations at the time of Sephardic immigration, and considered themselves part of White Australia even though Australians did not necessarily view them as part of the a homogeneous British and European Christian society. Anti-Semitism led the Ashkenazim to downplay their Jewish identity, since they could pass as Europeans. Thus, many responded to the Sephardim by denying that they were Jews and by attempting to avoid all contact with them.

The status anxiety arising out of fear of association with a subordinate group is not limited to Ashkenazi–Sephardic relations, but is also found among the different ethnic groups that constitute the Sephardic commu-nity. Thus, some Iraqi Jews (who went directly to Australia from Iraq or via Israel) refused to join either of the two Sephardic organizations because, as one of them put it, "They are Indians. You can never under-stand their language and they look peculiar."

A major concern of "ethnics" who have achieved high socio-economic status is having this status undermined by co-ethnics. It seems that most interaction between Sephardim and Ashkenazim in Sydney's Eastern suburbs can be viewed in this light. Ashkenazim who have reached the pinnacle of Australian society in terms of prosperity and position – and who have to some degree "de-ethnicized" themselves – are threatened by the manifestly unassimilated Sephardim. Similarly, upwardly mobile Sephardim often make a conscious decision to move from Sephardic areas and their Sephardic social circles to avoid being associ-ated with their more "tribal" or "primitive" brethren. Even more than the Ashkenazim, higher-status Sephardim feel threatened by associa-tion with their lower-status co-ethnics.

As has been demonstrated repeatedly in this work, Sephardic iden-tity is experienced as culturally and socially marginal. For example, the lack of Sephardic organizational success, particularly evident in the failure to establish a youth movement, has led a majority of Sephardic youth to avoid Sephardic youth oriented institutions in favor of Ashkenazi youth groups. In consequence, these youths also abandon Sephardic religious services, which they view as strange, noisy and primitive, and adopt the Ashkenazi version of Jewish ritual instead.

The attitudes of the Sephardim toward their own culture and ethnic background, coupled with the perceived negative Ashkenazi attitude toward them, has led to varying degrees of rejection of their culture. When this feeling of marginality is internalized by parents, it is transmitted to children. However, second-generation Sephardim, whose parents have already adopted Ashkenazi culture, and who attended Ashkenazi schools, do not develop the same sense of marginality. The situation at present in the 1990s is that most Sephardic children are in the process of being socialized into Ashkenazi culture through the Jewish day school system, and have at best limited familiarity with their ancestral heritage.

In the social-psychological sense, group marginality implies values and attitudes resulting from interaction among members of different groups.[3] Marginality implies awareness of differences between the groups as well as value judgments concerning the significance of these differences. As Gist and Wright (1973:32–33) put it:

> The individual may find a marginal situation conducive to internal strains and tensions because of the ambiguity concerning his status and expected role. There are two facets to ambiguity: one, the uncertainty in the individual's mind as to who he is or where he belongs; second, the uncertainty concerning his proper or expected role performance . . . If the person's identity is unclear, or his expected role confusing, such a situation is likely to be disturbing, especially if he is emotionally involved in an uncertain relationship with one or more groups. The individual in such a situation we shall consider as a marginal person.

Culturally and socio-economically, the Sephardim in Sydney are marginal to the Ashkenazim. They occupy the lower rungs of the status ladder and mobility scale among the Jewish community.[4] Most of them, including those who hold membership in Sephardic organizations, see the Ashkenazim as their reference group. Thus they desire and attempt to be identified socially and culturally with Ashkenazi culture.[5]

The Sephardic sense of marginality is manifested in negative ethnic self-identity and, in some cases, even in self-hatred. Just as they were and still are marginal to Middle Eastern societies they are marginal to Australian society as Jews and to both Ashkenazi and Australian society as "Asians" (Sephardic marginality *vis-à-vis* Ashkenazim and Australians also involves mis-categorization as Arabs. In short, they view their identity as a kind of stigma.[6]

These feelings of marginality, and the consequent development of a negative ethnic identity, are based on more than avoidance and outright discrimination. After immigration to Australia, the traditional community structures broke down, and seemed unamenable to recreation in the new society. Differences that divided the community and retarded the growth of positive identity included ethnic divisions, generational divisions, class divisions and old migrants *vis-à-vis* newcomers. Additionally the community is divided by degree of religious observance. However, the most important source of negative ethnic identity seems to be rooted in the Sephardim's relationships with each other and in the way they see themselves as a community.

For Sephardim, immigration to the Western world meant a move from a traditional autocratic society to one based on democratic principles. This change played havoc with their world view and resulted in cultural shock. Moreover, in the old country Sephardim associated mostly with members of their families and religious group. They usually worked and socialized with these same people and had little opportunity or need for outside friendships. As those brought up in ghetto-like environments began to engage in regular encounters with outsiders at work and through the educational system, new modes of behavior were called for. Many Sephardim, particularly those of the older generation, could not adapt to the new situation. But, a new pattern emerged among the young, in which most of them began to evince less and less interest in their community and in its continuity, instead attempting to follow Anglo-Saxon "popular culture" or its Ashkenazi version.

Acculturation into the new environment altered the structure of the Sephardic family by offering children and women more control over their lives. The outcome has been a serious diminution in parental authority – particularly of the father's. The father's attempts to exercise authority, and his children's refusal to submit to it, results in father–child conflict. Severe setbacks to the father's authority, both within and outside the family, accelerate the process of acculturation among the young. Children become the agents of cultural change, teaching the new culture to their parents.

When Sephardic fathers had to rely on their children for linguistic and cultural help in order to interact with the wider society, they were placed in a humiliating situation. This "degradation" was enhanced when wives began to work and gained some authority in the financial running of the household – a phenomenon almost unknown in the old world. Despite this, however, elderly and even young Sephardic wives still tend to accept their husband as the highest authority in the home. As has been demonstrated, even those wives who work outside the home are expected to care for the children and run the house without help from their husbands.[7] While young Sephardic wives have become somewhat acculturated to Ashkenazi or Australian culture, elderly women usually remain largely unacculturated to the social and cultural worlds outside the family and Sephardic community. But the acculturation of the young, aside from being a "threat to the integrity of the ethnic family", is also "the major factor in intermarriage".⁸ If one contrasts the number of divorces among Sephardim in the past with those in the present, it seems that much of the increase can be attributed to acculturation.⁹

In recent years, Sephardim have been rapidly moving away from the Sephardic components of their religion, not granting religion the prominence in their lives that it had had in the past. Thus, although religion is more resistant to acculturation than is ethnicity, there is considerable acculturation in religion as well. Acculturation to the new environment has also brought about a notable decline in the degree of religious observance of many Sydney Sephardim – a change that their more religious co-ethnics view as one of the worst ills that the modern world has brought upon the Sephardim. Those who cling to their religion, particularly those of the older generation, feel that religious change is being forced upon them, especially by those responsible for shaping their ritual observance in accordance with the generally less-observant Ashkenazi community, in an attempt to emulate and be accepted by the Ashkenazim. Spiro (1955:1245) notes that, for American migrants, "[U]nlike other aspects of culture, religious beliefs and rituals, when no longer observed, are not replaced by those of the dominant group." However, the majority of Sydney Sephardim do not seem to be experiencing religious "deculturation"; rather, they have reshaped their way of observing to suit the Ashkenazi religious institutions they aspire to be part of. But their Asian features and modes of behavior often prevent them from gaining full acceptance by the Ashkenazim. Consequently, many who feel unwelcome in Ashkenazi synagogues, at a time when they no longer find attendance at Sephardic services fulfilling, have become estranged from formal and informal Jewish rituals and religion.

The Sephardim hold ambivalent attitudes toward the Ashkenazim. On the one hand, they wish to be like them, and on the other, they resent them because they cannot truly become one of them. The disappointment of not being able to achieve acceptance by this elite group of Australian Jews is strong and enduring. Thus, one woman in a Sephardic discussion group said: "I would give ten years of my life to have been born Ashkenazi!" But when the conversation shifted to the subject of negative feelings toward the Ashkenazim, this same woman contributed her own litany of resentment.

The tension over Sephardic ethnicity among Sydney Sephardim contributes to their feeling of marginality, helplessness, anxiety, and denial of Sephardic identity. More importantly, it seems to have fostered a split ethnic personality in which "Sephardiness" is conveyed among Sephardim and downplayed in the presence of Ashkenazim.

Jewish identity is expressed by membership in the synagogue, but when it comes to attending services and rituals, fewer and fewer

Sephardim participate. This phenomenon must be examined within the context of the difference between degrees of religiosity in the country of origin – where social pressure to attend synagogue was quite strong, and the synagogue was the center of social and community life – and in Australia, where interaction with non-Jews is becoming the norm. For, as pointed out, Australian society itself has undergone a dramatic change in religious behavior and church attendance.

The majority of Sydney Sephardim do not belong to a Sephardic synagogue and only 17–20 percent of the community belongs to any congregation. On the other hand, some are members of two congregations: a Sephardic synagogue that they rarely attend, and an Ashkenazi synagogue that they attend more regularly. This dual membership seems to be a way of demonstrating their continuing connection to the Sephardic world in which they feel "at home" at the same time that they continue their efforts at upward mobility through Anglicized Ashkenazi community and into the mainstream culture.

The Jewish day schools in Sydney play an important part in this process of acculturation and "Ashkenization." But, while they play a crucial role in instilling Jewish identity and a sense of pride in that identity, these schools do little, if anything, to instill a sense of pride in Sephardic ethnic tradition and history. At school, Sephardic children become aware of, and come to prefer, the Ashkenazi aspect of Jewish identity, liturgy, heritage and traditions; they are taught Yiddish, and become accustomed to the Ashkenazi culture. Over time, these children become more resentful of their Sephardic identity. Thus, while attendance at Jewish day schools does put them in the company of other Jewish children, and enhances the chance that they will marry within the Jewish faith, it does little to instill pride in their Sephardic identity.

Economically, the Sephardic community can be rated lower-middle-class, whereas the majority of the members of the Ashkenazi community are concentrated in the middle- and upper-middle classes. Additionally, the Sephardim are largely clustered in the lower-status areas of the Eastern suburbs, while the majority of Ashkenazim live in higher-status areas near Sydney Harbor. In the eyes of the Sephardim, becoming "Ashkenized" is associated with socio-economic achievement within both Jewish and Australian society.

How does this small ethnic community participate in the Ashkenazi and Australian worlds? Does this participation help to perpetuate or weaken their identity? What kind of identity, if any, has emerged to represent Sephardic identity?[10]

The principal problem confronting the Sephardic community of Sydney is that the Sephardim constitute a social category rather than an ethnic group. Given the all-encompassing manifestation of their religion in the Middle East, however, its elders (at least) feel they "should" have the kind of solidarity generally associated with ethnic groups. However, they have not yet developed the formal or informal social and cultural strategies that would permit them to implement their distinctiveness within the general Jewish community. The ongoing tension is reflected in a personal and community-wide identity crisis. It sometimes seems that individual members of the community, as well as the community as a whole, maintain a kind of schizophrenic ethnicity, with concomitant feelings of marginality and worthlessness, some Sephardim even viewing their identity as a stigma. At other times, however, and mostly in restricted situations, a majority do find their Sephardic origin of instrumental or expressive benefit. Some even present myths of traditional Sephardic superiority, but such posturing is neither persuasive to outsiders nor seriously entertained by the community at large.

Although there is some evidence that an "endo-culture"[11] – involving the melding of Sephardic subcultures is emerging, it is not possible to predict its final form with any certainty. For the main sub-groups within the community – Iraqi and Iraqi-Indian, on the one hand, and the Egyptian, on the other – are still attempting to implant their own cultural values, norms and religious modes of behavior on the community as a whole, while resisting change themselves. The establishment of two Sephardic congregations further polarizes the group. From the beginning of the 1990s onward, the Iraqi-Indian segment seems to have become the dominant source of values and norms.

One may ask why, with so many serious internal and external problems, the Sephardic community of Sydney (and other ethnic communities in similar situations) continues to exist – what, if any, are the economic, political, psychological or cultural rewards inherent in Sephardic ethnicity? A look at possible economic rewards shows that there is little if any advantage in belonging to the group today other than those connected specifically with business, and even this area has declined as community members increasingly choose work they prefer over community-related positions. Nor is there any government funding of ethnic projects for Sephardim. As a community, the Sephardim do not generate political power or rewards within either the Ashkenazi or Australian political systems. Even within the "ethnic community" of New Australians, their community is too small to generate political power. This, together with disunity and lack of group political and social solidarity, prevents the Sephardic community from assuming a position of influence within the Jewish community. A. Cohen (1969:211) claims that different cultural variables are mobilized to provide solutions to organizational problems. The old and the new institutions adjust to one another, integrating to form a new sociocultural, political and economic system.

Perhaps, then, it is psychological factors that perpetuate Sephardic ethnic identity? Here, one must ask whether the Sydney Sephardim proclaim their identity to fulfill positive psychological needs, or whether they do so in order to keep from being identified by others as Indians, Asians or Middle Easterners – who have an even lower position on the Australian socio-economic scale. Almost all members of the community prefer to be associated with the Ashkenazim, who have achieved high status within Australian society, magnifying their Jewish identity while concealing its Sephardic components. Only a small segment of the community seems to accrue psychological and emotional support from their Sephardic identity. These are the elderly, who make little effort to adjust to the Australian environment and choose to live in the past.

As to cultural reward, the diversity of sub-groups within the Sephardic community would appear to negate this possibility. There seem to be few group-wide cultural similarities beyond their Jewishness. Their short history as a community in Sydney demonstrates a continuous struggle between, for example, the Iraqi and Iraqi-Indian groups, on the one hand, and the Egyptian group, on the other, over issues of culture and religion. Certainly, there does not seem to be much of a "cultural pay-off" or sense of cultural pride in maintaining the Sephardic identity. Moreover, they do not seem able to present those aspects of the culture that might appeal to non-Sephardim and gain them a more attractive identity within the wider Jewish or Australian communities.

In the absence of economic, political, psychological or cultural reasons to perpetuate their community, the Sephardic identity appears to persist because of their double rejection by both the Ashkenazi community and Australian society. It is this rejection that has resulted in the most crucial rejection: that from themselves as Sephardim and as a Sephardic community. For they have internalized external rejection to the point where this identity and culture have no positive value in their own eyes. One must conclude that the Sephardic ethnicity is perpetuated largely for negative reasons.[12]

The Sephardic community of Sydney must therefore be considered a paradoxical community – one defined by exclusion rather than by common ties. As a result, it lacks the clarity of purpose, shared community-specific and affect-laden symbols or the sense of common destiny necessary to guarantee that it will persist in future generations. This, together with the ongoing processes of acculturation and structural assimilation to Ashkenazi and Australian culture, will probably result in its disappearance as a viable "community" within a generation.

Appendix
Methods Used in the Collection of Data

Data for this research was collected through ethnographic research (participant observation and formal and informal interviews), and a "blind" questionnaire. Library research was accomplished at the Australian National Archives, in Canberra; the Judaica Archive of the Fisher Library, Sydney University; Tel Aviv University; and The Hebrew University of Jerusalem. In addition, data was collected from the Australian Bureau of Statistics.

Participant Observation:[1] I shared a similar cultural background with members of the community, as I am Jewish, was born in Iraq and raised in Israel. Early in my fieldwork, the congregants accepted me as a member of the community. Moreover, I speak the three languages most widely spoken by members of the Sydney Sephardic community: the Iraqi dialect of Arabic (my mother tongue); Hebrew (in which I was raised and educated); and English, a language we speak at home. I also understand and can speak (with some limitation) the Egyptian dialect of Arabic.

Older members of the community felt more at ease conversing in their native Iraqi-Arabic dialect. Some shifted from English to Iraqi during the course of the interviews. I understood their implications as well as their spoken language, and seldom felt the need to seek further clarification. Members of the group accepted me as one of them and they were seldom inhibited by my role as researcher.

The fact that I adhere to Jewish dietary laws made it possible for me to entertain members of the community in my home, particularly the elderly women of the Ladies Auxiliary Committee.

Early in my fieldwork, I discovered that gossip plays an important role in the collection of information. The data I collected about the Sephardim of Sydney from gossip complemented the formal and informal interviews and the questionnaires, and was a crucial factor in my study and analysis of the community. Another rich source of data that would not otherwise have been discovered came from information collected during interactions at localities and meetings frequented by Sephardim. For example, Orthodox members of the community patronize traders of Sephardic origin – who market oriental spices and foods, and who sell take-away Sephardic as well as Ashkenazi food. At these shops and in the other kosher stores, members of the community gossip about current market prices, social events and other topics of current interest such as the resignation of the first rabbi of the community, marriages and divorces, births and deaths. A. L. Epstein (1969:117–27), too, found the "gossip network" an important factor in his study of urban organization in modern Africa.

The behavior of community members during social interactions shed much light on the symbolic nature of ethnic behavior. Thus, although many Sephardim do not adhere to Jewish dietary laws, when a new acquaintance entertains them for the first time, they still inquire about the ingredients and preparation of the foods served. At first, I interpreted this as hypocritical. However, in time I came to understand that this represented a hidden element of their symbolic ethnic Jewish identity, a signal of their Sephardic Jewish identity, or their identification with their wider Jewish community. This type of behavior is typical of the symbolic nature of much of the ethnic identity in modern Western societies.

During the initial period of my research, I was often asked about my husband's origin. When I identified him as an English man, I was then asked directly whether he was Sephardic or Ashkenazi. When it became known that he is Ashkenazi, my status in the Sephardic community rose. This was my introduction to the phenomenon of marriage to an Ashkenazi lending the Sephardic partner higher status among the Sephardim.

As an active participant in community affairs, I volunteered to cook, bake and wash up at functions, and to type or drive elderly women to and from meetings when necessary. For the annual fête, a profitable social event for the Sydney Sephardic community, the Ladies Auxiliary always has trouble-finding volunteers to collect goods donated by the Jewish community. Many congregants are embarrassed to do this because they fear they will be viewed as beggars. However, the Ladies Auxiliary could always depend on my services. This, too, helped me gain respect and acceptance.

My participation as a volunteer was of great importance to my research because, through it, the community eventually accepted me as one of them and forgot my role as an anthropologist.

Participants in any social situation usually influence the outcome of the activities. For, even when an individual in a social interaction plays only a marginal role, his or her mere presence has an influence on the outcome. The position of the participant/observer differs only in that he/she is always aware of his/her situation as researcher and attempts to minimize this influence on the group being studied. In this context, there is always bound to be a certain amount of participation on the part of the anthropologist.[2]

At first, being a woman appeared to lower my status in the eyes of the Sephardic elders, since most married women remain at home to nurture their families for several years, after which they worked on a part time basis.

My relationship with the men in the community was of a quite different nature from my relationship with the women. Whereas the women tended to accept me from the outset, the men were mildly threatened by my research at first. With time, however, this situation improved greatly.

Two events that took place are crucial to understanding the male attitude and how males function as decision-makers on the all-male synagogue board and in the female domain of the home. My participation in various women's activities and committees allowed me a penetrating insight into the male domain. Prior to the Annual General Meeting of 1979, the Ladies Auxiliary Committee decided to nominate me as their representative on the Board of Management. Through no fault on the part of any individual, I did not receive a nomination form. When one of the elders was approached, his response was that I should seek election the following year. Another elder advised me not to seek election since "a woman's place is in the home". Disheartened, one of the women suggested that an elder be asked to co-opt me onto the Board. However, I tactfully refused because I did not want to do anything that might jeopardize my position as a researcher.

Prior to the 1980 Annual General Meeting, I was again asked to represent the Ladies Auxiliary on the Board of Management. I consented, and I was nominated. However, as I was absent during the meeting itself, my nomination was ignored. I was finally co-opted onto the board in a de facto manner, but not before there was exertion of pressure from the women on the Auxiliary committee on their board-member husbands to include me on the board.

After being co-opted onto the board, I discovered that a young member had nominated me, but had not been able to find an elder to second the nomination. He was requested to withdraw the nomination because other board members did not want a woman as their peer. This member – an academic who occupies important positions in the community and in society – informed me of these events months later. When I expressed surprise at nominations having to be seconded again, he replied, "This is how things are done."

My position as social chairperson on the Board of Management proved to be helpful in understanding the social processes of the group. It allowed me to witness the social struggle between different sub-groups and the power politics within the ruling elite. It also allowed me to identify the influential members of the board – who were not always one of the five executives of the board.

In addition to the participant observation technique, I distributed 140 questionnaires by mail, to randomly selected members of the community (25 percent of members of the community). The names were drawn from membership lists of the two Sephardic congregations, supplied to me by the presidents of each group.[3] Most of the questions in the survey were of a "closed" variety, and a few were "open". The object of the questionnaire was to examine the objective situation and subjective feelings of those who responded, and to shed light on the ethno-religious situation of the community.

The open questions were meant to assess the respondents' perspective on their ethnic identity; and how they viewed their position in Australian society. For example, whereas some congregants born in Iraq might consider themselves Australian citizens of Jewish heritage, others who went to Israel from Iraq before immigrating to Australia might still consider themselves Israelis even after having lived in Australia for more than thirty years. Interestingly, a stay in Israel of one to seven years influenced the respondents' definition of their identity. Such data was crucial to my attempt to define the identity of this particular group.

The major purpose of the questionnaire was to neutralize the effect of participant observation and formal interviews. It was my hope that respondents would feel more comfortable to reveal confidential information on a blind questionnaire. For example, some congregants felt awkward about revealing to me personally that they did not keep a kosher home, although they affirmed this on the questionnaire. I distributed the questionnaire two years after I began my research project, when I already knew many members of the community through my participation in community affairs.

The blind questionnaire facilitated detachment from the interviewees, and therefore maintained a degree of objectivity. It also enabled me to reach a larger cross-section of the community and to include a broader spectrum of the ethno-religious culture of the Sydney Sephardic community.

I delineated (arbitrarily) three sub-groups within the Sydney Sephardic community: (1) The NSW Association of Sephardim; (2) The Eastern Jewish Association; (3) "The Medley".

(1) The NSW Association of Sephardim is the group most extensively studied in terms of numbers. In mid-1981, when this survey was carried out, the NSW Association comprised 320 families and 442 registered

members. In 1984, there were 480 families and 530 registered members. Between 1984 and 1990 the number went down.

(2) The Eastern Jewish Association in 1981 comprised 79 families and 116 registered members. In 1984, there were 96 families and 132 registered members.

(3) "The Medley" consisted of over 2,000 individuals (estimated) who were not affiliated with either of the above groups. Some of these individuals and families became members of Ashkenazi synagogues when they moved to higher-status Ashkenazi neighborhoods.

Groups 1 and 2 were studied in depth. Members of Group 3, contacted through a network of acquaintances, were studied through extensive formal and informal interviews.

Notes

1 *Ethnicity, the Ethnic Group and Ethnic Identity*

1 Warner and Srole 1945; Gordon 1964; A. Cohen 1969, 1974; Barth 1969; Deshen 1975; Ben-Rafael 1982; Jupp 1984; Roosens 1989a.
2 Barth 1969.
3 De Vos 1975:17.
4 Peterson-Royce 1982:3; Spivak 1999:110; Rhedding-Jones 2001:146.
5 Glazer and Moynihan 1975:63, 72; Herzog 1984; Don-Yehia 1990; Dayan 1999; Lissak 1969; 1996.
6 Glazer and Moynihan 1963:13.
7 Luke and Luke 1999.
8 Glazer and Moynihan 1975:8; see also Gans 1979.
9 See Deshen 1972a:278–302, 1974:281–309; E. Cohen 1985:329–33; Lissak 1999.
10 Gale 1999; Australian Bureau of Statistics 1986, 1991.
11 I was amazed at the heavy representation of politicians at this Sephardic function.
12 One can draw some similarities between Leach's (1964:158–62) analysis of lineage and class in Highland Burma and our notions of ethnicity and class. A person in Burmese society is born into a lineage as in our society where one is born into an ethnic group.
13 O. Patterson 1975:30–56.
14 A. L. Epstein 1978; Gans 1979; Benson 1981; Roosens 1989a.
15 Glazer and Moynihan 1963, 1975; A. Cohen, 1969, 1974; Habel and Zuesse (1992) found similar trends in Australian society.
16 Peterson-Royce 1982. Ayalon, Ben-Rafael and Sharot 1985.
17 A. L. Epstein 1978:95; A. Cohen 1969, 1974; Glazer and Moynihan 1975.
18 Barth 1969: 11, 14–15; see also Hicks and Leis 1977:11.
19 For similarity in Isael see Lissak 1999; Ram 1993, 2002.
20 Parsons (1975) attempted to find a balance between group organic reality and the individual's place in the social structure. He defined a societal community as an ethnic entity, with solidarity, where its collectivity is a major point of reference in defining the identity of its members. See also Durkheim 1977, 1961.
21 Gordon 1964: 72.

22 Gordon 1964:99, 102, 107.
23 Rhedding-Jones 1996: 2–14, 2001:150–53; Kringas 1984:114–25; Zameret 1993; Shuval and Leshem 1998:3–50.
24 Cultural assimilation refers to changes in behavioral and world view only. Structural assimilation suggests the disappearance of the minority at the group level, consequent to the adoption of the cultural and structural patterns of the majority (Gordon 1964:60–83). Spiro (1955:12–44) viewed the acculturation process as an "exclusive function of the group's desire and capacity for acculturation", and assimilation as "a function of both dominant and ethnic group behavior" (see Medding 1968; Porter 1965).
25 Goldberg 1939:327–36.
26 Klaff 1980:102–18.
27 See Palfreeman 1967; Yarwood 1964, 1968; de Lepervanche, 1984a, 1984b; Rhedding-Jones 2001.
28 See Stannard 1987; de Lepervanche 1984a; Jupp, 1995.
29 Eisenstadt 1989:7–15; See also Matras 1985:1–23; Peres 1985:39–56, Lissak 1999; Meir-Glizenstein 2000; Shetrit 2004.
30 Lissak 1999; 1996.
31 Warner and Srole 1945:67–102; Spiro 1955:12–43; Gans 1979:3, 1962:229–46.
32 See also Weingrod 1985 ;Weingrod and Gurevitch 1977:67–78; Raphael 1983:42–43; E. Cohen 1985:320–33; Lissak 1999.
33 Herberg 1955:85; Glazer and Moynihan 1963, 1975.
34 These figures are based on my counts of attendance at the Sephardic synagogue for the period from 1981 to 1984 in the normal day-to-day course of events.
35 Lissak 1999; Kop 2000; Klaff 1980.
36 For an elaboration of "new ethnicity", see Novak 1971, 1977, 1979; Weed 1973; Greeley 1974; Glazer and Moynihan 1975.
37 Klaff (1980:102) notes that "ethnic residential segregation is an established fact in the U.S.". The same element of segregation exists in Israel. Eisenstadt (1954:48) speaks of "ecological distribution". And Klaff (1977:112) demonstrated that residential patterns of foreign-born populations across thirteen settlement communities in Israel were based on the country of origin. See also Smooha 1993; Lissak 1999; Kop 2000.
38 See Gordon 1964:159; Barth 1969:14.
39 Quoted in Parsons 1975:65. See also Schneider 1969:116–25.
40 Zubrzycki 1968; Grassby 1973a, 1973b; Martin 1976, 1978; Australian Government, the Immigration Council 1978; an excellent review of the literature by de Lepervanche 1984a:170–228; Jupp 1995 and more; Short 1995.
41 For further analysis, see de Lepervanche 1984a:187.
42 Gans 1979:14.
43 Zameret 1993; Eisenstadt 1954, 1971; E. Cohen 1969, 1985.
44 Amir, Sharon and Ben-Ari 1978; Also see Suarez-Orozco (1990a:265–87).
45 See Spivak 1999.
46 Price 1957, 1962.
47 Blainey 1987:26; Stannard 1987:76; Jupp 1984:179, 1995, 1999; see also ABS 1981; 1986; 1991.
48 Martin 1976; de Lepervanche 1984b; Jupp 1984; Kelley and Bean 1988.

49 J. Zubrzycki, – 1995 Global Cultural Diversity Conference.
50 A. G. Guillermo, – 1995 Global Cultural Diversity Conference.
51 Spivak 1999 speaks against the "them and us" dichotoies. For Israel see Baba 1994; Haver and others 2002; E. Cohen 2003; Lissak 1999; Ram 2002.
52 Gordon 1964:53. See also De Vos and Suarez-Orozco 1990a:246–64. With regard to horizontal and vertical stratification in Israel, see M. Hartman and Ayalon 1975; Peres 1989:949–65.
53 De Vos 1990; A. L. Epstein 1978; Van den Berghe 1974; Smooha 1993.
54 Peterson-Royce 1982; Jupp 1984; Roosens 1989a; De Vos 1990b.
55 Rhedding-Jones 2001:151.
56 A. L. Epstein 1978:96, 99–102.
57 Herman 1979:86–87; Peterson-Royce 1982.
58 Deshen 1972a:278–302; P. Cohen 1968:103–10.
59 Weber 1961.
60 For analysis of personality development and identity definition, see Barth 1969, Benson 1981:95–115, and De Vos 1990a:17–74.
61 Kwen Fee (1982:46) suggests that: "Collective and individual management of identity and adaptation on the part of minority group . . . " may involve "modifications of existing social reality interpreted in terms of the ideology of the ethnic group . . . "
62 See similar situation (Whyte 1943; Gallo 1974) among Italians in Cornerville who developed a negative ethnic identity.
63 Similarly, in his study of Italians and Germans in Australia, Borrie (1959) stated that structural assimilation did not occur and ethnic identity was still strong.
64 Quoted in Peterson-Royce 1982:19.

2 *The Sephardim of Sydney*

1 The 1981 census suggests that well over 2,500 Jews residing in New South Wales were born in Asia or Africa (see also Chapter 5).
2 Australian Archive of Judaica, Fisher Library, University of Sydney, Sephardic File No. 4 and Aaron's book, 1979.
3 Aaron 1979:69.
4 The event was reported in the *Sydney Morning Herald*, the *Sydney Jewish News* and in the *Australian Jewish Times*.
5 Lewis 1984b; Roumani 1983:1; Ben-Ya'acob 1986.
6 Hunt and Walker 1974:241; Sitton 1974:65–87.
7 Lewis 1984a:45, quoted from the British Consul in Mosul, 1909.
8 Hunt and Walker 1974; Lavendar 1981.
9 Quoted in Roumani 1983:24.
10 Sitton 1974:73.
11 Lavendar 1981:26. See also Stillman (1979:388) who quoted from the Public Record Office (London), 10.10.1860. FO 195/624 No. 31 of 1860. where there is a description of an anti-Jewish incident that was prevented by "a zealous Turkish official."
12 Schmelz and Della Pergola 1993:442; Lewis 1984a:54; H. Cohen 1973. It is difficult to state accurately the size of the Jewish population of Iraq, despite

the censuses carried out by Iraqi authorities in 1904, 1919, 1932. In 1947, the official estimate was 118,000 Jews. Yet, during the period 1948–51, some 123,500 Iraqi-born Jews immigrated to Israel. Not all the emigrants went to Israel and no accurate data exist on Jewish emigration from Iraq to India, the Far East and to Europe, which began in the 1830s.

13 Gilbert 1976; Ben-Ya'acob 1985.
14 Hunt and Walker 1974:244; Sitton 1974:77–80; Lewis 1984a:44–56; H. Cohen 1996:204–8.
15 Deshen 2001:30–44; Roumani (1983:78) estimates that the number of Jewish and Arab refugees in the Middle East between 1948 and 1975 was almost identical: 786,268 Jews emigrated – 586,268 to Israel and 200,000 to other countries – while some 789,000 Arabs were displaced in 1948. Also see Kedourie 1978.
16 Aldridge 1969:314; M. R. Cohen 1980.
17 Schweitzer 1971:132.
18 H. Cohen 1973:81; Sacher 1974:29–30.
19 Sitton 1974:81; Patai 1981:133.
20 Landau 1969:6.
21 Landau 1969.
22 Lewis 1984b; Schmelz and Della Pergola 1993.
23 Lewis 1984b; Schmelz and Della Pergola 1993:441.
24 Landau 1969:8.
25 Aharoni 1983:69
26 Aldridge 1969; Aharoni 1983; Landau 1973:99–142.
27 Sitton 1974:83; Lewis 1984a:53.
28 Roumani 1983:6; Sacher 1974:567.
29 Landau 1969:115–25; interviews with members of the Sephardic community of Sydney.
30 Sitton 1974:83–85; H. Cohen 1973:51.
31 Aldridge 1969:257; H. Cohen 1973:52–53.
32 Landau 1969:9–10; H. Cohen 1973:87–91.
33 Sitton 1974:83; Aldridge 1969:312.
34 Lewis 1984a:48.
35 Patai 1981:143; Ben-Ya'acob 1985:9–21.
36 Patai 1981:142.
37 Kedourie 1978:175–223; Ben-Ya'acob 1985:19.
38 Sacher 1974:108.
39 For further elaboration, see Sitton 1974:32–33; Ben-Ya'acob 1983:24.
40 Sitton 1974:33; Patai 1981:144; Kedourie 1978:204–14.
41 M. J. Cohen 1982:266.
42 Sacher 1974:66–108; Sitton 1974:31–38; Lewis 1984a:45–46; Ben-Ya'acob 1985; interviews with members of the Sydney community.
43 H. Cohen 1973:32–33; also Sitton 1974:32–37.
44 Sitton 1974:37.
45 H. Cohen 1973:37; Gilbert 1976.
46 Aharoni 1983; Sitton 1974:32; Patai 1981:145–49.
47 H. Cohen 1973:89.
48 Lewis 1984a:50.

49 H. Cohen 1973:90
50 Sitton 1974:32; also Aldridge 1969; Kedourie 1978; Kedourie and Haim 1982.
51 H. Cohen 1973:161.
52 Kedourie 1971:355–61; Sacher 1974:108.
53 Gaby 1999:94–118; Patai 1981; H. Cohen 1973:169.
54 Landau 1969; Aharoni 1983.
55 H. Cohen 1973:25–26, 42–48.
56 H. Cohen 1973:108–16.
57 Sacher 1974:7; H. Cohen 1973:109.
58 Landau 1969:71–79.
59 Patai 1981:133; Landau 1969:93–105.
60 Strizower 1971:6, 79; Stillman 1979:374–76.
61 Ben-Ya'acob 1985:22; Kushner 1973; W. J. Fischel 1962; Tugend 1994:7.
62 Kushner 1973.
63 Ben-Ya'acob 1985:23, 30, 141; Schmelz and Della Pergola 1993:440.
64 Strizower 1971:19.
65 Kehimkar 1937; Strizower 1971; Ben-Ya'acob 1985; Isenberg 1989.
66 Sassoon 1949, Kehimkar 1937; Strizower 1971:128–44.
67 Strizower 1971:42; Sassoon 1949:203.
68 Kehimkar 1937:166–68; Strizower 1971:137; Musleah 1975.
69 Kehimkar 1937:226–49; Israel 1984; Isenberg 1989.
70 Israel 1984:88–97, The Chief Rabbinate of Israel 1964, Bene-Israel: An Inquiry into Their Origin.
71 Sasson 1949; Abraham 1973:3, 16; Musleah 1975:26–39, 270–332; Elias and Elias-Cooper 1974.
72 Abraham 1973:22. Until then Jewish children had attended Christian institutions.

3   The Immigration of Sephardic Jews to Australia

1 Rutland (1991:225–56) discussed Jewish migration between 1945–1960.
2 Price 1964; Medding 1973; Poulsen and Spearritt 1981; Federal Census 1981; Lippman 1986; H. Rubinstein 1993:322, Schmelz and Della Pergola 1993:443.
3 See Rutland 1991:237. Also File AA ACT CRS A434 Item 47/3/21 deals with refugees in Shanghai, the majority of whom escaped from the war in Europe. Only a few Sephardim arrived in Sydney from Shanghai, due to the White Australia policy (Bartrop 1990).
4 Abraham 1973; Musleah 1975; Ben-Ya'acob 1985.
5 Immigration to Australia from India was not so difficult in 1947, as the Australian authorities knew little about Indian Jewry. The problem began, in my informant's words, "when an influx of Jews from Asia began to flood the Australian consulates in Asian countries, particularly in India. Just then the Australian Immigration Department started to wake up".
6 Lippman 1979:37; Wilton and Basworth 1984:35; Rutland 1991:35–58.
7 Stannard 1987:76.
8 Markus 1983:19–22; Bartrop 1990:77–80; Rutland 1991:231–40.

9   ACT CRS A433, Item 47/2/4/1; Bartrop 1990:69–78; Rutland 1991:241.
10   ACT CRS A461, Item 349/3/5/ p.2 PM's file M.349/3/5/ WB/SMCM; Bartrop 1988:611–82.
11   ACT CRS A461, Item 349/3/5/P.2 PM's File M.349/3/5/WB/SMCM; The New Policy for Enemy Aliens, Part II CRS A445 Item 235/1/24.
12   Lippman 1979:38.
13   Australian Archives ACT CRS A461, Item MA349/3/5.
14   ACT A432, Item 38/01425; CRS A445, Item 235/5/9; ACT CRS A434, Item 49/3/3196.
15   ACT CRS A433, Item 47/2/4/1 and AA ACT CRS A434, Item 49/3/3196.
16   Rutland 1991:228–30.
17   Wilton and Bosworth 1984:31; W. D. Rubinstein 1986.
18   Hammond 1954:54–55, 92–112. See also Chapman 1956:232–46; Guyatt 1967; Ray 1972:207–13; Markus 1983:20; W. D. Rubinstein 1985:131–38, 1986:1–52; Bartrop 1990:76. For similar trends in America see Ginsburg 1981.
19   CRS A445, Item 235/1/24.
20   In the same letter, Heyes did not reveal that the Department of Immigration defined the Jews as a race rather than a religious group or nationality. These policies prevailed before and after the war (Markus 1983:21; Rutland 1991:51).
21   Ref. No. 7/5/1954, Mr. Nutt BVK., CASI Department of Immigration, Central Office Correspondence File, AA CRS A446, Item 077857/72.
22   Ibid. Ref. No. 58 2 8691; CRS A446, Item 077857/72.
23   Kondapi 1951; Price 1966; Palfreeman 1974:164–72; De Lepervanche 1984b:57–78.
24   CRS A445, Item 140/2/25. p.6.
25   Lippman 1979:93.
26   *The Sydney Morning Herald*, 2 May 1972.
27   Australian Government: Migrant Attitudes Survey 1986:60–69; W. D. Rubinstein 1986.
28   AA CRS A446, Item 077857/72, CA51; May 1949, Melbourne.
29   AA CRS A446, Item 077857/72, Ref. 49/2/8111, 10 June 1949; Ref. No. 49/2/3771.
30   AA CRS A446, Item 077857/72 copy No. 50/3/23237, letter written on 4 July 1950, Ref. No. 49/2/8111.CA51.
31   AA CRS A446, Item 077857/72, Ref. No. 50/3/23237, 49.2.8111. CA51.
32   AA CRS A446, Item 077857/72, Ref. 51/24.3, 11 July 1951.
33   AA CRS A446, Item 077857, 72, File No. 50/40, Imm. No. 114 Copy: IW, Original on 50/3/10401. The holder of a *British passport* is someone born in England or to British parents; the holder of a *British Subject passport* is a person of other nationality granted the right only to travel on a British document. Indian Jews who opted for British nationality after independence were provided with British Subject passports and were unaware that this status did not permit unrestricted travel and residence within the Commonwealth. (Information provided by the British Consulate in Sydney and the British High Commissioner's officer in Canberra.)
34   See note 33.

35   Ref. No. 3596(27/6/79).
36   Ref. No. 51/243; (22 February 1952), AA CRS A446, Item 077857,72, CA51; see also Rutland 1991:342.
37   AA CRS A446, Item 077857/72.51/13/9029, June 1952.
38   AA CRS A446, Item 077857/72, Ref. No. 51/243, December 1952.
39   AA CRS A446, Item 077857/72, Ref. No. 7/5/1954, Mr. Nutt. BVK.
40   AA CRS A446, Item 077857/72, Ref. 235/5/5 14.8.1953.
41   AA ACT CRS A445, Item 140/4/23 and AA ACT CRS A433, Item 47/2/4/1.
42   Ref. No. 234/5/8 in answer to Ref. No. B46/1/3/2, AA CRS A446, Item 077857/72.
43   AA CRS A446, Item 077857/72, Ref. No. SR.CA51.
44   AA A433, Item 077857/72, Ref. No. SR.
45   AA CRS A446, Item 077857/72, File No. 53/1/3/29, Memorandum No. 62, 11/1/1954.
46   AA ACT CRS A461, Item 349/3/5, p.1.
47   AA ACT CRS A461, Item 349/3/5; Roumani 1983:3; *New York Times*, 19 February 1947; *Manchester Guardian*, 25 November 1947.
48   Aaron 1979:64–65.
49   *Eastern Herald*, 13 February 1986, pp. 12–13.
50   AA CRS A446, Item 077857/72, Ref. No. SR.
51   AA CRS A446, Item 077857/72, Copy No. 50/3/23237, Ref. No. 49/2/8111.

4   The Sephardic Family

1   Wirth 1938; Parsons 1943; Bott 1955; Firth 1956, 1969; Young and Willmott 1973; Smelser 1959; S. Benson 1981.
2   Dumont 1980:26–28; Beteille 1971:46; Layish 1994.
3   Patai 1981; Stahl 1993.
4   Buber-Agassi 1993 explains gender inequality within the family in Israel. See also Martin 1957:29–50; Layish and Shaham 1991:1–10.
5   D. H. J. Morgan 1975:87–101.
6   L. M. Epstein 1973:89–106.
7   Zelditch 1956:377–90; Deshen and Zenner 1982.
8   J. Katz 1982:40; Layish and Shaham 1991.
9   Shokeid (1980:127–47) speaks of the anguish of the husband and the way he perceived his position in the community as a barren man.
10   Patai 1960:71.
11   Patai 1981:151; H. Cohen 1973:173; Layish and Shaham 1991:1–10. Bigamy (and polygamy) was more prevalent among Sephardim and Oriental Jews, whereas among Ashkenazim it was forbidden by *Herem* (the ban) of Rabbi Gershom since 1240, but not among the Sephardim. In the Muslim world Islam permitted polygamy (Elon 1975:368).
12   Deshen and Zenner 1982:194–99; Solomon 1983:131–40.
13   M. Elon 1975:414–24: A *get* is a *bill of divorcement*. A woman can ask for a *get*, but the husband is the only one who can issue it; the rabbinical courts can sometimes force him to give one but usually do not want to use extreme measures.
14   L. M. Epstein 1973:53, Bulka 1986:23–33.

15   H. Cohen 1973:176; Shokeid and Deshen 1974:135; Layish and Shaham 1991:2.
16   Bulka 1986:79.
17   Blood and Blood 1978:118–49; Filsinger 1983:145–57; Martin 1957:24–53.
18   D. H. J. Morgan 1975:146.
19   Rudy divorced his wife in 1991 and was granted custody of the children on the grounds that his wife is an alcoholic that demonstrated incompetence and negligence in the care for their children.
20   M. Hartman 1980:225–55.
21   For similar patterns in Australia see Huber 1977; Isaacs 1980.
22   Elon 1975:403–9.
23   See Zelditch 1956; Fallding 1957; Sarantakos 1980; Layish and Shaham 1991.
24   R. Katz 1983:98.
25   For similar situations in Israel see H. Cohen 1973; Smooha 1978; Swirski 1981; Deshen and Zenner 1982.
26   Parsons and Bales 1956:124; see also Bar-Yoseff 1991:169–96.
27   M. Hartman 1980:225–55.
28   See Azmon and Izraeli (1993:395–421); See also Sagy and Sharon 1983 and Schrift 1989.
29   Basham 1978:90.
30   Zelditch 1956:377–78; Bell and Newby 1975:159.

5   Residence, Social Mobility and Ethnic Identity

1   McAllister 1991; Maman 1993; Eisenstadt, Lissak and Nahon 1993; Duncan 1993; Bleda 1979.
2   Cadwallader 1992; De Vos 1975; Glazer and Moynihan 1970.
3   M. Hartman and Ayalon 1975; DeSantis and Benkin 1980; Ayalon, Ben-Rafael and Sharot 1985.
4   Gundars (1982:81–82.
5   Lee (1977:23).
6   Duncan 1982, 1993.
7   Fromm-Reichmann 1975; Freud 1977.
8   Kardiner and Ovesey 1951:335
9   Gist and Wright 1973:32–33.
10   Kardiner and Ovesey 1951:337–88; De Vos and Wagatsuma 1967:228–57.
11   Johnston 1976:145–47, Geyer 1980:xvii.
12   Geyer 1980:84; Germani 1980:49–90.
13   Gale 1994a, 1999; see also Stivens 1985.
14   Bott 1957: Stivens 1985; Gale 1999; Silverman 1988.
15   Bott 1955: Young and Willmott 1957, 1973; Osterriech 1965; Martin 1976; Lee 1977; Rapoport 1982; Gale 1994a, 1999.
16   Bott 1957; Young and Willmott 1957. Like Gans, Ginsburg and Marans (1980) considers this cohesiveness to be a working-class phenomenon. See also Litwak 1960.
17   Gale 1997, 1999; DeSantis and Benkin 1980:137–43.
18   Martin 1976, 1978; Lippman 1979; Blainey 1987; Gale 1994b.

19 Jupp 1984, 1988, 1995, 1999; Aaron 1979; Australian Archives CRS A446, 077857/72, SR.
20 Australian Government MAS 1986:62; Kelley and Bean 1988; Evans, Jones and Kelley 1988; Gale 1994b; Lippman 1979; W. D. Rubinstien 1986. For similar trens in USA see Long 1988; Varady 1983. In Israel see Kraus and Hodge 1990; Gonen 1995; Ben-Rafael 1985; Lazerwitz and Tabory 1993.
21 Gale 1988:332; 1997.
22 Gale 1988:205–23.
23 Aaron 1979:174–82.
24 Ginsburg and Marans 1980.
25 Poulsen and Spearritt 1981:4; Sydney Market Homes 1996.
26 Lenski 1961:306; Deshen 1979:99; Gale 1988:355, 1997: 321–33.
27 Basham 1977:179; Gale 1999:152–55.
28 Weingrod 1965, 1985; Porter 1965.
29 Glazer and Moynihan 1975:15–16.
30 Martin 1978:213.
31 Ginsburg and Marans 1980; Ben-Rafael 1985.
32 Shuval 1966:101; For further analysis see, Peres 1985:39–56, Matras 1985:1–23; Weingrod 1985 for a similar situation between blacks and whites in the United States, see Varady 1979:38–66; Dashefsky 1981.
33 A. L. Epstein 1978; De Vos 1975, 1990b; Driedger 1980:78–79.
34 Porter 1965; Driedger 1980, 1990.
35 Though Weingrod's study was written in 1965, and it can be assumed that much has changed in 30 years, nonetheless as Ben-Rafael (1985, 1991) found, the ethnic factor in Israeli society remains fundamental in upward mobility. Furthermore, the immigration of over 600,000 Russian and Ethiopian Jews in the early 1990s highlighted the rift and the split of Israeli society along ethnic and class lines.
36 Gale 1997.

6 *Religious Organization and Secular Power*

1 A. Cohen 1969; Deshen 1972b:81.
2 Deshen and Shokeid (1974:149) discuss the role of rabbis in North Africa.
3 Hirschberg 1969:196–97; Hunt and Walker 1974:242.
4 Hunt and Walker 1974:243–44; H. Z. Hirschberg 1969:198.
5 Lewis 1984a, 1984b; Deshen and Zenner 1982:166–67, 187–92.
6 Deshen and Shokeid 1974.
7 Geertz 1973:131; Gale 1997:323.
8 Austin 1984:54–5; See also Geertz 1973; M. Bloch 1977; Connell 1977.
9 Stahl 1979:116.
10 A. Cohen 1969, 1974; Aronoff 1973; Smooha 1978:112; Deshen 1982:340–97, 1979:99; For further elaboration on the emergence of ethno-grouping and the use of religious idioms and symbols to gain political power, see Deshen 1970, 1972b:62, 82, 1978:397–409, 1979:98–110; Glazer and Moynihan 1970; eds, 1975; Aronoff 1973:145; Geertz 1973; ; Gans 1979:1–20.
11 Song of Songs (chapter I verse 14: "O my dove, who art in the clefts of the rock, in the secret places of the cliff, let me see thy countenance, let me thy voice; for sweet is thy voice, and thy countenance is comely").

12   Psalms (Tehilim) chapter 122, verse 8. "Peace be within thy walls, and pros-
     perity within thy palaces. For my brethren and companions' sakes, I will
     now say, peace be within thee, for the sake of the house of the Lord our God
     I will seek thy good."
13   Traditional Sephardic leadership was not characterized by democratic
     rules.
14   De Vos 1975:18.
15   Freidman 1992.
16   Deshen 1970; Gans 1979.
17   Mol 1969; Habel 1992; Charlesworth 1992; Sharpe 1984, 1992.
18   Bloch 1977:289; Levy 1972:14.
19   See Deshen 1979, 1982.
20   Herberg 1955:72–73, De Vos (1990a: 31, 70) also writes of the need to
     preserve ethnic identity and the role of religion in psycho-ethnic stability.
21   A. L. Epstein 1978.
22   Goitein 1982:200; Deshen 1970; Gans 1979.
23   Deshen 1979:99; Gale 1997:321–33.
24   See Turner (1982:79–82) who argues that ritual performances are separated
     in time and space from everyday action. Thus the elders created a theatre
     wherein they can manipulate rituals to gain power in the synagogue.
25   Dushkin 1964/5:109–10; De Vos and Suarez-Orozco 1990a.
26   Gans 1979:1–20; Gale 1988:35–47; 1990:40–65.
27   N. Glazer 1983.
28   See Mol 1969; Wilson 1967:233; Gillman 1992:92–105; Charlesworth 1992.
29   Dushkin 1964:108.

7   Conclusion: A Paradoxical Community

1   In Israel there is only Ashkenazi mobility ladder for Sephardim.
2   See Chapter 3.
3   Johnston 1976:145–47.
4   Sephardim and Ashkenazim each encompass numerous ethnic groups;
     however, each recognize the divisions within their own group but see the
     other one as a homogeneous group.
5   Ashkenazi culture is "Australianized" into the Anglo-Celtic-Irish culture.
6   See Goffman 1972; Eidheim 1969:39–57.
7   See Chapter 4.
8   Spiro 1955:1247.
9   See S. Benson 1981; Roosens 1989a.
10   Sephardim are accepted as a separate group within the Australian ethnic
     scene.
11   See A. Cohen 1974.
12   Many Ashkenazim I interviewed insisted that they do not discriminate
     against Sephardim and were quite upset by the notion that they might.
     Nevertheless, I must emphasize that, throughout my fieldwork, the feeling
     that came across repeatedly in interviews with Sephardim and at social and
     religious gatherings was that of rejection by the Ashkenazim.

Appendix: *Methods Used in the Collection of Data*

1   Simmons 1969.
2   For further discussion of "reflexivity" in fieldwork, see Hammersey and Atkinson 1983:14–23; for the study of the researcher's role identity, see Wax 1971; for role conflict between insider/outsider researcher position, see Seteney 1988:115–38.
3   Survey Questionnaire Adapted from Encel and Buckley 1972:107–14.

Bibliography

Books

Aaron, A. 1979: *The Sephardim of Australia and New Zealand.* Sydney: Aaron Aaron.

Abraham, I.S. 1973: *Origin and the History of the Calcutta Jews.* Calcutta: Dawson and Co.

Abramson, H.J. 1973: *Ethnic Diversity in Catholic America.* New York: Wiley Interscience.

Aharoni, A. 1983: *The Second Exodus.* Pennsylvania: Dorrence.

Aldridge, J. 1969: *Cairo.* Boston and Toronto: Little Brown.

Austin, D.J. 1984: *Australian Sociologies.* Sydney, London and Boston: George Allen and Unwin.

Azmon, Y. and, D.N. 1993: Women in Israel: A Sociological Overviews. In Y. Azmon and D.N. Izraeli (eds.), *Women in Israel: Studies of Israeli Society*, New Jersey: Transaction Publishers, 6, 1–24.

Barth, F. (ed.) 1969: *Ethnic Groups and Boundaries: The Social Organization of Culture Difference.* Boston: Little Brown.

Bar-Yosef, R. 1991: Household Management in two types of Families in Israel. In L. Shamgar-Handelman and R. Bar-Yosef (eds), *Families in Israel*, Jerusalem: Akademon, 169–196 [Hebrew].

Basham, R. 1977: Ethnicity as a Total Institution. In R. Gordon and B. William (eds), *Exploring Total Institutions*, Ill.: Stripes Publishing co, 176–185.

———— 1978: *Urban Anthropology: The cross-cultural study of complex societies.* California: Mayfield Publishing Company.

Bell, C. and H. Newby 1975: Ethnicity and Social Change. In N. Glazer and D.P. Moynihan (eds), *Ethnicity: Theory and Experience*, Cambridge, MA: Harvard University Press, 141–176.

Ben-Maimon, Moses Maimonides (Harambam) *Ha'yad Ha'Hazakah, Halakhot Ishut: Perek Nashim* (vol. 14: chap. 15), Halakhah 4 (1135–1204 CE) [Hebrew].

Ben-Rafael, E. 1982: *The Emergence of Ethnicity: Cultural Groups and Social Conflict.* London: Greenwood Press.

———— 1991: *Ethnicity, Religion and Class in Israeli Society.* Cambridge: Cambridge University Press.

———— 1985: Social Mobility and Ethnic Awareness: The Israeli case. In A.

Weingrod (ed), *Studies in Israeli Ethnicity After the Ingathering*, Montreux: Gordon and Breach, 57–79.

Benson, L. 1979: Marx's General and Middle-Range Theories of Social Conflict. In R.K. Merton *et al.* (eds), *Qualitative and Quantitative Social Research*, New York: Free Press, 189–209.

Benson, S. 1981: *Ambiguous Ethnicity*. Cambridge: Cambridge University Press.

Ben-Ya'acob, A. 1985: *Babylonian Jewry in the Diaspora*. Jerusalem: Rubin Mass [Hebrew].

Beteille, A. 1971: *Harmonic and Disharmonic Social Systems*. Sydney: Sydney University Press, Great Britain, Europe, and North America: International Scholarly Book Services.

Blood, R.O. and Blood, M. 1978: *Marriage*. New York: Free Press.

Borrie, W.D. 1959: *Immigration: Australia's Problems and Prospects*. Sydney: Angus and Robertson.

Bott, E. 1957: *Family and Social network: Roles, Norms and External Relationships in Ordinary Urban Families*. London: Tavistock.

Buber-Agassi, J. 1993: Theories of Gender Equality: Lessons from the Israeli Kibbutz. In Y. Azmon and D.N. Izraeli (eds), *Women in Israel: Studies of Israeli Society*, New Brunswick: Transaction Publishers, 135–146.

Bulka, R.P. 1986: *Jewish Marriage: A Halachic Ethic*. New York and Hoboken: Ktav Publishing House Inc. and Yeshiva University Press.

Cadwallader, M.T. 1992: *Migration and Residential Mobility: Macro and Micro Approaches*. Madison: The University of Wisconsin Press.

Cass, B. 1977: Family. In A.F. Davis *et al.* (eds), *Australian Society*, Melbourne: Longman Cheshire, 138–176.

Chapman, B.B. 1956: *The Complete Anti-Semite: An Inoculation Against Infection*. Sydney: Associated General Publications.

Charlesworth, M. 1992: Religion and Ethics in a Multicultural Society. In N. Habel (ed.), *Religion and Multiculturalism in Australia*, Adelaide: AASR (Australian Association for the Study of Religions).

Chief Rabbinate of Israel 1964: *Bene Israel*. Jerusalem: Israel Rabbinate Press [Hebrew].

Cohen, Abner 1969: *Custom and Politics in Urban Africa: A Study of Hausa Migrants in Yoruba Towns*. London: Routledge & Kegan Paul.

——— 1974: *Two-Dimensional Man: An Essay on the Anthropology of Power and Symbolism in Complex Society*. London: Routledge & Kegan Paul.

Cohen, Erik 1969: *Population Dispersion and Integration of Immigrants as Contradictory Objectives*. Jerusalem: The Magnes Press [Hebrew].

——— 1985: Ethnicity and Legitimization in Contemporary Israel. In E. Krausz (ed.), *Politics and Society in Israel: Studies of Israeli Society*, 3, 320–333.

Cohen, Ethan. 2003: *The Moroccans – The Negatives of the Ashkenazim*. Tel Aviv: Rasling [Hebrew].

Cohen, Haim J. 1973: *The Jews of the Middle East, 1860–1972*. New York and Toronto: Wiley.

Cohen, Mark R. 1980: *Jewish Self-Government in Medieval Egypt, 1065–1126*. Princeton: Princeton University Press.

Cohen, Michael J. 1982: *Palestine and the Great Powers 1945–1948*. Princeton: Princeton University Press.

Connell, R.W. 1977: *Ruling Class, Ruling Culture.* Cambridge: Cambridge University Press.

Cooley, C.H. 1902: *Human Nature and the Social Order.* New York/ Chicago/Boston: Scribner's.

Coult, A.D. and Habenstein, R.W. 1965: *The Function of Extended Kinship in Urban Society.* Kansas City: Community Studies.

Dayan, A. 1999: *The Story of Shas.* Jerusalem: Keter Publishing House.

Deshen, S.A. 1972a: Is the Business of Ethnicity Finished?: The Ethnic Factor in a Local Election Campaign. In A. Arian (ed.), *The Election in Israel–1969,* Jerusalem: Academic Press, pp. 278–302.

———— 1974: Ethnicity in Israel during the 1960s. In A. Cohen (ed.), *Urban Ethnicity.* London: Tavistock, 281–309.

———— 1975: "Political Ethnicity and Cultural Ethnicity during the 1960s," in ASA Monographs-*Urban Ethnicity,* London and New York: Tavistock, 281–309.

———— 1982: Israel: Searching for Identity. In C. Caldarola (ed.), Religion and Societies, Asia and the Middle East. Berlin-New York: Mouton, 85–118.

Deshen, S. and Zenner, W.P. (eds) 1982: *Jewish Societies in the Middle East: Community, Culture and Authority.* Washington, D.C.: University Press of America.

Devereux, G. 1975: Ethnic Identity: Its Logical Foundations and its Dysfunctions. In G. De Vos and L. Romanucci-Ross (eds.), *Ethnic Identity: Cultural Continuities and Change,* Palo Alto: Mayfield, 42–70.

De Vos, G.A. 1975: Ethnic Pluralism: Conflict and Accommodation. In G. De Vos and L. Romanucci-Ross (eds.), *Ethnic Identity: Cultural Continuities and Change,* Palo Alto: Mayfield, 5–41.

—— 1990: Self in Society: A Multilevel Psycho-cultural Analysis. In G.A. De Vos and M. Suarez-Orozco (eds.), *Status Inequality: The Self in Culture*, London: Sage Publications, 17–74.

De Vos, G. and Wagatsuma, H. 1967: *Japan's Invisible Race: Cast in Culture and Personality.* Berkeley–Los Angeles: University of California Press.

De Vos, G.A. and Romanucci-Ross, L. 1975: Ethnic Identity: Cultural Continuities and Change. In G.A. De Vos and L. Romanucci-Ross (eds.), *Ethnic Identity: Cultural Continuities and Change,* Palo Alto: Mayfield.

De Vos, G.A. and Suarez-Orozco, M.M. 1990: Ethnic Belonging and Status Mobility. In G.A. De Vos and M. Suarez-Orozco (eds.), *Status Inequality: The Self in Culture*, London: Sage Publications, 246–264.

Driedger, L.1990: *Ethnic Demography: Canadian Immigrants, Racial and Cultural Variations.* Ottawa: Charleton University Press.

Dumont, L. 1980: *Homo Hierarchicus: The Caste System and Its Implications.* Chicago: Chicago University Press.

Duncan, J.S. (ed.) 1982: *Housing and Identity: Cross-Cultural Perspectives.* New York: Holms and Meier.

———— 1993: *Place, Culture and Representation.* London: Routledge.

Durkheim, E. 1961: *The Elementary Form of the Religious Life.* New York: Free Press of Glencoe (1st edition 1912).

———— 1977: Religion as a Product of Social Need. In J. Needleman *et al.* (eds.), *Religion for a New Generation.* New York: Macmillan

Dushkin, A.M. 1964/1965: *Analysis of Some Recent Developments in Jewish Education in the Diaspora: Survey and Monographs on the Jewish World.* Jerusalem: World Zionist Organization, 101–115.

Eidheim, H. 1969: When Ethnic Identity is a Social Stigma. In F. Barth (ed.), *Ethnic Groups and Boundaries: The Social Organization of Culture Difference.* London: George Allen and Unwin, 39–57.

Eisenstadt, S.N. 1954: *The Absorption of Immigrants.* London: Routledge & Kegan Paul.

——— 1971: Israeli Society – Major Features and Problems. In H.H. Ben-Sasson and S. Etinger (eds.), *The Jewish Community Through the Ages.* London: Vallentine Mitchell, 313–328.

——— 1989: *The Transformation of Israeli Society.* Jerusalem: The Magnes Press (1st edn 1985, Weidenfeld and Nicolson Ltd, London)

Eisenstadt, S.N., M. Lissak and D. Nahon 1993: *Ethnic Groups and Their Social Status in Israel.* Jerusalem: The Jerusalem Institute for Social Research.

Elias, F. and Elias-Cooper, J. 1974: *The Jews of Calcutta: The Autobiography of a Community, 1798–1972.* Calcutta: The Jewish Association of Calcutta.

Elkin, A.P. 1957: The Family – A Challenge. In A.P. Elkin (ed.), *Marriage and the Family in Australia,* Sydney: Angus and Robertson, 199–215.

Elon, M. (ed.) 1975: The Principles of Jewish Law. In *Encyclopedia Judaica.*

Encel, S. and Buckley, B. 1972: *The New South Wales Jewish Community: A Survey.* Kensington: New South Wales University Press.

Epstein, A.L. 1969: Gossip, Norms and Social Network. In J.C. Mitchell (ed.), *Social Networks in Urban Situations,* Manchester: Manchester University Press, 117–127.

——— 1978: *Ethos and Identity: Three Studies in Ethnicity.* London: Tavistock.

——— 1981: *Urbanization and Kinship: The Domestic Domain of the Copperbelt of Zambia, 1950–1956.* London-New York: Academic Press.

Epstein, L.M. 1973: *The Jewish Marriage Contract: A Study in the Status of the Woman in Jewish Law.* New York: Arno Press Inc.

Erikson, E.H. 1968: *Identity: Youth and Crisis.* New York: Norton.

Evans, M.D.R. *et al.* 1988: Job Discrimination Against Immigrants. In J. Kelley and C. Bean (eds.), *Australian Attitudes: Social and Political Analyses from the National Social Science Survey.* Sydney: Allen and Unwin, 111–127.

Fallding, H. 1957: Inside the Australian Family. In A.L. Elkin (ed.), *Marriage and the Family in Australia,* Sydney: Angus and Robertson, 54–81.

Firth, R. 1956: *Two Studies of Kinship in London.* London: Athlone.

Firth, R. *et al.* 1969: *Families and Their Relatives.* London: Routledge & Kegan Paul.

Freud, S. 1977: (c. 1959). *Inhibition, Symptoms and Anxiety.* New York: Norton.

Fromm-Reichmann, F. 1975: *Principles of Intensive Psychotherapy.* Chicago: University of Chicago Press (c. 1950).

Gale, N. 1988: *From the Homeland to Sydney: The Sephardi Jews.* Unpublished Ph.D. dissertation, University of Sydney.

Gallo, P.J. 1974: *Ethnic Alienation: The Italian-Americans.* Rutherford: Fairleigh Dickinson University Press.

Gans, H.J. 1962: *The Urban Villagers: Group and Class in the Life of Italian Americans.* New York: The Free Press of Glencoe.

Geertz, C. 1973: The *Interpretation of Culture: Selected Essays.* New York: Basic Books.

Germani, G. 1980: *Marginality*. New Brunswick, New Jersey: Transaction Books.

Geyer, R.F. 1980: *Alienation Theories: A General System Approach*. New York: Pergamon Press.

Gilbert, M. 1976: *Jewish History Atlas*. London: Weidenfeld and Nicolson.

Gillman, I. 1992: The 'Culture' Within which Religion has been Found in Australia. In N.C. Habel (ed.), *Religion and Multiculturism in Australia*, Adelaide: Australian Association for the Study of Religion, 92–105.

Gist, N.P., and Wright, R.D. 1973: *Marginality and Identity: Anglo-Indians and Racially-Mixed Minority in India*. Leiden: Brill.

Glazer, N. 1983: *Ethnic Dilemmas*. Cambridge, MA: Harvard University Press.

Glazer, N. and Moynihan, D.P. 1963: *Beyond the Melting Pot*. Cambridge, MA: MIT Press (2nd ed. 1970).

Glazer, N. and Moynihan, D.P. (eds.) 1975: *Ethnicity: Theory and Experience*. Cambridge: Harvard University Press.

Goffman, E. 1959: *The Presentation of Self in Everyday Life*. New York: Doubleday Anchor.

———— 1972: The Presentation of Self to Others. In G.J. Manis and B.N. Meltzer (eds.), *Symbolic Interaction*. Boston–London: Allyn and Bacon, 234–244.

Goitein, S.D. 1982: The Social Structure of Jewish Education in Yemen. In S. Deshen and W.P. Zenner (eds.), *Jewish Societies in the Middle East: Community, Culture and Authority*, Washington, D.C.: University Press of America, 211–234.

Gonen, A. 1995: *Between City and Suburbs: Urban Residential Patterns and Processes in Israel*. Aldershot: Avenbury.

Gordon, M. 1964: *Assimilation in American Life: The Role of Race, Religion, and National Origins*. New York: Oxford University Press.

———— 1978: *Human Nature, Class and Ethnicity*. New York: Oxford University Press.

Grassby, A.J. 1973a: A Multi-Cultural Society for the Future. *Immigration Reference Paper*, Australia: Department of Immigration, AGPS, Canberra.

———— 1973b: *Australia Decade of Decisions: A Report on Migration, Citizenship, Settlement and Population*. A.J. Grassby, the Minister for Immigration, Tabled in the House of Representatives, 11 October 1973.)

Gray, J. 2000: "Is The Assertion of Minority Identity Compatible with the Idea of a Socially Inclusive Society?" In P. Askonas (ed.), *Social Inclusion: Possibilities*. USA: Palgrave Macmillan, 169–185.

Greeley, A.M. 1974: *Ethnicity in the United States: A Preliminary Reconnaissance*. New York: Wiley.

Grunebaum G.E. Von. 1970: *Classical Islam: A History 600–1258*. Chicago: Aldine Publishing Co. (Published also by Barnes and Noble 1997.)

Gundars, R. 1982: *Residential Location Determinants of the Older Population*. Chicago: University of Chicago Press.

Guyatt, J. 1967: *A Study of Attitudes to Jews and of the Jewish Stereotype in Eastern Australia, 1938–1948*. MA thesis University of Queensland.

Habel, N.C.(ed.) 1992: *Religion and Multiculturalism in Australia*. Adelaide: Australia Association for the Study of Religion.

Hammersley, M. and Atkinson, P. 1983: *Ethnography: Principles in Practice*. London: Tavistock.

Hammond, S.B. 1954: Attitudes of Gentiles to Jews. In S.B. Hammond and O. Adolf Oeser (eds.), *Social Structure and Personality in a City*, London: Routledge & Kegan Paul, 92–112.

Haver, H. Shenhav, Y. and Muzafi-Haler P. (Eds.) 2002: *Orientals in Israel*. Jerusalem: Hakibbutz Hameuhad and Van Leer Institute.

Herberg, W. 1955: *Protestant-Catholic-Jew: An Essay in American Religious Sociology*. Garden City, New York: Doubleday.

Herman, H.V. 1979: Dishwashers and Proprietors: Macedonian in Toronto's Restaurant Trade. In W. Wallman (ed.), *Ethnicity at Work*. London: Macmillan, 71–93.

Hicks, G. and Leis, P. (eds.) 1977: *Ethnic Encounters: Identities and Contexts*. North Scituate, MA: Duxbury Press.

Hirschberg, H.Z. 1969: The Oriental Jewish Communities. In A.J. Arberry (ed.), *Religion in the Middle East*, Vol. 1. Cambridge: Cambridge University Press, 119–235.

Huber, R. 1977: *From Pasta to Pavlova: A Comparative Study of Italian Settlers in Sydney and Griffith*. St. Lucia: Queensland University Press.

Hunt, C.L. and Walker, L. 1974: *Ethnic Dynamics: Patterns of Intergroup Relations in Various Countries*. Illinois: The Dorsey Press.

Isaacs, E. R. 1980: *The Greek Community in Sydney: A Contribution to the Sociology of Ethnicity*. Unpublished Ph.D thesis, University of NSW.

Isenberg, S.B. 1989: *India's Bene Israel: A Comprehensive Inquiry and Sourcebook*. Bombay: Popular Prakashan.

Israel, B.J. 1984: *Bene Israel of India: Some Studies*. Bombay: Orient Longman.

Johnston, R.J. 1971: *Urban Residential Patterns: An Introductory Review*. London: Bell.

Jupp, J. (ed.) 1984: *Ethnic Politics in Australia*. Sydney: Allen and Unwin.

———— 1988: Immigration and Ethnicity. In J.M. Najman and J.S. Western (eds.), *A Sociology of Australian Society*, Melbourne–Sydney: Macmillan, 162–181.

Kardiner, A. and Ovesey, A. 1951: *The Mark of Oppression: Explorations in the Personality of the American Negro*. Cleveland–New York: Meridian.

Katz, Jacob 1982: Traditional Society and Modern Society. In S. Deshen and W.P. Zenner (eds.), *Jewish Societies in the Middle East: Community, Culture and Authority*, Washington, D.C.: University Press of America, 35–48.

Kedourie, E. 1978: *England and the Middle East: The Destruction of the Ottoman Empire 1914–1921*. Sussex: Harvester.

Kedourie, E. and Haim, S.G. (eds.) 1982: *Palestine and Israel in the 19th and 20th Century*. London: Frank Cass.

Kehimkar, H.S. 1937: *The History of the Bene-Israel of India*. Tel Aviv: Schocken.

Kelley, J. and Bean, C. (eds.) 1988: *Australian Attitudes: Social and Political Analyses from the National Social Science Survey*. Sydney: Allen and Unwin.

Kondapi, C. 1951: *Indians Overseas 1838–1949*. New Delhi: Oxford University Press.

Kopp, Y. 2000: *Pluralism in Israel: From Melting Pot to 'Jerusalem Mixture*. Jerusalem: The Center for the Social Research Policy [Hebrew].

Kraus, V. and Hodge, R.W. 1990: *Promises in the Promised Land: Mobility and Inequality in Israel*. New York: Greenwood Press.

Kringas, P. 1984: Really Educating Migrant Children. In J. Jupp (ed.), *Ethnic Politics in Australia*, Sydney: Allen and Unwin, 114–125.

Kushner, G. 1973: *Immigrants from India to Israel: Planned Change in an Administered Community*. Tucson, Arizona: University of Arizona Press.

Landau, J.M. 1969: *Jews in Nineteenth-Century Egypt*. London: London University Press.

——— 1973: *Middle Eastern Themes: Papers in History and Politics*. London: Frank Cass.

Layish, H. 1994: *Islamic Law in the Contemporary Middle East*. England: Lang.

Leach, E.R. 1964: *Political System of Highland Burma*. London: G. Bell and Sons.

Lee, T. 1977: *Race and Residence: The Concentration and Dispersal of Immigrants in London*. Oxford: Oxford University Press.

Lenski, G. 1961: *The Religious Factor: A Sociological Study of Religion's Impact on Politics, Economics and Family Life*. Garden City, New York: Doubleday.

de Lepervanche, M. 1984a: Immigrants and Ethnic Groups. In S. Encel and L. Bryson (eds.) *Australian Society*, Melbourne: Longman Cheshire, 170–228. (4th ed.)

——— 1984b: *Indians in a White Australia: An Account of Race, Class and Indian Immigration to Eastern Australia*. Sydney/London/Boston: George Allen and Unwin.

Levy, A. 1972: *The Sephardim: A Problem of Survival?* London: Rabbi Abraham Levy, The Spanish and Portuguese Jews' Congregation.

Lewis, B. 1984b: *The Jews of Islam*. New Jersey: Princeton University Press.

Lippman, W.L. 1986: *Australian Jewry*. Victoria: Macmillan.

Lissak, M. 1969: Integration of Oriental Ethnic Groups in the Political and Social Structure in Israel. In M. Lissak (ed.), *The Integration of Immigrants*. Jerusalem, pp. 51–65 [Hebrew].

———, 1999: *The Mass Immigration in the Fifties: The Failure of the Melting Pot Policy*. Jerusalem: The Biyalik Institute [Hebrew].

———, 1996: Ethnics and Ethnicity in Israel in a Historical Perspective. In M. Lissak and B. Kanie-Zahav (eds.) *Israel Towards the Year 2000: Society Politics and Culture*. Jerusalem: Magness, The Hebrew University Press, 74–89 [Hebrew].

Litwak, E. 1965: Extended Kin Relations in an Industrial Democratic Society. In E. Shanas and G. Streib (eds.), *Social Structure and the Family Relations*, Englewood Cliffs, NJ: Prentice-Hall, 290–325.

London, H.I. 1970: *Non-White Immigration and the "White Australia" Policy*. Sydney: Sydney University Press.

Long, L. 1988: *Migration and Residential Mobility in the United States*. New York: Sage.

Maman, D. 1993: *Ethnic Social Status and Social Networks: Priliminary Findings*. Jerusalem: The Jerusalem Institute for Social Research.

Martin, J.I. 1957: Marriage, the Family and Class. In A.P. Elkin (ed.), *Marriage and the Family in Australia*, Sydney: Angus and Robertson, 24–53.

——— 1976: Ethnic Pluralism and Identity. In S. Murray-Smith (ed.), *Melbourne Studies in Education*, Melbourne: Melbourne University Press, 11–27.

——— 1978: *The Migrant Presence: Australian Responses 1947–1977. Research Report for the National Population Inquiry*. Sydney: George Allen and Unwin.

Matras, J. 1985: Intergenerational Social Mobility and Ethnic Organization in the Jewish Population of Israel. In A. Weingrod (ed.), *Studies in Israeli Ethnicity after the Ingathering*, Montreux: Gordon and Breach Science Publishers, 1–23.

McAllister, I. 1991: *Immigrant Social Mobility: Economic Success Among Lebanese, Maltese and Vietnamese In Australia*. Sydney: University of Wollongong.

Mead, G.H. 1934: *Mind, Self and Society*. Chicago: University of Chicago Press.

Medding, P.Y. 1968: *From Assimilation to Group Survival*. Melbourne/Canberra/Sydney: F.W. Cheshire.

—— 1973: *Jews in Australian Society*. Melbourne: Macmillan.

Meir-Glizenstein, E. 2000: The immigrants from Iraq and the Israeli Policy in the Early Fifties and their Struggle for Integration. In A. Shapira, Y. Rhienhertz and Y. Hariss (eds.), *The Zionism Era*, Jerusalem: Zalman Shazar Institute, 271–295 [Hebrew].

Mercer, B.E. and Wanderer J.J. 1970: *The Study of Society*. Belmont, CA: Wadsworth.

Mol, H. 1969: *Christianity in Chains: Sociologist's Interpretation of the Church's Dilemma in a Secular World*. Australia: Thomas Nelson.

Morgan, D.H.J. 1975: *Social Theory and the Family*. London and Boston: Routledge & Kegan Paul.

Musleah, E.N. 1975: *On the Banks of the Ganga: The Sojourn of Jews in Calcutta*. MA: The Christopher Publishing House.

Novak, M. 1971: *The Rise of the Unmeltable Ethnics*. New York: Macmillan.

—— 1977: *Further Reflection on Ethnicity*. Middleton, Penn.: Jednota Press.

—— 1979: The New Ethnicity. In D.R. Colbourn and G.E. Pozzetta (eds.), *America and the New Ethnicity*, Port Washington/New York/London: National University Publications, Kennikat Press, 15–28.

Osterreich, J. 1965: Geographical Mobility and Kinship: A Canadian Example. In R. Piddington (ed.), *Kinship and Geographical Mobility*, Leiden: Brill, 131–165.

Palfreeman, A.C. 1967: *The Administration of the White Australia Policy*. Melbourne: Melbourne University Press.

—— 1974: The White Australia Policy. In F.S. Stevens (ed.), *Racism: The Australian Experience*, Sydney: ANZ Book Co. (3 vols.), Vol. I 164–172.

Parsons, T. 1965: The Normal American Family. In S.M. Farber *et al.* (eds.), *Man and Civilization: The Family's Search for Survival*, New York: McGraw-Hill, 31–50.

—— 1975: Some Theoretical Considerations on the Nature and Trends of change of Ethnicity. In N. Glazer and D. Moynihan (eds.), *Ethnicity: Theory and Experience*, Cambridge, MA: Harvard University Press, 53–83.

Parsons, T. and Bales, R.F. 1956: *Family, Socialization and Interaction Process*. London: Routledge & Kegan Paul.

Patai, R. 1960: *Family, Love and the Bible*. London: MacGibbon and Kee.

—— 1981: *The Vanished World of Jewry*. London: Weidenfeld and Nicolson.

Patterson, O. 1975: Context and Choice in Ethnic Allegiance: A Theoretical Framework and Caribbean Case Study. In N. Glazer and D. Moynihan (eds.), *Ethnicity: Theory and Experience*, Cambridge, MA: Harvard University Press, 305–349.

Peres, Y. 1985: Horizontal Integration and Vertical Differentiation among Jewish Ethnicities in Israel. In A. Weingrod (ed.), *Studies in Israeli Ethnicity after the Ingathering*, Montreux: Gordon and Breach Science Publishers, 39–56. [Also in M. Lisak (ed.), (1989) *Stratification in Israeli Society: Ethnic National and Class Cleavages*. Tel Aviv: The Open University of Israel, 965–979.]

Peterson-Royce, A. 1982: *Ethnic Identity: Strategies of Diversity*. Bloomington: Indiana University Press.

Porter, J. 1965: *The Vertical Mosaic*. Toronto: University of Toronto Press.

Porush, I. 1977: *The House of Israel*. Melbourne: The Hawthorn Press.

Poulsen, M. and Spearritt, P. 1981: *Sydney: A Social and Political Atlas*. Sydney/London/Boston: George Allen and Unwin.

Ram, A. 1993: Society and Social Science in Israel. In A. Ram (ed.), The Israeli Society: A Critical Analysis. Tel Aviv: Bneh Brerot, 7–39 [Hebrew].

Rapoport, A. 1982: Identity and Environment: A Cross-Cultural Perspective, In J.S. Duncan (ed.), *Housing and Identity: Cross-Cultural Perspectives*, New York: Holms and Meier, 6–35.

Roosens, E.E. 1989 *Creating Ethnicity: The Process of Ethnogenesis*. London: Sage Publications.

Roumani, M.M. 1983: *The Case of the Jews from Arab Countries: A Neglected Issue*. Tel Aviv: World Organization of Jews from Arab Countries.

Rubinstein, H. 1993: Australia. In D. Singer and R.S. Seldin (eds.), *The American Jewish Year Book*. New York and Philadelphia: The American Jewish Committee and Jewish Publication Society, 93:314–328.

Rubinstein, W.D. 1985: The Politics of Anti-Semitism: The Australian Experience. In S. Liberman (ed.), *Anti-Semitism and Human Rights*. Melbourne: Australian Institute of Jewish Affairs, 1131–1138.

—— 1986: *Attitudes and Opinions towards Australian Jews and Jewish Affairs*. Melbourne: (A detailed research report on the McNair Anderson survey of March 1984).

Rutland, S.D. 1991: *Edge of Diaspora*. Sydney: Allen and Unwin.

Sacher, H.M. 1974: *Europe Leaves the Middle East 1936–1954*. New York: Knopf.

Sandberg, N.C. 1974: *Ethnic Identity and Assimilation: The Polish-American Community*. New York: Praeger.

Sarantakos, S. 1980: *Marriage and the Family in Australia*. Sydney: Budget Publishing Books.

Sassoon, D.S. 1949: *A History of the Jews in Baghdad*. Letchworth Herts: D.S. Sassoon.

Schmelz, V.O. and DellaPergola, S. 1993: World Jewish Population 1991. In D. Singer and R.S. Seldin (eds.), *American Jewish Year Book*, New York and Philadelphia: The American Jewish Committee and Jewish Publication Society, 93:423–448.

Schneider, D.M. 1969: Kinship, Nationality and Religion in American Culture: Toward a Definition of Kinship. In R.F. Spencer (ed.), *Forms of Symbolic Action*, Seattle and London: University of Washington Press, 116–25.

Schrieft, R. 1989: Marriage – Optional or a Trap. In D. Izraeli (ed.), *Trapped Women*, Tel Aviv: Hakibbutz Hameuhad Press [Hebrew].

Schweitzer, F.M. 1971: *A History of the Jews since the First Century AD*. New York: Macmillan.

Selvin, H.C. 1975: The Formalizing Theory. In L.A. Coser (ed.), *The Idea of Social Structure*, New York: Harcourt Brace Jovanovich, 339–354.

Seteney, S. 1988: Studying Your Own: The Complexities of Shared Culture, In S. Altorki and C. Fawzi El-Salh (eds.), *Arab Women in the Field*, Syracuse: Syracuse University Press.

Sharpe, E.J. 1992: Multiculturalism and the Study of World Religions. In N. Habel (ed.), *Religion and Multiculturalism in Australia*, Adelaide: Australian Association for the Study of Religion.

Shetrit, S.S. 2004: *The Mizrahi Struggle in Israel: Between Oppression and Liberation, Identification and Alternative 1948–2003*. Tel Aviv: Am Oved Publishers Ltd.

Shokeid, M. and Deshen, S. 1974: *The Predicament of Homecoming: Culture and Social Life of North African Immigrants in Israel*. Ithaca and London: Cornell University Press.

————— 1982: *Distant Relations: Ethnicity and Politics among Arabs and North African Jews in Israel*. South Hadley, MA: J.F. Bergin.

Shokeid, M. 1980: Changes in Male–Female Division of Labour in Morrocan Families. In M. Shokeid *et al.* (eds.), *Social Anthropology*, Jerusalem: Schoken Publishing Co., 141–149.

Shuval, J. and Leshem, E. 1998: The Sociology of Migration to Israel. In M. Shuval and E. Leshem (eds.) *Immigration to Israel: Sociological Perspectives*. Vol III Studies in Israeli society. New Brunswick (USA) and London: Transaction Publishers, pp. 3–50.

Silverman, M. 1988: Family Kinship and Ethnicity: Strategies for Upward Mobility. In M. Silverman (ed.), *Persistence and Flexibility*, Albany: State University of New York Press.

Simmons, M. (ed.) 1969: *Issues in Participant Observation: A Text and Reader*. Reading, MA: Addison-Wesley.

Sitton, D. 1974: *The Sephardi Jewish Communities in Contemporary World*. The Council of the Sephardi Community, Jerusalem: Ahva Cooperative Press [Hebrew].

Smelser, N.J. 1959: *Social Change in the Industrial Revolution*. Chicago: University of Chicago Press.

Smooha, S. 1978: *Israel: Pluralism and Conflict*. London: Routledge & Kegan Paul.

————— 1993: Social, Ethnic and National Differences and Democracy in Israel. In A. Ram (ed.) *The Israeli Society: A Critical Analysis*. Tel Aviv: Brerot, 172–202 [Hebrew].

Spivak, G.C. 1999: *A Critique of Postcolonial Reason: Toward a history of the vanishing present*. Cambridge, MA: Harvard University Press.

Stahl, A. 1993: *Family, and Child Upbringing in Oriental Jewry*. Jerusalem: Akademon Press.

Stillman, N.A. 1979: *The Jews of Arab Lands: A History and Source Book*. Philadelphia: The Jewish Publication Society of America.

Stivens, M. 1985: The Private Life of the Extended Family: Family, Kinship and Class in a Middle Class Suburb of Sydney. In L. Manderson (ed.), *Australian Ways: Anthropological Studies of an Industrialized Society*, Sydney/London/Boston: Allen and Unwin, 15–32.

Strizower, S. 1971: *The Children of Israel: The Bene-Israel of Bombay*. Oxford: Basil Blackwell.

Suarez-Orozco, M.M. 1990: Migration and Education: United States- Europe Comparisons. In G.A. DeVos and M.M. Suarez-Orozco (eds.), *Status Inequality: The Self in Culture*, Newbury/London/New Delhi: Sage Publications, 265–287.

Swirski, S. 1981: *Orientals and Ashkenazim in Israel: The Ethnic Division of Labour.* Haifa: Mahbarot Le-Machkar Ulebikoret [Hebrew].

Sydney Market Homes 1996: *Home Price Guide.* Sydney: Australian property Monitors.

Turner, V. (ed.) 1982: *Celebration: Studies in Festivity and Ritual.* Washington: Smithsonian Institution Press.

Van den Berghe, P.L. 1974: *Race and Ethnicity: Essays in Comparative Sociology.* New York-London: Basic Books.

——— 1981: *The Ethnic Phenomenon.* New York-Oxford: Elsevier.

Varady, D.P. 1979: *Ethnic Minorities in Urban Areas: A Case Study of Racially Changing Communities.* The Hague: Nijhoff.

Warner, W.L. *et al.* 1963: *Yankee City.* New Haven: Yale University Press.

Warner, W.L. and Srole, L. 1945: *The Social Systems of American Ethnic Groups.* New Haven: Yale University Press.

Wax, R.H. 1971: *Doing Fieldwork: Warning and Advice.* Chicago: University of Chicago Press.

Weber, M. 1961: Ethnic Groups. In T. Parsons *et. al.* (eds.), *Theories of Society: Foundations of Modern Sociological Theory,* New York: Free Press, Vol. 1, 305–309.

Weed, P.L. 1973: *The White Ethnic Movement and Ethnic Politics.* New York: Praeger.

Weingrod, A. 1965: *Israel: Group Relations in a New Society.* London: Pall Mall Press.

Weingrod, A. (ed) 1985: *Studies in Israeli Ethnicity After the Ingathering,* Montreux: Gordon and Breach

Whyte, W.F. 1943: *Street Corner Society.* Chicago: University of Chicago Press.

Wilson, B.R. 1967: *Religion in Secular Society.* Watts: Penguin.

Wilton, J. and R. Bosworth 1984: *Old Worlds and New Australia: The Post-War Migrant Experience.* Victoria: Penguin Australia.

Yarwood, A.T. 1964: *Asian Migration to Australia: The Background to Exclusion 1896–1923.* London and New York: Cambridge University Press.

Yarwood, A.T. (ed.) 1968: *Attitudes to Non-European Immigration.* Australia: Cassell Ltd.

Young, M. and Willmott, P. 1957: *Family and Kinship in East London.* London: Routledge & Kegan Paul (1st edn 1957).

——— 1973: *The Symmetrical Family: a study of work and leisure in the London region.* London: Routledge & Kegan Paul.

Zameret, Z. (1993) *The Melting Pot: The Frumkin Commission on the Education of Immigrants Children (1950).* Be'er-Sheva: Ben-Gurion University Press [Hebrew].

Zangwill, I. 1908: *The Melting Pot.* New York: Macmillan.

Zelditch, M. 1956: Role Differentiation in the Nuclear Family: A Comparative Study. In T. Parsons and R.F. Bales (eds.), *Family, Socialization and Interaction Process,* London: Routledge & Kegan Paul, 307–351.

Zuesse, E.M. 1992: From Assimilation to Affirmation: The Jews of Australia. In N.C. Habel (ed.), *Religion and Multiculturalism in Australia*, Adelaide: Australian Association for the Study of Religion, 172–198

Journals

Abramson, H.J. 1975: The Religioethnic Factor and the American Experience: Another Look at the Three-Generation Hypothesis. *Ethnicity* 2, 163–177.
Amir, Y. *et al.* 1978: Asymmetry, Academic Status, Differentiation and the Ethnic Perceptions and Preferences of Israeli Youth. *Human Relation* 31 (2), 99–116.
Aronoff, M.J. 1973: The Politics of Religion in a New Israeli Town: The Manipulation of Religion in the Political System of Sephardim in Israel. *Eastern Anthropologist* 26 (2), 145–171.
Ayalon, H. *et al.* 1985: Variations in Ethnic Identification among Israeli Jews. *Ethnic and Racial Studies* 8 (3), 389–407.
Babah, H. 1994: The Question of the Other: Differences, Discrimination and the Colonial Discourse. *Critical Theory* 5, 144–157 [Hebrew].
Bartrop, P. 1988: The Australian Government's 'Liberation' of Refugees Immigration Policy in 1938: Fact or Fiction? *Menorah: Australian Journal of Jewish Studies* 2 (1), 66–82.
────── 1990: The 'Jewish Race' Clause in Australian Immigration Forms. *Australian Jewish Historical Society Journal* 11 (1), 69–78.
Bleda, S.E. 1979: Socio-economic, Demographic, and Cultural Bases of Ethnic Residential Segregation. *Ethnicity* 6, 147–167.
Bloch, M. 1977: Past and Present in the Past. *Man* 12, 378–393.
Bott, E. 1955: Urban Families: Conjugal Roles and Social Networks. *Human Relations* 8, 345–384.
Breton, R. and Pinard, M. 1960: Group Formation among Immigrants: Criteria and Processes. *Canadian Journal of Economics and Political Science* 26, 465–477.
Cahnman, W.J. 1965: Role and Significance of the Jewish Artisan Class. *The Jewish Journal of Sociology* 7 (2), 207–220.
Cohen, Haim J. 1996: Note on the Social Change Among Iraqi Jews 1917–1950 *Jewish Journal of Sociology* 8, 204–208.
Cohen, P.S. 1968: Ethnic Groups Differences in Israel. *Race* 9, 103–110.
Dashefsky, A. 1975: Theoretical Frameworks in the Study of Ethnic Identity: Toward a Social Psychology of Ethnicity. *Ethnicity* 2, 10–18.
────── 1981: Theory, Method, and Social Policy in Ethnicity: Developmental Trends in Study of Jews. *Ethnicity* 8 (2), 196–205.
DeSantis, G. and Benkin, R. 1980: Ethnicity without Community. *Ethnicity* 7 (2), 137–143.
Deshen, S.A. 1970: On Religious Change: The Situational Analysis of Symbolic Action. *Comparative Studies in Society and History* 12 (3), 260–274.
────── 1972b: Ethnicity and Citizenship in the Ritual of an Israeli Synagogue. *Southwestern Journal of Anthropology* 28 (1), 69–82.
────── 1978: Two Trends in Israeli Orthodoxy. *Judaism: A Quarterly of Jewish Life and Thought* 27 (4), 397–409.
────── 1979: The Judaism of Middle Eastern Immigrants. *The Jerusalem Quarterly* 13, 98–110.

———— 2001: The Jews of Baghdad in the Nineteenth Century: The Growth of Social classes and multicultural groups. *Zemanim* 73, 30–44 [Hebrew].

Don Yiheya, E. 1990: Religiosity and Ethnicity in the Israeli Politics. *State, Government and International Relations* 32, 11–54.

Driedger, L. 1980: Jewish Identity: The Maintenance of Urban Religious and Ethnic Boundaries. *Ethnic and Racial Studies* 3 (1), 67–88.

Faur, J. 1972: The Sephardim: Yesterday, Today and Tomorrow. *The Sephardic World* 1 (1), 5–8.

Filsinger, E.E. 1983: Love, Liking, and Individual Marital Adjustment: A Pilot Study of Relationship Changes within One Year. *International Journal of Sociology of the Family* 13 (1), 145–157.

Fischel, W.J. 1944: The Jews of Kurdistan. *Commentary* 8, 554–559.

Friedman, J. 1992: The Past in the Future: History and Politics of Identity. *American Anthropologist* 94, 837–859.

Gaby, N. 1999: The Education of Women in the Jewish Community of Bagdhad (1894–1951). *Pe'amim, Studies in Oriental Jewry* (82), 94–118 [Hebrew]

Gale, N. 1990: The History of Immigration of Sephardi Jews to Australia. *Australian Journal of Jewish Studies* 4 (1–2), 40–65.

———— 1994a: Love and Marriage, Past and Present: The Case of the Oriental Jews in Sydney. *International Journal of Sociology of the Family* 24, 61–86.

———— 1994b: A case of double rejection: The immigration of Sephardim to Australia. *New Community* 20 (3), 269–286.

———— 1997: Religious Involution: Sacred and Secular Conflict among Sephardic Jews in Australia. *Ethnology* 36 (4), 321–333.

———— 1999: Residence, social mobility and practice theory: the case of Sephardic Jews of Sydney. *Journal of Sociology* 35 (2), 149–168

Gans, H.J. 1979: Symbolic Ethnicity: The Future of Ethnic Groups and Cultures in America. *Ethnic and Racial Studies* 2 (1), 1–20.

Ginsburg, Y. 1981: Jewish Attitudes toward Black Neighbours in Boston and London. *Ethnicity* 8 (2), 206–218.

Ginsburg, Y. and R.W. Marans 1980: Social Mix in Housing: Does Ethnicity Make a Difference? *The Journal of Ethnic Studies* 7 (3), 101–112.

Goldberg, J.A. 1939: Jews in the Medical Profession – A National Survey. *Jewish Social Studies* 1 (3), 327–336.

Hartman, M. 1980 The Role of Ethnicity in Married Women's Economic Activity in Israel. *Ethnicity* 7 (3), 225–255.

Hartman, M. and Ayalon, H. 1975: Ethnicity and Class in Israel. *Megamot* 21 (2), 124–139 [Hebrew].

Herzog, H. 1984: Ethnicity as a Product of Political Negotiation: The Case of Israel. *Ethnic and Racial Studies* 7 (1), 517–533.

Hirst, J. 1990: Australia's Absurd History: A Critique of Multiculturalism, *Overland* 117, 5–10.

Johnston, R.J. 1976: The Concept of the 'Marginal Man': A Refinement of the Term. *A.N.Z.J.S.* 12 (2), 145–157.

Katz, Ronald 1983: Conjugal Power: A Comparative Analysis. *International Journal of Sociology of the Family* 13 (1), 79–101.

Kedourie, E. 1971: The Jews of Baghdad in 1910. *Middle Eastern Studies* 7, 355–361.

Klaff, V.Z. 1977: Residence and Integration in Israel: A Mosaic of Segregated People. *Ethnicity* 4, 103–121.

───── 1980: Pluralism as an Alternative Model for the Human Ecologist. *Ethnicity* 7 (1), 102–118.

Kwen Fee, L. 1982: Identity in Minority Group Relations. *Ethnic and Racial Studies* 5 (1), 42–52.

Lavendar, D.A. 1981: Arabic-Islamic and Spanish-Mediterranean Influences on 'The Jewish Mind': A Comparison to European-Christian Influence. *The Journal of Ethnic Studies* 8 (4), 23–35.

Layish, H. and Shaham, S. 1991: Islamic Law in the Middle East. *The Journal of Middle Eastern Studies*, 1–29.

Lazerowitz, B. and Tabory, E. 1993: Religion and Ethnicity Among Jews. *Journal of Jewish Communal Service* 69. (2/3), 39–49.

Lewis, B. 1984a: The Decline and Fall of Islamic Jewry. Commentary 77 (6), 44–54.

Lippman, W.L. 1979: Current Attitudes to Asian Immigration into Australia. *Journal of Ethnic Studies* 3(1), 37–45.

Litwak, E. 1960: Geographical Mobility and Extended Family Cohesion. *American Sociological Review* 25, 385–394.

Luke, C. and Luke A. 1999: Theorizing Interracial Families and Hybrid Identity: an Australian perspective. *Educational Theory* 29, 223–249.

Markus, A. 1983: Jewish Migration to Australia 1938–1947. *Journal of Australian Studies* 13, 18–31.

Parsons, T. 1943: The Kinship System of the Contemporary United States. *American Anthropologist* 45, 22–38.

Patterson, G.J. 1979: A Critique of 'the New Ethnicity'. *American Anthropologist* 81, 103–105.

Price, C.A. 1957: The Effects of Post-War Immigration. *Australian Quarterly* 29, 28–40.

───── 1962: Overseas Migration to and from Australia 1947–1961. *Australian Outlook* 16, 160–174.

───── 1964: Chain Migration and Immigrant Groups, with Special Reference to Australia Jewry. *The Jewish Journal of Sociology* 6 (2), 157–170.

───── 1966: 'White' Restriction on 'Coloured' Immigration. *Race* 7, 217–234.

Ram, U. 2002: Mizrahim or Mizrahiyut? Equality and Identity in Israeli Critical Social Thought. *Israeli Studies Forum* 17 (2), 114–130.

Raphael, C. 1983: Jewish History and the Sephardim. *Commentary* 75 (5), 39–44.

Ray, J.J. 1972: Anti-Semitism: A Cognitive Significance? Some Observations on Australian Neo-Nazis. *Jewish Journal of Sociology* 2 (2), 207–213.

Rhedding-Jones, J. 1996: Researching Early Schooling: poststructural practices and academic writing in an ethnography. *British Journal of Education* 17, 21–37.

───── 2001: Shifting Ethnicities: 'natives informants' and other theories from/for early childhood education. *Contemporary Issues in Early Childhood* 2 (2), 135–156.

Sagy, A. and Sharon, N. 1983: The Male's Role in the Family: Change in Perceptions and Influence. *Society and Welfare* 5 (1), 3–14 [Hebrew].

Shuval, J.T. 1966: Self-Rejection Among North-African Immigrants in Israel. *The Israeli Annals of Psychiatry and Related Disciplines* 4(1), 101–110.

Skinner, K.A., and G.L. Hendricks 1979: The Shaping of Ethnic Self-Identity Among Indochinese Refugees. *Journal of Ethnic Studies* 7 (3), 25–41.

Solomon, N. 1983: Jewish Divorce Law and Contemporary Society. *The Jewish Journal of Sociology* 25 (2), 31–140.

——— 1994: Judaism and Modernity: The Whole Agenda. *The Jewish Journal of Sociology* 36 (2), 119–132.

Spiro, M.E. 1955: The Acculturation of American Ethnic Groups. *American Anthropologist* 57, 1240–1252.

Stahl, A. 1979: Ritualistic Reading Among Oriental Jews. *Anthropological Quarterly* 52 (2), 115–120.

Stein, H.R. and Hills, R.F. 1977: The Limit of Ethnicity. *The American Scholar* 46, 181–189.

Turner, F.J. 1893: The Significance of the Frontier in American History. The Proceedings of the State Historical Society of the Wisconsin, Dec. 14.

Varady, D.P. 1983: Determinants of Residential Mobility Decision. *Journal of the American Planning Association* 49, 184–199.

Weingrod, A. and Gurevitch, M. 1977: Who Are the Israeli Elites? *The Jewish Journal of Sociology* 19 (1), 67–78.

Wirth, L. 1938: Urbanism as a Way of Life. *American Journal of Sociology* 44, 1–24.

Zubrzycki, J. 1968: The Questing Years. *Digest* (Australia, Department of Immigration, Canberra).

Official Documents

Australian Archives Australian Capital Territory CRS: A432 Item 38/01425; A433 Item 47/2/4/1; A434 Item 49/3/3196; A445 Items: 140/2/25; 140/4/23; 140/4/26; 235/5/9; CRS A461 Items: 349/3/5; MA 349/3/5; J349/1/6PI; A1067 Item IC46/31/1/14; A1838 Item 861/5/7.

CA 51 Department of Immigration, Central Office Correspondence Files, Annual Single Number Series, with Block Allocations, Australian Archives CRS A446 Item **077857/72:** Copy No. 50/3/23237, Ref. No. 49/2/8111; Ref. No. 49/2/3771; Ref. No. 11.7.1951, 51/24.3; File No.50/40, Imm. No.114. Copy: IW, Original on 50/3/10401; Minute No.339 (Agendum Item No.6) Ref.No. 51/24/3; Ref.No. 3596(27/6/79); Ref.No.51/13/9029; Ref.No.7/5/1954, Mr. Nutt. BVK.; Ref. No. 235/5/5, 14.8.1953; File No. 53/1/3/29, Memorandum No. 62, 11 January 1954; Ref. No. SR.;

Australian Archive of Judaica File No. 4 (Sephardim) Newspaper Cuttings from 1959–1965, Fisher Library, University of Sydney, Sydney, NSW.

Australian Bureau of Statistics (ABS), 1981: *Census of Population and Housing: Jewish Population of NSW* by Place of Birth. Sydney: Australian Government; (1981) 492[f8]. Jews in Cross Tabulation Between Religion and Birthplace.

Australian Government 1986: *Migrant Attitudes Survey.* Vol. 2: Overall Findings. Canberra: Australian Government Publishing Service.

Australian Population and Immigration Council 1976: A Decade of Migrant Settlement, Report on the 1973 Immigration: Survey. Canberra: Australian Government Publishing Service.

Australian Population and Immigration Council 1978: "Australia as a Multicultural Society: Submission to the Australian Population and Immigration Council on the Green Paper," Immigration Policies and Australia's Population. Canberra: Australian Government Publishing Service (1st edn 1977).
Diary and Directory of the Jewish Community of New South Wales, 1983–1984.

Papers in Conferences, Newspapers, and Other Documents

The Australian Jewish Times 1979: Book Launch Supports Sephardic School, The Statistics, School for Thought, Experts Cautious on Proposal, 28 June, p. 5.
Blainey, G. 1987: Reaction to Stone: A Clue to Illness in Our Society, *The Weekend Australian*, 5–6 December, p. 26.
Guillermo, A.G. 1995: Arts Culture and Identity. *Global Cultural Diversity Conference Proceedings*, Sydney.
Jupp, J. 1995: Public Policy and Diversity – Migration Patterns and Policy Selection and Rejection – Twenty Years of Australian Immigration. *Global Cultural Diversity Conference Proceedings*. Sydney.
———— 1999: The Snowy Mountains Scheme and Multicultural Australia, *The Spirit of the Snowy – Fifty Years on, Academy Symposium* November 1999.
Sharpe, E. 1984: Literature, Religion and Culture – Trio, Triad or Trinity. *Conference on Literature, Religion and Culture: An Australian Perspective.* The University of Sydney, 8–10 February.
Sheehan, P. 1983: Israel: Tears of Blood. *The Sydney Morning Herald, Good Weekend*, Saturday, 11 June, p. 33.
Short, Jim. 1995: Multiculturalism and Australian Identity. *Global Cultural Diversity Conference Proceedings*, Sydney.
Stannard, B. 1987: Migration Wrangle Heats Up: Asian Inflow Revives Old Phobias. *The Bulletin*, 24 November, pp. 72–75.
Tugend, T. 1994: Indian Jews Predict the End of Their Millennium. *The Jerusalem Post*, 23 February, in Features, p. 7.
Zubrzycki, J. 1995: The Evolution of the Policy of Multiculturalism in Australia 1968–95. *Global Cultural Diversity Conference Proceedings*, Sydney.

Index

Aaron, Aaron, 26, 58, 60
Aaron, Miss E., 53
Aaron family, 26, 53–4
Aaron, Jacob, 26, 27
Aaron, Reuben, 53
Abed-al-Hamid, 29–30
Abed-Al-Magid, 29
Abramson, H.J., 9, 131
acculturation, 6–11, 141, 156*n*
  Ashkenazi family, 95
  generation gap, 128-9
  immigrants, 117
  intermarriage 145-6
  Jewish day school, 147
  power control, 119
  and the rabbi, 121-2
  and religion, 94, 139, 146
  residential factors, 99
  Sephardim of Sydney, ix, x, 46, 94, 96,
    99, 132, 145–6, 147
  synagogue attendance, 132
  of the young, 94, 145-6
  see also assimilation
Adam, H., 54
alienation, ix, 98
Alliance Israelite Universelle, 31, 40,
  41
Anglo-conformity, 6–7, 11
anti-Semitism, 49–50, 60, 143
anxiety *see* status anxiety
Arab nationalism, 30
ascription by others, 2
Ashkenazi community
  acculturation, 95
  lack of assistance to Sephardim, 58,
    60, 61, 142
  as reference group to Sephardim, x,
    47, 96, 107, 108–16,
      135–6, 141–2, 143–4, 146–7
  ritual observances, 132–6

  status anxiety *vis-à-vis* Sephardim, 53,
    143
Ashkenazi conformity, 12
assimilation, 3, 6–11, 141–2, 156*n*
  immigrants, 117
  intermarriage, 81–2
  residential factors, 96–7
  see also acculturation
Aston, William J., 58
Australia
  acculturation, ix, 6–8
  Anglo-conformity, 6–7
  assimilation, 6–7
  ethnic diversity, 12–13
  immigration policy, 47, 48–57
  immigration of Sephardic Jews, 47–61
  Jewish population, 3, 47
  Melbourne Jewish community, 18–19
  multiculturalism, 13, 16
  the "native" metaphor, 14
  pluralism, 12–13
  quota system, 47, 52
  role of ethnicity in elections, 3
  strength of ethnic pride and identity,
    9
  White Australian policy, 47, 52, 106–7
  see also Sephardim of Sydney
Australian Jewish Times, 3
Australian Jewish Welfare Society
  (AJWS), 48, 49, 55, 57–8,
  59–60
Bales, R.F., 62, 78
Barth, F., 2, 4–5, 141
Basham, R., 20, 62, 93
behavioral acculturation, 7–8
behavioral assimilation, 7
Bell, C., 94
Bell, D., 3
Bene-Israel community, 24, 42, 43–4,
  142–3

Benson, L., 20
Benson, S., 63
Beyond the Melting Pot (Glazer and Moynihan), 2
Blainey, G., 12
B'nai Brith, 7
Bombay Group, Sephardim of Sydney, 23–4
Bombay Jewish community, 43–4, 48
Breton, R., 20
Buckley, B., 133
Burma Group, Sephardim of Sydney, 23, 42
Burmese Jewish community, migration to Australia, 48

Cahnman, W. J., 7
Calcutta Group, Sephardim of Sydney, 23–4
Calcutta Jewish community, 43, 45, 48, 52–3
Calwell, Arthur, 50, 51, 52, 53
Canada
    multiculturalism, 13
    strength of ethnic pride and identity, 9
Cass, B., 88
children, 65–7
    father–child relations, 82–5, 86, 87, 88, 145
    socialization of, 87–9
Chinese Jewish community
    choosing a partner, 76
    migration to Australia, 48, 54
    see also Shanghai Group
Christian community, Ottoman Empire, 28
Clark, A. G., 54
class
    and anxiety, 97–8, 114–16
    ethclass subculture, 15–16
    residential factors, 102–6
    Sephardim of Sydney, 8, 22, 102–6
    social stratification, 5–6
    straight-line theory, 8
    traditional Sephardic communities, 88
class mobility, 114–16
Cochin Group, 42–3
    Sephardim of Sydney, 24
Cohen, A., 4, 141
Cohen, Moses Duek, 24, 45
Cohen, P., 17
communal groups, 20
Connell, R.W., 115
Cooley, C.H., 18

Coult, A.D., 93
cultural assimilation, 6, 10, 141, 156*n*
cultural difference, 15, 16
cultural diversity, 9–11, 14
cultural erosion, 17, 21
cultural groups, 20
cultural markers, 10
cultural pluralism, 10–11
cultural symbols *see* symbolic ethnicity
culture, 64–5
    Barth's position, 4–5, 141
    as important concept, 4, 6
    see also acculturation
Curtin, John, 58

Dashefsky, A., 19
De Vos, G.A., 2, 18, 21
Deshen, S.A., 16, 17
Devereux, G., 18
dietary laws, 133, 134, 151
divorce
    Sephardim community, 64, 67
    Sephardim of Sydney, 67–75, 146
dominant groups, 1, 10, 14
Duek, Elias Moses, 45
Duwayk, Chief Rabbi Hayyim, 34

Eastern Herald, 3
Eastern Jewish Association (EJA), 22, 23, 25–6, 27, 47, 154
Egyptian Group, Sephardim of Sydney, 23, 24, 25, 130
Egyptian Jewish community, 27–8, 30–5, 45–6, 143
    authority and legitimacy of rabbis, 118
    education, 41–2
    marriage age of women, 40
    migration to Australia, 48, 59–60
    religious orientation, 42
Einfeld, S., 58
EJA *see* Eastern Jewish Association (EJA)
Emanuel School, viii
emasculated pluralism, 11
Encel, S., 133
Epstein, A.L.
    assimilation and modernization, 15
    culture, 64
    ethnic behavior, 4
    ethnic identity, 2, 4, 18, 19
    gossip networks, 151
Erikson, E.H., 19
ethclass subculture, 15–16
ethnic boundaries, 4–5, 15, 141

ethnic classifications, 5–6
ethnic groups
  boundaries, 4–5, 15, 141
  defined, 1, 4–5
  emotional attachment to, 3
  identity switching, 1–2, 114
  as interest groups, 2, 4, 141
  Sephardim, x, 5, 20–1
Ethnic Groups and Boundaries (Barth), 4
ethnic identity, 2–6
  defined, 2
  and education, 108
  genuine ethnic pluralism, 11
  identity crisis, 17–19, 114
  persistence of, 3
  political mobilization, 2
  residential factors, 96–7, 102
  Sephardim of Sydney, x–xi, 17, 18, 21,
    102, 108, 143–9
  shifting, 2–3, 16
  society's power structure, 1–2
  symbolic ethnicity, 11–12
ethnic minorities, 12, 16
  Jewish communities in India, 42–5,
    46
  Jewish communities in Ottoman
    Empire, 27–42, 45–6
  see also Ashkenazi community;
    Sephardim of Sydney
ethnic revival, 12
ethnic solidarity, 11
ethnic symbols *see* symbolic ethnicity
ethnicity
  decline through generations, 8
  defined, 1, 3, 6
  as extension of kinship, 6
  as major academic concern, 1
  political and economic aspects, 4, 16,
    141
  and religion, 4, 28, 117
  residential factors, 102
  role in elections, 3
  shifting, 2–3, 16
  "traditional" versus "new", 10, 16
  as working-class phenomena, 8
  see also symbolic ethnicity
Executive Council of Australian Jewry
  (ECAJ), 49, 55–6,
    57–60
Ezra, Mr., 54

families, 62–3
  relationships between members, 82–9
  residential factors, 98–106
  Sephardim in Israel, 86

Sephardim of Sydney, 83–4, 86–95,
  98–106, 145–6
  traditional Sephardim community,
    63–5, 82–6, 88, 94–5,
    98–9
Faruk, King of Egypt, 34
Faur, J., 40
Federation of Orthodox Synagogues of
  NSW, 27
Feisal, King of Iraq, 36, 37
Ferrier, Peter, 49
frontier thesis, 8

Gale, N., 102, 123
Gans, H.J., 8–9, 11, 12, 102, 141
Geertz, C., 119
generation thesis, 9
German Jewish community, 49
Ginsburg, Y., 108
Gist, N.P., 43, 142, 144
Glazer, N., 2, 3, 4, 9, 81–2, 141
globalizations, 3
Goffman, E., 18
Goitin, S.D., 130
Gordon, M., 10, 15–16
gossip, 150–1
Grassby, A.J., 10–11, 13
Gray, J., 14
Grunebaum, G.E. von, 28
Guest, L., 53–4
Guilleremo, A.G., 10, 13–14
Gullett, H.B., 49–50

Habenstein, R.W., 93
Haganah, 37, 38
HagiHasan RaficPasha, 29
Hakham, 27
Hakham Bashi, 28, 118–19, 137
halakhah, 76, 85–6, 121–2, 124, 125
halizah ceremony, 86
Harrison, E.J., 54
Hayim family, 54
Hechalutz Zionist movements, 38
Hendricks, G.L., 2, 18
Herberg, W., 9, 18, 138
Heyes, T.H., 51, 53, 55, 56–7
Hill, R.F., 12
Hirst, J., 14
Holt, Harold, 51, 54, 55, 56
Hong Kong Group, Sephardim of
  Sydney, 42
Horgan, J., 52
Hungarian Jewish community, 57,
  59–60
Hunt, C.L., 28

identification by others, 2, 17
identity *see* ethnic identity; national
   identity
identity crisis, 17–19, 114
Indian Jewish community, 42–5, 46
   authority and legitimacy of rabbis,
      118
   barriers between, 143
   Bombay community, 43–4, 48
   Calcutta community, 43, 45, 48, 52–3
   choosing a partner, 76
   Cochin community, 42–3
   migration to Australia, 47, 48, 51–3,
      159*n*
   survival of community, 138
Indian–Iraqi Group, Sephardim of
   Sydney, 23–5, 27, 42, 130,
   148
individualism, 97
Indonesia Group, Sephardim of
   Sydney, 23, 42, 68
industrialization, 92
interest groups, 2, 4
intermarriage, 8, 10
   forbidden under Islamic law, 39
   Jewish community in Cochin, 42
   Sephardim of Sydney, 81-2, 93, 145-6
Iraqi group, Sephardim of Sydney, 23,
   24–5, 143
Iraqi Jewish community, 27–8, 29–30,
   35–9, 45, 157–8*n*
   authority and legitimacy of rabbis,
      118
   education, 40, 41
   halakhah, 85–6
   migration to Bombay, 44
   naming ceremony for baby girls, 125
   religious orientation, 41
   secularization, 39
   status of women, 40
   survival of community, 138
   yeshivot, 41
Isaac, E., 55
Ismael Pasha, 31, 32
Israel
   acculturation, 6–8
   Ashkenazi conformity, 12
   assimilation, 6–7
   attitudinal study, 115
   Bene-Israel immigration, 44
   class factors, 8
   Cochin Jewish immigration, 42–3
   education system, 12
   emergence of new ethnicity, 3
   ethnic factors, 115, 165*n*

ethnic pluralism, 12
ethnicity as political issue, 16
generation gap, 139
Iraqi Jewish immigration, 37
Jewish allegiance to, 3
Law of Return, 56
Melting Pot theory, 12
mutual assistance, 108
residential factors, 115
Sephardim community, 14, 17, 18, 86
strength of ethnic pride and identity,
   9
symbolic ethnicity, 12

Jack, W., 54
Jacob, B.V., 52–3
Jewish Board of Education, viii–ix
Jewish hospitals, 7
Jewish Welfare Board of Singapore, 55
jizya, 28
Johnston, R.J., 97
Jupp, J., 3

al-Kabir, Abraham, 36
Kadourie family, 45, 54
Ketubah, 75
kinship, 6, 62
   residential factors, 98–106
   Sephardim of Sydney, 92–5, 98–106
Kondapi, C., 52

Ladies Auxiliary, 25, 150, 151, 152
Landa, A., 58, 59
Layish, H., 86
Lenski, G., 9, 136, 137
leverate marriages, 86
Lewis, B., 46
Lippman, Walter, 11
Litwak, E., 63

McGinness, H., 56
Madhat Pashas, 29
Marans, R.W., 108
marginality, 1, 16, 47, 114
   agnostics, 135
   and multiculturalism, 13
   Sephardim of Sydney, ix, x, 96, 98,
      116, 142–9
Martin, J.I., 11, 13
Marx, K., 19–20
Massada College, viii
Mead, G.H., 18
Medding, P.Y., 18–19
"The Medley", 154
Melbourne Argus, 49–50

Melbourne Jewish community, 18–19
Melbourne Sun, 50
Melting Pot theory, 8, 11, 12
Mercer, B.E., 20
millets, 28–9, 30, 46
Mills, C. Wright, 136
minyan, 117–18, 138
modernization, 15, 46, 92
mohar, 75
Moriah College, vii, 109
Mount Sinai College, viii
Moynihan, D.P., 2, 3, 4, 9, 81–2, 141
Mujtahid, 37
A Multicultural Society for the Future
    (Grassby), 10
multiculturalism, 6, 10, 13–15, 16
    "soft" versus "hard", 14
Musleah brothers, 25
Musleah, Myer, 26
Muslim Brotherhood, 33
Muslims, attitude to Jewish commu-
    nity, 28
Mustafa Azem Pasha, 29

Nagib, General Muhammad, 34
Nagid, 29
al-Nasser, Gamal Abd, 34
national identity, 3, 13
New South Wales (NSW) Association
    of Sephardim, 22, 23,
    24–5, 26–7, 47, 119, 153–4
New South Wales (NSW) Hebrew
    Association, 26
New South Wales (NSW) Jewish Board
    of Deputies, 27
Newby, H., 94
Nutt, Mr. (immigration officer), 56

Opperman, Hubert, 52
Orthodox Beth-Din (Jewish
    Ecclesiastical Court), 22
Osterreich, J., 94
the "other", 14, 16
Ottoman Empire
    ethnic minorities, 27–42, 45–6
    Hakham Bashi, 28, 118–19

Paerach, 45
Parsons, T, 62, 63, 78, 93, 155*n*
participant observation, 150–3
Passover, as a social function, 4
Patterson, G.J., 10
Patterson, J.G., 141
Patterson, O., 3
Peterson-Royce, A., 2, 5, 114

Pinard, M., 20
pluralism, 6, 9–13
Polish Jewish community, 49
polygamy, 67, 161*n*
Porush, Rabbi Israel, 73, 74
The Presentation of Self in Everyday Life
    (Goffman), 18
psychological identification, 15–16
psychological reality, 5

questionnaires, 153

rabbis, 118–27, 136, 139–40
race, as extension of kinship, 6
racial discrimination, 52, 106–7, 114
"racial" minorities, 16
Rassaby, Hugh, 58–9
Rassaby, Maurice, 59
Rassaby, Musel, 59
religion, 117–40
    acculturation, 94, 139, 146
    Egyptian Jewish community, 42
    and ethnicity, 4, 28, 117
    importance of, 8–9
    Iraqi Jewish community, 41
    loss of vitality, 94
    naming ceremony for baby girls,
        124–5
    rabbis, 118–27, 136, 139–40
    religious attendance, 117–18, 130–2,
        146–7
    religious observance, 130–6, 146
    rituals for the birth of a boy, 126
    segregation of sexes in synagogue,
        121–3
    Sephardim of Sydney, 117–18, 119–28,
        130–40, 146–7
    Sunday school, ix, 25, 123–4
religious rituals, 4, 119, 124–6, 132–6
religious symbols *see* symbolic ethnicity
residential factors, viii, 96–106, 107–11,
    116
    voluntary and involuntary segrega-
        tion, 97
residential mobility, 96–7, 99–106,
    108–11, 116
Reuben, Mrs., 56
Rhedding-Jones, J., 2, 12, 14, 16
rituals, 124–6, 132–6
    and Jewish identity, 146
    and Jewish practices, 21, 144
    and migrant societies, 3–4
    observance, 121, 146, 164*n*
    and rabbis, 119
    and social power, 117, 164*n*

robust pluralism, 11
Roosens, E.E., 2, 11, 12
Rosh Hashana, 25
Rutland, S.D., 51

al-Said, Nuri, 37
Samra, David, 36
Sandberg, N.C., 8
Sassoon, David, 44
Sassoon family, 54
Schneider, D.M., 10
Schrift, R., 78
Seder, 133
self-ascription, 2
self-identification, 2, 17
Selvin, H.C., 20
Sephardim community
  children, 65–7
  division into classes, 88
  divorce, 64, 67
  education, 63–4
  in Egypt, 27–8
  family life, 63–5, 82–6, 88, 94–5, 98–9
  father–child relations, 82–5
  husband–wife relations, 82–4
  in Iraq, 27–8
  marriage, 64, 65
  in Middle East and Asia, 27–45
  migration to Australia, 47–61
  naming ceremony for baby girls,
    124–5
  polygamy, 67, 161*n*
  women, 40, 63–4, 82, 88
Sephardim in Israel
  dichotomy of "us" and "other", 14
  ethnic identity, 17, 18
  family life, 86
Sephardim of Sydney
  acculturation, ix, x, 46, 94, 96, 99, 132,
    145–6, 147
  Ashkenazi community, x, 47, 96, 107,
    108–16, 135–6,
    141–2, 143–4, 146–7
  Australianization, 111–12
  authority and legitimacy of rabbis,
    119–27, 136, 139–40
  Bene-Israel Group, 24
  Bombay Group, 23–4
  Calcutta Group, 23–4
  children, 66–7
  Cochin Group, 24
  communal institutions, 94
  dichotomy of "us" and "other", 14
  divorce, 67–75, 146
  education, 88, 108

Egyptian Group, 23, 24, 25, 130
ethnic division and organizational
    structure, 24–7
ethnic group issue, x, 5, 20–1
ethnic identity, x–xi, 17, 18, 21, 102,
    108, 143–9
executive committee power struggle,
    126–7
family life, 83–4, 86–95, 98–106, 145–6
father–child relations, 86, 87, 88, 145
first synagogue, 27
generation gap, 128–9, 137, 139
husband–wife relations, 86–7, 88,
    89–92, 99, 145–6
Indian-Iraqi Group, 23–5, 27, 42, 130,
    148
inter-ethnic conflict, 129–30
intermarriage, 81–2, 93, 145-6
Iraqi Group, 23, 24–5, 143
kinship relations, 92–5, 98–106
marginality, ix, x, 96, 98, 116, 142–9
marriage, 67–82
measures of success, 108
modernization, 46
mutual assistance, 108
numbers of, ix, 22, 47
occupations, 22–3, 89–92
polygamy, 67
religion, 117–18, 119–28, 130–40,
    146–7
religious attendance, 117–18, 130–2,
    146–7
religious committee power struggle,
    127–8
religious observance, 130–6, 146
residential factors, viii, 96–106,
    107–11, 116
ritual observances, 132–6
rituals for the birth of a boy, 126
segregation of sexes in synagogue,
    121–3
social class, 8, 22, 102–6
socialization of children, 87–9
socio-ethnic structure, 22–4
status anxiety, 114–15, 143–9
Sunday school, 25, 123–4
synagogue membership, 24, 132,
    146–7
women, 22–3, 25, 88–92, 95
Seri Camal Pasha, 29, 30
Shaham, S., 86
Shahat, Moshe, 36
shamash, 124, 125, 126
Shanghai Group, Sephardim of Sydney,
    23, 42, 159*n*

Shanghai Jewish community, migration to Australia, 54
Shta'al, 66
Silas, Rabbi Simon, 27
Singapore Group, Sephardim of Sydney, 23, 42
Singapore Jewish community, migration to Australia, 48, 52
Skinner, K.A., 2, 18
Smooha, S., 65, 86
social groups, x, 19–21, 64–5
social mobility, 8, 97–8, 99–112, 113–16
social stratification, 5–6
socialization, 87–92, 93–4
Solomon, A., 59
Solomon, N., 123
Spiro, M.E., 8, 146
Srole, L., 8
Stannard, B., 13, 57
State Zionist Council, 26
status anxiety, 97–8, 142–9
    Ashkenazi community, 53, 143
    Sephardim of Sydney, 114–15, 143–9
Stein, H.R., 12
straight-line theory, 8–9
structural assimilation, 6–7, 10, 141, 156n
structural pluralism, 10, 11
structural reality, 5
Suarez-Orozco, M.M., 21
subsistence anxiety, 97
Sydney Beth-Din, 27
Sydney Jewish News, 58
Sydney Morning Herald, 3
symbolic ethnicity, 3, 6, 9, 11–12, 141
    defined, 11
synagogues
    membership, 24, 131–2, 146–7
    religious attendance, 117–18, 130–2, 146–7
    segregation of sexes, 121–3

Tarzi, Salim, 36
Trelore, Mr. (immigration officer), 56
Turkish Jewish community
    marriage age of women, 40
    secularization, 39
Turner, Frederick Jackson, 8

unconscious, and ethnic behavior, 19
United Israel Appeal (UIA), 110
United States
    acculturation, 6–8
    Anglo-conformity, 6–7
    assimilation, 6–7
    ethnicity as political issue, 16
    strength of ethnic pride and identity, 9

Van den Berghe, P.L., 5, 6, 20

Walker, L., 28
Wanderer, J.J., 20
Warner, W.L., 5, 8
Weber, M., 17–18
Weingrod, A., 8, 115
Weisman, Chaim, 36
Wentworth Courier, 3
Willmott, P., 62
Withall, 54
women
    husband–wife relations, 82–4, 86–7, 88, 89–92, 99, 145–6
    segregation in synagogue, 121–3
    Sephardim of Sydney, 22–3, 25, 88–92, 95
    status in Jewish world, 40, 123
    traditional Sephardim community, 40, 63–4, 82, 88
working-class, 8, 102
Wright, R.D., 43, 142, 144

Yehezkel, Sir Sasoon, 36
Yeshiva College, viii, 109, 135
Yom Kippur, 25
Young Egypt movement, 33
Young Ladies Guild, 25
Young, M., 62
Youth Organization, 128–9

Zangwill, I., 8
Zelditch, M., 94
Zionism, 33
Zionist Conference, 26
Zionist Record, 7
Zubrzycki, J., 10, 13